The Irreversible Decision
1939 — 1950

THE

Irreversible Decision

1939 – 1950

By Robert C. Batchelder

THE MACMILLAN COMPANY, NEW YORK

The material in this book, in essentially this form, was submitted as a dissertation to the Graduate School of Yale University in partial fulfillment of the requirements for the degree of Doctor of Philosophy.

Grateful acknowledgment is due the following authors and publishers for permission to quote selections from the works cited:

Life Magazine: *Year of Decisions* by Harry S. Truman. Copyright © 1955, 1956 by Time, Inc.

Oxford University Press: *Atomic Quest* by Arthur H. Compton. Copyright © 1956 by Oxford Unversity Press.

Harper & Brothers: *On Active Service in Peace and War* by Henry L. Stimson and McGeorge Bundy. Copyright 1947, 1948 by Henry L. Stimson. Selections reprinted by permission of Harper & Brothers. *Speaking Frankly* by James F. Byrnes. Copyright 1947 by Donald S. Russell, Trustee of the James F. Byrnes Foundation. Selections reprinted by permission of Harper & Brothers.

Catholic Association for International Peace: *Peace in the Atomic Age*, CAIP pamphlet No. 38.

To my wife

Acknowledgments

I AM INDEBTED to Professor H. Richard Niebuhr for whatever insights into Christian ethics I have had; to Professor William Lee Miller for encouragement and incisive criticism; to Alexander Sachs, James B. Conant, Elting E. Morison, and Arthur H. Compton for kindly consenting to grant personal interviews; to Yale University Divinity School and the National Council on Religion in Higher Education for generous financial aid; to Mrs. John A. Russell for timely aid in proofreading; and most of all to my wife for patience under many trials, and gracious help in many ways.

Contents

The Irreversible Decision

1939 — 1950

1. Prologue

On August 2, 1939, Dr. Albert Einstein signed a paper addressed to President Franklin D. Roosevelt on which were these words:

> Some recent work by E. Fermi and L. Szilard, which has been communicated to me in manuscript, leads me to expect that the element uranium may be turned into a new and important source of energy in the immediate future. Certain aspects of the situation which has arisen seem to call for watchfulness and, if necessary, quick action on the part of the Administration. I believe therefore that it is my duty to bring to your attention the following facts and recommendations.
>
> . . . it may become possible to set up a nuclear chain reaction in a large mass of uranium, by which vast amounts of power and large quantities of new radium-like elements would be generated. Now it appears almost certain that this could be achieved in the immediate future.
>
> This new phenomenon would also lead to the construction of bombs, and it is conceivable — though much less certain — that extremely powerful bombs of a new type may thus be constructed. A single bomb of this type, carried by boat and exploded in a port, might very well destroy the whole port together with some of the surrounding territory. . . .[1]

Thus began a chain reaction of events. President Roosevelt appointed a committee and provided $6000. Scientists broke hallowed tradition by imposing secrecy upon themselves and withholding the results of their research from publication. Football players at Columbia University spent hours stacking and unstacking and restacking shiny black bricks of graphite in

1

the basement of the physics building, and emerged looking like coal miners. A swarthy Italian ordered a metal rod to be withdrawn one more foot from its slot in a pile consisting of uranium lumps imbedded in a matrix of carbon bricks; neutron counters clicked faster and faster — and the first self-sustaining release of atomic energy was accomplished. The Assistant Secretary of the Treasury, accustomed to thinking in terms of *ounces* of silver, was dismayed when an Army officer asked to borrow "about fifteen thousand tons" of the Treasury's silver bullion — half a billion dollars' worth — to wire a monstrous electromagnet. A Tennessee village known colloquially as "Dogpatch" swelled to a city of 78,000 persons; work went on night and day in a huge factory nearby, from which no visible "product" ever emerged. A boom town of 60,000 erupted on the banks of the Columbia River, a huge industrial plant was erected, and the boom town was as suddenly deserted. Then at 5:30 one lightning-streaked morning, a group of men in the desolation of the New Mexico desert watched in awe as a "huge multi-colored surging cloud boiled to an altitude of over 40,000 feet" from a blinding explosion that climaxed years of theorizing and labor. The next day newspapers reported that a munitions dump had blown up in New Mexico "with remarkable light effects," and President Truman received at the Potsdam Conference a message describing the birth of a new baby. Three weeks later an American B-29 flew over the city of Hiroshima as it busily settled into its early morning routine; and then, within a single second, the city was transformed into an agonized pile of bodies and burning rubble. The atomic bomb had become a reality.

II

Even before the atomic bomb had become a reality, it had become a burning problem to the consciences of the human beings who knew of its possibility. Could it be right under any circumstances to use against a city a weapon of such great and indiscriminate destructiveness? Could massive slaughter of women and children by an atomic bomb be justified if use of the bomb saved more lives than it took? What impact would its use have upon other nations, and upon the prospect for an enduring peace after the war? Such were the questions with which a handful of scientists, soldiers, and statesmen wrestled in the strictest secrecy during the days which led up to Hiroshima.

Once the bomb had burst into public consciousness, the debate intensified. Vice-President Truman, when told of the death of President Roosevelt, is reported to have said that he felt like a man upon whom a load of hay had fallen. Much the same feeling was common among thinking men in the first days of the atomic age. There was widespread questioning whether man's "scientific development" had not outstripped his lagging "moral development," making him unfit to cope with the challenge of this newest technological advance. Could the theory of the "just war," long maintained by Christian moralists, be upheld in the future? Would it be possible to abolish these new weapons so that acceptable wars might continue to be fought with "conventional" weapons — or did the horror of the new bombs and the likelihood of their use in any future conflict mean that war itself had to be abolished? How was it possible to maintain any longer the distinctions, hard enough to maintain in World War II's mass-bombing attacks with incendiaries, between combatant and noncombatant, military and civilian targets, industrial and residential areas? Were there any possible circumstances in which it would be justifiable to use atomic bombs against an enemy? Might not the extreme horror of the new bomb be a blessing in disguise, forcing men by shock and fear to give up war and create a world government that would settle international differences peacefully? If America kept her supply of atomic bombs as a "sacred trust," what was to prevent a disastrous atomic arms race? Such were the questions that filled men's minds and troubled their hopes for the future.

An oyster, into whose shell an irritating bit of sand has intruded, cannot rest until the foreign particle has been covered over and made smooth with layers of mother-of-pearl; in this state, the irritating bit does no damage to the ordinary processes of life — it can be lived with. In somewhat the same manner, atomic energy was suddenly injected into the life of man in 1945. Despite its potentialities for good, its main impact thus far has been irritation of the conscience and a mortal threat to man's very life on earth. Since 1945 men have been struggling to find a way to live with atomic energy (since apparently it will not go away by itself) by smoothing over its rough edges, trying to incrust it with political controls and moral inhibitions. It might be possible, if the overlay of morality, discipline, and control is thick enough and smooth enough, to transform what is now a threatening intrusion into a thing of beauty, usefulness, and inestimable value.

It is this process of accommodation that is the subject of this study: man — with his inescapable sense of having a moral claim laid upon him, with his compulsion to seek the good and the right — confronted with nuclear weapons and their capacity for massive and indiscriminate destruction. Man's continued existence and development on earth depend in large measure upon the relation between his morality and the weapons now available to him.

III

We shall approach the general problem of ethics and nuclear weapons by starting with events rather than with ethical theory. The focus will be upon certain crucial decisions and debates centering around the atomic bomb, and we shall analyze the role played by ethical considerations.

Part I describes the interaction between ethics, physics, and politics which led to the decision to make the atomic bomb. Part II tells the story of the decision to use the atomic bomb against Japan. After the war a vigorous debate sprang up between those who condemned the bombing of Hiroshima and Nagasaki and those who defended the decision to use the atomic bomb. In Part III we shall examine the arguments on both sides of this debate and attempt to reach a valid judgment on whether the atomic bombing of Japan was right or wrong. Part IV considers the more general discussion that arose after the war concerning the nature and morality of atomic warfare, and notes how the impact of men's experiences during World War II shaped their thinking about the moral problems of the "next war."

The final chapter outlines some general conclusions about ethics and war in the atomic age. By identifying some of the errors of the past we may contribute to the development of a constructive way of thinking about war and atomic weapons for the future.

I

The Decision to Make
the Atomic Bomb

1939-1941

2. The Campaign of the Exiled Scientists

IF ONE WERE ASKED the question "Shall we make an instrument which can destroy a whole city and wipe out tens of thousands of lives in an instant?" one's response would be an emphatic "No!" Yet conscientious and humanitarian scientists — Nobel Prize winners among them — persuaded the United States government, in time of peace, to undertake a full-scale attempt to make such an instrument. As a result, all mankind lives under the daily possibility of annihilation: enough nuclear weapons now exist to kill within an hour most of the people between Moscow and Los Angeles, wreck Western civilization, and perhaps (through radioactive fallout) to erase human life from the face of the earth.

When presented as an abstract example from an ethics textbook, the question can be given a simple answer that is clearly either "right" or "wrong." However, when the question of making an atomic bomb appeared in the flux of history, in the lives of real men, it was transformed in such a way that conscientious men felt impelled, in the concrete situation confronting them, to affirm as the best possible alternative (indeed, as their moral duty) the choice which in the abstract would appear wrong. Unraveling the process by which this transformation took place leads to a fascinating tale, and some understanding of the interplay between historical events and ethics.

How was the decision to produce an atomic bomb reached? Who decided, and for what reasons? To answer such questions it is necessary to focus attention upon a small group of scientists — nuclear physicists and chemists — and particularly upon a handful who had been trained in western Europe and during the 1930's had made their way to the United States. Except for the vision, initiative, and perseverance of these men the decision would not have been made as it was. The decision to make the atomic bomb was essentially their decision.*

A double question plagued the scientists during the three years from the discovery of nuclear fission to the final decision to make a full-scale effort to produce an atomic bomb. The first aspect was scientific and technical: was it theoretically and actually possible to produce a fast-fission chain reaction (i.e., an explosive release of nuclear energy) in a mass of uranium? If so, could engineers overcome the formidable tech-

---

* It may seem at first glance an oversimplification to call the decision to make the atomic bomb almost exclusively the scientists' — surely, in a decision that committed the United States government to large-scale action and expenditure, government officials must have played an important role. It is true that the final decision had to be made by the highest elected official in the land, the President himself. Yet in this case the President was not guided by any specific mandate from Congress; that body as a whole knew nothing about the atomic bomb project; a few Congressmen were informed *after* the decision had been made, when it became necessary to appropriate large sums of money for construction of the Hanford and Oak Ridge plants. Secrecy made it impossible for the press or public opinion to have any influence in the debate leading to the decision. In its formative stages it was essentially a dialogue between scientists and the government; and those who spoke most authoritatively for the government were themselves scientists. Vannevar Bush was a professor of electrical engineering, later vice-president of Massachusetts Institute of Technology, then president of the Carnegie Institution of Washington (a sponsor of basic scientific research); in 1940 he was given over-all responsibility for directing the government's program of scientific research relating to World War II, first as Chairman of the National Defense Research Committee, and later as Director of the Office of Scientific Research and Development. James B. Conant, a chemist and president of Harvard University, had primary responsibility under Bush for determining *on behalf of the government* whether the atom bomb project should be expanded into a full-scale effort. So intimately interconnected were the political and the technical scientific aspects of the decision — the probability that the chain reaction would work, the progress of the German scientists and therefore the degree of threat posed by Hitler, the effectiveness of the proposed bomb and hence the priority it should be given over other research projects — that political leaders could only rely upon the judgment of the scientists (and the scientists in government). Thus the decision was peculiarly the scientists'.

nical obstacles involved in producing fissionable materials in large amounts? The second aspect was the moral one: even if scientists and engineers agreed that a bomb *could* be made, would it be right to make and to use such an instrument of destruction? Scientists struggled with these questions in the midst of a historical situation which itself had profound influence upon the answers that they finally reached. It is to the historical context of the decision that we turn first.

II

One of the fateful ironies of the twentieth century is that the crescendo of discovery in nuclear physics and the crescendo of Hitler's ambitions in Europe reached the point of climax at the same time. The years from 1932 to 1939 witnessed the scaling of one of the highest pinnacles of human intellectual achievement in the discovery of the key for releasing the unlimited energy hitherto locked within the nucleus of the atom. The same years witnessed the swift rise of Hitler to military dominance, the fall of Austria and Czechoslovakia, and the rising tension that brought Europe to the brink of world war. The development of nuclear physics not only paralleled the development of Hitler's power but was significantly influenced by it.

The key piece to the puzzle of the atom's nucleus was revealed in 1932 when Sir James Chadwick discovered a new subatomic particle which he called the neutron. Within a few months of this discovery, Hitler gained power in Germany. Both events had important repercussions in the scientific world. Hitler's coming to power vitally affected the lives of many of the most brilliant scientists of Europe. Barely a month passed before seven professors, including Max Born and Nobel Prize winner James Franck, were forced to leave their posts in the Natural Science Faculty at the University of Göttingen. Many

eastern Europeans studying in Germany, including physicists
Edward Teller, Leo Szilard, and Eugene Wigner, were subjected
to abuse and persecution because of their Jewish ancestry; they
departed the country and sought refuge in Denmark, England,
and the United States. In the autumn of 1933, Albert Einstein,
whose theory of relativity had been denounced as "Jewish
physics," left Berlin for the Institute of Advanced Studies at
Princeton.[1]

The identification of the neutron had an impact no less profound. Enrico Fermi undertook in 1934 to follow up Chadwick's discovery with a series of experiments at Rome in which
he systematically bombarded all known elements with a beam
of neutrons. By this means he achieved the alchemists' dream
of transforming one element into another, and produced a whole
new family of artificially radioactive isotopes. The resulting
isotope usually turned out to be a new form of a neighboring
element, with an atomic number one or two higher or lower
than the element originally bombarded. Fermi found that turning neutrons against uranium, the heaviest of all metals and
the last element (No. 92) in the periodic table, also produced
a new radioactive isotope. Unable to identify this new isotope
with elements 90 or 91, Fermi concluded that he must have produced an element of atomic number 93 or 94, which did not
exist in nature. This conclusion was later discovered to be an
illusion. What Fermi had done, without realizing it, was to split
the uranium atom into two roughly equal parts.[2]

During the years 1935 to 1937, while Hitler was rearming
Germany and marching into the Rhineland in direct violation
of the Versailles treaty, Professor Otto Hahn and his Viennese
colleague, Fräulein Lise Meitner, duplicated Fermi's experiments and subjected the resulting new isotopes to exhaustive
chemical tests. It was while they were puzzling over the strange
results of bombarding uranium with neutrons that Hitler, in
March 1938, marched into Vienna and annexed Austria. Fräulein Meitner, who had hitherto been exempt from Hitler's anti-

Semitic laws because of being an Austrian, now became subject to them. Despite protests by Hahn, his collaborator in twenty-five years' labor was forced to leave her position at Berlin's Kaiser Wilhelm Institute, and to slip secretly across the border.[3]

Shortly thereafter, another leading physicist joined the ranks of the exiles. In November 1938 Enrico Fermi left Italy, ostensibly to go to Stockholm to receive a Nobel Prize in recognition of his 1934 experiments. However, he had quietly determined not to return to Italy, where Mussolini's aping of Hitler's anti-Semitism had created difficulties for Fermi's wife, who was Jewish. From Stockholm, the Fermis sailed to New York, where he became professor of physics at Columbia University in January 1939.[4]

While Fermi was on his travels, Professor Hahn continued his analysis of the radioactive products of uranium bombardment. The new isotope resembled both lanthanum and radium, but was clearly neither. Using the most precise and delicate chemical analysis, Hahn and his assistant F. Strassmann were led shortly before Christmas 1938 to the conclusion that the new element was barium, element No. 56, which occupies a position in the center of the list of elements and weighs little more than half as much as uranium. Such a conclusion was impossible to explain by means of the existing theories of nuclear physics, but the chemical evidence was incontrovertible. Because of the importance of their discovery, Hahn and Strassmann decided to publish their results despite their inability to account for them theoretically. In their report they stated that "as chemists, we are bound to affirm that the new bodies are not radium but barium." Yet they could not bring themselves positively to affirm that barium was produced by the bombardment of uranium by neutrons, for this conclusion would be "in contradiction to all previous experience in nuclear physics." Mailing his manuscript to the journal for publication, Hahn was assailed by doubts as he realized that his results flew in the face of established theory. Had he made an error that would make him a laughingstock? "The whole thing once more seemed so improbable to me that I wished I could get the document back out of the mailbox." [5]

Hahn immediately sent the results of his experiments to Professor Meitner, who had taken refuge in Sweden. In conversation with her nephew, Otto R. Frisch, also a refugee from Germany, who was spending the Christmas holidays with her, she came to the correct and astounding interpretation of Hahn's results. The uranium atom must have been split into two smaller pieces. If such splitting were actually taking place, it should be accompanied by the release of energy unparalleled by any other atomic event. Using Einstein's formula, $E = mc^2$, Frisch and Meitner calculated that the amount of energy which should be released would be of the order of 200 million electron volts. Upon his return to his Copenhagen laboratory, Frisch conducted experiments showing that the fragments of the uranium atom indeed flew apart with the unheard-of amount of energy his calculation had predicted. Atomic fission had been discovered.[6]

The discovery of atomic fission came three months after the Munich agreement. Both events were hailed as achievements of great promise for the future, yet both events raised haunting questions. While the world wondered whether Hitler would abide by his solemn agreements, the scientists wondered whether nuclear fission would be restricted only to isolated atoms in laboratories, or whether the fission of one atom might lead to fission of many, thus releasing energy in usable amounts. The question of whether significant amounts of energy could be produced by fission of the uranium atom depended upon the answer to another question: does the breakup of the uranium atom, caused by its being hit by a neutron, produce more neutrons? If so, then these neutrons might in turn serve as bullets to hit other uranium atoms, and the fission process might become a self-sustaining chain reaction.

Within another three months both the scientific and the political questions had been answered. Szilard and Fermi, working independently in New York, undertook experiments which showed that on the average each uranium atom, as it fissions, releases from one to three neutrons; thus the release of nuclear energy by a chain reaction was seen to be theoretically possible.[7] And, on March 15, 1939, German troops marched into Prague in arrogant violation of the Munich pact — less than six months after Hitler had solemnly agreed to it. Hitler's ambitions and ruthlessness were now clear to all.

The point of climax had been reached, both in physics and in international relations. The impact of the one upon the other had resulted in the gathering together in the United States of a small group of men having in common a unique combination of characteristics and experience. Born in Europe, trained in science at German universities, all had experienced persecution (or the threat of it) under Nazi and Fascist regimes, and had left their homes rather than live under totalitarianism — and they also knew the secret of the atom and its energy. As scientists they exulted over the discoveries that promised to unlock the unlimited energy of the atom for the benefit of mankind. Yet, as the oppressive summer of 1939 wore on, they found that their exhilarating hopes for the future were being invaded by fears of what this new energy would mean in the hands of a fanatical and ruthless dictator whose thirst for power was insatiable. The unique combination of their experience, their knowledge, and their fears was destined to give them a decisive role to play in the wartime affairs of their adopted country.

III

The vision of Hitler in possession of an atomic bomb filled with alarm the group of refugee scientists, which centered on

Leo Szilard, and included Eugene Wigner, Edward Teller, Enrico Fermi, and Victor Weisskopf. Early in 1939 they took the
initiative. Even before his experiments which showed that a
chain reaction was theoretically possible, Szilard attempted to
persuade his fellow scientists to refrain from publishing the results of their research in the nuclear field, out of fear that the
publication of encouraging results might lead to the development of atomic bombs that would be exceedingly dangerous
"in the hands of certain governments." This attempt at voluntary censorship was undercut when Frédéric Joliot-Curie, working
in Paris, independently discovered the possibility of a chain reaction and published his findings. This setback, combined with
the objections of many American scientists, temporarily frustrated Szilard's efforts. Agreement was not reached until a year
later on a mechanism for restricting publication of articles in
the fission field which had military importance.[8]

This secrecy undoubtedly hid from the Nazis the progress
in uranium research being made by American scientists — but
it also hid information from their American fellow scientists.
The attempt of each university to keep its research secret for
security reasons meant the retarding of fission studies elsewhere
in the country, for research had to be duplicated in several
places, and vital cross-fertilization of ideas was hampered. Arthur H. Compton reports that during the summer of 1940,
while Fermi was visiting lecturer at the University of Chicago,
the atmosphere of secrecy was so prevalent that despite the
vital interest of both men in uranium research and "almost
daily contacts neither he nor I once raised the question of how
the atomic chain reaction might be made to work." [9]

Mere secrecy among scientists, however, was not enough
without more positive action. Steps should be taken to alert
the government to both the dangers and the possibilities inherent in the discovery of nuclear fission. On March 16, 1939,
the day after Hitler marched into Prague (and only ten weeks

after arrival in the United States), Enrico Fermi traveled to Washington to bring to the attention of the United States Navy the tremendous implications of the possibility that "uranium might be used as an explosive that would liberate a million times as much energy per pound as any known explosive." The Navy's response was less than enthusiastic. As an attempt to stimulate active government support of expanded nuclear research, Fermi's venture failed.[10]

As the summer of 1939 wore on, evidence began to accumulate indicating that the Germans were actively engaged in atomic energy research. Shortly after Hitler took over Czechoslovakia — which possessed one of the world's three major uranium deposits — exports of uranium ore from that country were cut off. Reports were received that at the Kaiser Wilhelm Institute in Berlin (where Hahn had discovered nuclear fission), nuclear physicists had been meeting together under the auspices of the German Army. Apparently Hitler was actively pursuing research in atomic energy for military purposes.[11]

Reports such as these increased the anxiety of men like Szilard, and stimulated their determination to awaken the government to the real danger of an atomic bomb in the hands of Germany. Wracking their brains for a method of accomplishing this, Szilard and his friends brought their problem to Dr. Alexander Sachs, an economist who had gained President Roosevelt's confidence and had access to the White House. Together they finally hit on the idea of getting Albert Einstein, whose reputation would surely carry weight, to write a letter direct to the President of the United States. Szilard and Wigner, in consultation with Dr. Einstein, drafted the famous letter to the President, which Einstein signed on August 2. The letter pointed out that the possibility of a chain reaction implied the possibility of constructing "extremely powerful bombs," which, if exploded in a port, "might very well destroy the whole port together with some of the surrounding territory."

Einstein also reported the signs of German activity, and urged quick action by the government to speed up experimental work on uranium and to secure a supply of uranium ore for the United States.[12]

Sachs was entrusted with the letter, but before he could bring it personally to the attention of the President war broke out in Europe with Hitler's invasion of Poland on September 1, 1939. During the next hectic weeks Roosevelt was preoccupied with the campaign to repeal the arms embargo provisions of the Neutrality Act. It was not until October 11 that Sachs managed to secure an appointment and to present the letter from Einstein. Although Roosevelt was impressed, he was not at first convinced that substantial government action was called for. However, Sachs was persistent, and raised the subject again at breakfast the next morning. Finally Roosevelt said, "Alex, what you are after is to see that the Nazis don't blow us up." Sachs replied, "Precisely." The President then called in his military aide and told him, "This requires action."[13]

The "action" taken was the formation of an Advisory Committee on Uranium, which studied the problem and reported on November 1, 1939, that further investigation of uranium fission was "worthy of direct financial support by the Government." The committee qualified its recommendation by stating that "the military and naval applications . . . must at present be regarded only as possibilities . . ."[14] No further action took place for several months; government interest lagged. The establishment of the government's Advisory Committee seemed to "retard rather than to advance the development of American uranium research. Its appointment seemed to imply that the nation's interests with regard to fission would be looked after."[15] Yet the committee did nothing substantial to advance the work. Einstein felt compelled to write a second letter for submission to the President, in March 1940, emphasizing the importance of uranium work and pointing out that nuclear research was being expanded and intensified at the Kaiser Wilhelm Institute in Berlin.[16] About this time, the first United States government grant of funds for uranium work was made: $6000 for the purchase of graphite and uranium.[17] Still, progress was slow. Washington had no agency that could recognize the importance of new scientific discoveries or adequately support their development for the purposes of national defense. Only after the fall of France in June 1940 was the National Defense Research Committee formed. The Advisory Committee was reconstituted as a subcommittee of the NDRC.[18]

During 1940 and 1941 the scientists labored to clarify the many intricacies of the uranium problem. Although the problems with which they struggled were highly technical and complex, they had immediate military and political implications — for the more easily could the difficulties be overcome the closer to an atomic bomb must Hitler be, and the more urgent became prompt action to expand our own uranium program. It is appropriate to describe briefly at this point the nature of the problems facing the scientists.

Natural uranium consists of a mixture of two isotopes (atoms chemically identical but having different atomic weights). By far the greatest part of uranium as it occurs in nature (99.3%) consists of atoms weighing 238 atomic units; the remainder (0.7%, or one part in 140) consists of atoms of weight 235. It is only the uranium-235 atom that fissions when hit by a neutron; the U-238 merely absorbs the neutron and becomes U-239 without fissioning. Thus the possibility of a chain reaction, implied in the fact that each fissioning U-235 atom releases several neutrons, was apparently rendered impossible again by the fact that most of these neutrons would be absorbed by the plentiful U-238 atoms, thus quenching the chain reaction. It seemed certain that if sufficient U-235 could be separated from the more abundant U-238, the former would sustain an explosive chain reaction in itself. However, separation of measurable amounts of U-235 from U-238 is an exceedingly difficult process, since the two isotopes are chemically identical and their weight is so nearly equal. (Faced with these tantalizing frustrations, Fermi is reported to have sighed, "The sheer cussedness of nature!")[19]

If only the problem of separating U-235 from U-238 could be solved, then construction of a bomb would be a comparatively simple matter. In a sufficiently large mass of U-235 (where the number of neutrons escaping from the surface of the lump into the surrounding air becomes small compared with the number confined within the lump), neutrons released by the fission of one U-235 nucleus must inevitably hit and fission other nuclei. Thus a simple bomb may be constructed by arranging a device that will bring quickly together two pieces of U-235, each smaller than the "critical mass," but together exceeding it. A fast chain reaction will ensue, releasing tremendous amounts of energy within a split second.

A possibility of establishing a nuclear chain reaction without having to separate U-235 was opened up by the discovery that it is fast-moving neutrons, such as those emitted by a fissioning atom, which tend to be absorbed by U-238, while slow-moving neutrons tend to be absorbed by U-235 atoms (which then fission). Fermi hit upon the idea of embedding small lumps of uranium throughout a matrix of graphite; fast neutrons released by fission of a U-235 atom would escape from the small lump of uranium, bounce around in the graphite until a series of collisions with carbon atoms reduced their speed drastically, and might then be absorbed by U-235 atoms, which would in turn fission and release more neutrons.* If for every atom that fissioned, something more than one neutron (on the average) could be absorbed by another U-235

* Fermi chose graphite as a moderator because it is reasonably effective, and also readily available. Heavy water is a much better moderator, but was not available in sufficiently large amounts.

atom, the fission process, and its attendant release of energy, would be self-sustaining. Fermi's experiments and calculations showed that such a chain reaction could be achieved, given a large enough pile and sufficiently pure graphite and uranium.[20]

While the scientists wrestled with these problems, further new evidence continued to point to increasing German activity in the field of fission research. The Dutch-born chemist Peter Debye was forced to leave his position as Director of the Kaiser Wilhelm Institute for Physics in Berlin; upon his arrival in the United States, he reported that his former laboratory was being turned over to research on uranium. After Germany had occupied Norway, British intelligence units began to receive reports that the Germans had ordered the Norsk Hydro plant, the world's largest producer of heavy water, to increase its output sharply. The fact that heavy water is the most efficient moderator for a controlled nuclear chain reaction, combined with the fact that German scientists had publicly announced in 1939 that heavy water might become vitally important to Germany's war effort, pointed to German development of atomic energy for war purposes. This seemed to be confirmed by the fact that Germany, despite wartime stress, was continuing the operation of Joliot-Curie's cyclotron in occupied Paris.[21]

In spite of these ominous warnings of Hitler's intentions, the scientists found themselves increasingly frustrated in their attempts to stimulate active United States government concern for the exploration and development of atomic energy. Recalling the inertia and resistance to the theories of the scientists, Wigner later remarked, "We often felt as though we were swimming in syrup." [22] As late as September 1941, more than a year after the transfer of uranium work to the NDRC, James Conant, who headed the NDRC's division responsible for nuclear fission, felt that government support for nuclear research should be dropped until after the war. There was substantial agreement among the scientists that if a sufficient amount of uranium isotope 235 could be separated from its "twin," uranium 238, a fission explosion of enormous destructiveness would be possible — but no one could suggest a method that would be feasible for separating the two isotopes on a sufficiently large scale. Most of the uranium research thus far had been directed toward achievement of a controlled-fission chain reaction as a source of power, e.g., for driving ships. The consensus was that such a nuclear power source could be perfected, but only after many years of developmental engineering. Hence Conant had decided to urge that "the uranium project be put in wraps for the war period," and that the available scientific talent be used on projects that promised immediate wartime results.[23]

The tide of opinion both in government and among scientists turned in the latter part of 1941. One reason for the change was the receipt of a very optimistic report from "British" nuclear scientists (many of whom were Continental refugees from Hitler). Results of their research indicated that an atomic bomb could be made with much less uranium 235 than had hitherto been thought; it now seemed "quite probable that the atom bomb may be manufactured before the end of the war." [24]

A second reason was the discovery by Ernest O. Lawrence at the University of California Radiation Laboratory that in a pile made of ordinary uranium, the plentiful U-238 would be transformed by the chain reaction into the new element plutonium. Like U-235, plutonium would fission under neutron bombardment, emitting extra neutrons, and hence would be as suitable as U-235 for making an atomic bomb. Furthermore, the gathering of a sufficient amount of fissionable material for an atomic bomb would be much easier in the case of plutonium, since it could be separated from uranium by straightforward chemical means. It now appeared that uranium-238, which had hitherto been an obstacle to producing fissionable material, could now itself be converted into material for an atomic bomb; the uranium pile was no longer a detour, but a main road leading to the bomb.

These new developments were discussed in September 1941 by Lawrence, Conant, and Arthur H. Compton at a meeting that Compton describes as the real "start of the wartime atomic race."

> We in the United States then saw for the first time that exploration of the possibility of atomic bombs was a military necessity for the safety of the nation. It was then that American scientists began to throw themselves into this exploration with everything they had.[25]

A special committee of the National Academy of Sciences, under the chairmanship of Arthur H. Compton, was appointed to review the situation in the light of these new developments. And, in the fall of 1941, government officials at the highest level were for the first time brought together formally to advise the President on the future of the atomic energy project. This Top Policy Group included Vice-President Wallace, Secretary of War Stimson, Army Chief of Staff Marshall, and, inevitably, Conant and Bush. In November 1941 Compton's review committee submitted to the Top Policy Group a highly favorable report — the first report to the government focusing primarily on the possibility of a U-235 bomb — estimating that bombs could be made "within three or four years." At last, firm action was taken. On December 6, 1941, the day before Pearl Harbor, the crucial decision was approved by the President. The possibility of obtaining atomic bombs for use in the present war was deemed good enough to justify throwing the full support of the government, both financial and technical, behind the project, which should be reorganized for an all-out effort. If the atomic bomb could be made at all, the United States was now officially committed to making it first.[26]

It is significant to note that although the technical problems
with which atomic energy confronted scientists, both in England and America, were identical, the British had early focused
their whole uranium program upon the one end of producing
a specific weapon, the atomic bomb. The Americans did not
reach this position until November 1941 — more than a year
after the British, and two and a half years after Fermi's first
attempt to interest the United States government. Why the
delay? Apparently because for the scientists in Britain the war
was a present reality and Hitler an immediate threat separated
from them by only twenty miles of water. For their American
counterparts, on the other hand, the war was somewhat remote,
echoing only faintly within the walls of their laboratories.
While they were tremendously excited by the discovery of fission and the possibilities of releasing nuclear energy, they found
it difficult to concentrate their enthusiasm upon the construction of a weapon of war. The two groups of scientists — sharing
the same information, faced with the same technical problems,
and holding essentially the same moral ideals — differed in their
conclusions because of the differing historical situations within
which they were working. As it became more and more evident
that the United States would inevitably become actively involved in the war against totalitarianism, her scientists moved
closer to the position of the British scientists. Once America
was actually at war, the British and American atomic projects
were merged into a unified all-out effort to make the atomic
bomb.[27]

IV

We have seen that the imagination and enthusiasm of a small
group of nuclear physicists, centered about Enrico Fermi and
Leo Szilard, were the primary factors leading to the decision to
make an atomic bomb. These men did much more than simply give willing obedience to orders given them by the govern-

ment. Although outside the government, they repeatedly took the initiative in urging government officials to take the possibility of an atomic bomb seriously. Official skepticism, inertia, and the countless administrative and technical obstacles that blocked the road to the release of atomic energy were finally overcome almost entirely by their determination and persistence. They instituted a precedent-breaking system of censorship of their own research; they dragged many of their American colleagues out of the isolation of their private research into the campaign to produce a weapon of mass destruction.

What were the motives which lay beneath their sense of urgency? What moral claim did they feel which led them to drop their own research projects and give up the cherished scientific tradition of free exchange of ideas in the conviction that they were obeying the call of a higher duty?

Evidence is abundant that the primary force driving Szilard's group, and finally gaining the support of the American scientists and government, was the fear of Hitler's prior achievement of the atomic bomb. Even before the possibility of a nuclear chain reaction was confirmed, Szilard, in a letter to Joliot-Curie urging him to withhold publication of his research, justified his request by a thinly veiled reference to the extreme danger of fission bombs in the hands of "certain governments." Einstein's letters specifically mentioned Germany's activities. Arthur Compton reports that Wigner's "lively fear that the Nazis would make the bomb first" caused him to plead with Compton "almost with tears" to establish an active bomb project in the United States. What finally convinced Compton, Conant, and Lawrence of the urgency of our making the bomb was "the evidence that the Nazis were making a major effort" to do so. "We just could not afford to let the Nazis beat us to the making of atomic weapons. This would be inviting disaster." [28]

It was this same fear of Hitler that motivated the government's support of the atomic bomb project. President Roosevelt's initial understanding was that government action was necessary to make sure that "the Nazis don't blow us up." Secretary of War Stimson, who was "directly connected with all major decisions of policy on the development and use of atomic energy" during the war, describes the continuing motive behind government action thus:

> The policy adopted and steadily pursued by President Roosevelt and his advisers was a simple one. It was to spare no effort in securing the earliest possible successful development of an atomic weapon. The reasons for this policy were equally simple. The original experimental achievement of atomic fission had occurred in Germany in 1938, and it was known that the Germans had continued their experiments. In 1941 and 1942 they were believed to be ahead of us, and it was vital that they should not be the first to bring atomic weapons into the field of battle.[29]

The scientists' sense of urgency did not grow out of the positive desire to obtain nuclear weapons, or a thirst for military power. On the contrary, it grew out of fear of what might happen to the civilized world if Hitler were the first to achieve such weapons. These men had experienced Hitler and his devices at first hand, and had become refugees rather than submit to him. They were convinced that the German leader had no scruples whatsoever, and would not hesitate to use an atomic bomb in his quest for world domination. It was to prevent the nightmarish possibility that Hitler might at some point in the future have a monopoly of atomic bombs that these scientists undertook their campaign. Many indeed hoped against hope that in the course of their investigations they would stumble upon a wrinkle of nature that would make a chain reaction, and hence a nuclear explosion, inherently impossible, both for Hitler and for them. However, they could not rest comfortably in the *mere hope* that an atomic bomb would prove to be impossible. They had to push forward with their experiments either until it was proved to be impossible, or until they had created the bomb themselves. "If such a weapon is going to be made, we must do it first. We can't afford not to." [30]

Was it victory and glory for their nation which motivated the scientists? In large part the answer must be no. In the days when the crucial decision was being made, the initiative was not being taken by Americans on behalf of their own country (which was not yet at war); the initiative was taken by scientists who had only recently come to this country. Their motives were hardly "patriotic" or nationalistic, although they were grateful for the hospitality and freedom of the land that welcomed them. They cherished the broader values of Western civilization, which Europe and America shared but fascism was threatening to destroy. Professionally they prized the scientific endeavor itself, freedom of inquiry, free publication and exchange of ideas, uninhibited search after the truth no matter what its implications might be. These had been subverted by Hitler's attack on "Jewish physics" and his attempt to promote in its place "German physics." The scientists were further appalled at Hitler's anti-Semitism (some had tasted persecution personally) and by his totalitarian invasion of personal privacy and freedom. While they were acutely aware of their burden of responsibility in trying to create a weapon capable of killing thousands of persons, they felt constrained to do so in order to protect the best achievements of Western civilization.

They were under no illusions that their course was perfectly righteous; it was the choice of a lesser evil. Nevertheless, the *relative* goodness of this alternative was so clear to them that they undertook their task with a sense of high calling. To it they devoted their fullest energies — often with dislocation to their private lives and at sacrifice of time from other projects more personally satisfying to them — in order to prevent a great evil from enveloping the world and obliterating all they held dear.

3. Germany's Quest for the Atomic Bomb

WHEN THE DECISION was made in December 1941 to put the United States' atomic bomb project on an all-out basis, it was with the understanding that the Germans had initiated their major uranium effort at least two years earlier. "The Germans have a big head start, and we must come from behind in order to prevent a catastrophic victory by Hitler"; this thought provided a constant sense of urgency to the whole atomic energy project. Indeed the assumption of German proficiency turned our every success into a spur to increased effort: if we have been able to progress this far, how much further must the Germans have gone! [1]

In December 1942 a rumor spread among the atomic scientists in Chicago that Hitler might attempt to bomb Chicago, the center of United States atomic research, on Christmas Day — and that the attack would be with radioactive dust which would poison the city's air and water. So real seemed the threat that certain physicists evacuated their families to the countryside.[2]

Leaders like Compton felt that Germany might well be able to produce enough plutonium by the end of 1943 to make bombs, which would mean the devastation of London and a turn of the military tide in Germany's favor. "So acute was our concern about the Germans' progress that when the Allies landed on the Normandy beaches on 6 June 1944, certain of the American officers were equipped with Geiger counters," in the fear that the Germans might possess large quantities of radioactive materials for use as a very effective poison gas against our troops.[3]

With the Allied invaders of Europe was a special scientific-military intelligence unit called Alsos, which was charged with the urgent task of discovering how close the Germans were to the atomic bomb. As the armies swept across Europe, Alsos members followed close behind the front-line troops, and in fact sometimes preceded them, capturing documents, laboratory samples, Rhine River water, scientists — anything that might indicate the location of the German atomic energy laboratories and the extent of their progress.[4]

Results were inconclusive until Strasbourg was captured in November 1944. Here, in an office of the Physics Institute of the University, Alsos investigators found documents left behind by Dr. C. F. von Weizsacker, a leader in the German atomic energy program. Samuel Goudsmit, chief scientific officer of Alsos, sitting far into the night poring over Weizsacker's papers by candlelight, suddenly gave a shout. He had found a whole bundle of papers dealing with uranium research. These documents provided conclusive evidence that the German atomic research project was not ahead of the American but, rather, was far behind. Germany "had no atom bomb and was not likely to have one in any reasonable time." The Germans had been unsuccessful in their attempts to separate U-235; neither had they succeeded in constructing a chain-reacting uranium pile. By mid-1944 they had reached about the point where the Americans had stood in 1940!

As the armies invaded Germany, Alsos units captured laboratories and interrogated scientists; all that they learned merely confirmed the conclusion indicated by Weizsacker's papers. Germany had never been within striking distance of an atomic bomb.[5]

II

What were the causes of Germany's lack of progress in nuclear energy? The primary factor was economic: Germany could not, under wartime conditions, make the tremendous investment in large-scale industrial plants necessary to produce substantial amounts of fissionable material. Professor Werner Heisenberg, the key physicist in the German uranium project, explained after the war that Germany had made no attempt to produce an atomic bomb because such a large project "could not have succeeded under German war conditions. . . . In 1942, German industry was already stretched to the limit . . ." (This was before Allied bombing had had any significant effect upon the German economy.) Even had the limitations imposed upon the economy by the war been absent, German scientists estimated that the purely technical problems were of such magnitude that a bomb could not be produced in time to be of use in the present war. Weizsacker and Heisenberg later justified this estimate by pointing out that the European war ended before the Americans, working under the most favorable conditions, had been able to construct a bomb.[6]

The decisive turning point in the German atomic program came in June 1942, when Professor Heisenberg submitted a progress report on atomic energy research to Albert Speer, Hitler's Minister of Supply. Speer decided that construction of an atomic bomb was too remote a possibility and should be dropped as a wartime project. He directed that work on construction of a uranium pile for energy purposes should go forward with a high priority, but on a limited scale.[7] Even work in this restricted area was hampered by Allied sabotage and bombing attacks, which seriously curtailed heavy-water production at the Norsk Hydro plant and interrupted production of uranium metal for the pile.[8] By the end of the war the German scientists had not yet achieved a self-sustaining chain reaction — a feat achieved by Fermi and his associates in December 1942.

German scientists were fully aware that a bomb could be constructed if adequate amounts of U-235 could be separated; their recognition of the impracticality of attempting to separate

U-235 was a recognition of the limitations of their economy in wartime. But there was a *scientific* failure in addition to the economic one. As a result of research paralleling that of Lawrence at the University of California, Fritz Houtermans had concluded as early as 1941 that a new metal heavier than uranium (plutonium) could be produced in a pile, that it probably would have the same explosive properties as U-235, and that it could be easily separated by chemical means. And so German physics had achieved the theoretical knowledge that plutonium could be produced in a pile; but the scientists actively working on the German uranium project never really grasped the basic idea that a chain-reacting pile could be used to produce plutonium as *material* for an atomic bomb. The idea persisted that the bomb would consist of a *pile itself* in which the fission chain reaction went so fast as to be out of control.[9]

Several other factors contributed to the lag in German atomic research. Early in the war Hitler apparently believed that Germany could win using the presently existing types of weapons. Later he encouraged development of new weapons but forbade major effort on scientific research projects that did not promise to result in usable weapons within a few months. Both decisions worked against uranium research.[10]   The German scientists shared with their American counterparts the assumption of German scientific superiority; as a result the German program lacked a sense of urgency. In America this assumption produced fear, which stimulated concerted and imaginative effort; in Germany it produced overconfidence (if we, the leaders in science, have not been able to produce an atomic bomb, how could the Americans be expected to do so?). Weizsacker admitted after the war, "We had such a precise knowledge of the difficulties inherent in the production of an atom bomb and considered them so formidable that it had never occurred to us that America would be in a position to produce atom bombs during the war." [11]

Hitler's Nazi ideology worked against German success in

atomic research in several ways. It drove out of Germany during the 1930's the very scientists who were responsible for creating the bomb for the United States during the 1940's. Although there were several first-rate scientists left in Germany, Alsos found that their effectiveness was diminished by the Nazi policy of putting into key research positions men who were first-rate Nazis but second-rate physicists.[12]   Finally, it is known that certain leading scientists still in Germany were personally opposed to Hitler and all that he stood for, and reportedly felt that it would be a crime against humanity to present to Hitler a weapon as dangerous as the atomic bomb.[13] Whether such conscientious opposition to Nazism produced an actual conspiracy to delay atomic research in order to keep the bomb away from Hitler (as has been suggested by some)[14] or simply a lack of enthusiasm, the contrast with the united and enthusiastic American effort is striking. Whether German scientists, faced with an explicit command to produce an atomic bomb for Hitler, would have refused on conscientious and humanitarian grounds cannot now be determined. In effect the wartime economic situation took the choice out of their hands before the bomb was a live possibility; ". . . German physicists were spared the last, hard decision." [15]

III

The crowning irony of the German atomic energy program is that it was initiated in 1939 in the belief — in the fear — that the Americans were already active in atomic research and that the Germans must take the initiative to stay ahead. Professor Heisenberg wrote after the war:

Almost simultaneously with the outbreak of the war, news reached Germany that funds were being allocated by the American Military authorities for research on atomic energy. In view of the possibility that England and the United States

might undertake the development of atomic weapons, the
Heereswaffenamt created a special research group . . . whose
task it was to examine the possibilities of the technical exploi-
tation of atomic energy.[16]

If Heisenberg's statement is an accurate account, it would appear that the Germans began their program on the basis of
mistaken information. The meeting at the Heereswaffenamt
(Army Weapons Department) which organized the German
uranium project was held on September 26, 1939,[17] two weeks
before Alexander Sachs brought Einstein's letter to the attention of President Roosevelt. It was November 1 before the
Advisory Committee on Uranium recommended to President
Roosevelt that expanded uranium research was "worthy of direct financial support by the Government." The first transfer
of funds did not take place until February 1940, by which time
German research was being intensified under military auspices.[18]

The Germans, in their early attempt to stay ahead of the
feeble American program, which they overestimated, established a research project that the Americans in turn overestimated. The end result was to stimulate the Americans to
such efforts that they accomplished the very feat the Germans
were sure no one could accomplish. Without the Americans'
fear that the Germans were ahead of them in the race for an
atomic bomb, it is very doubtful that the bomb would have
been produced during World War II. Thus ignorance and miscalculation, as well as prophetic vision, scientific genius, and
brilliant research, played important roles in the decision to
make the atomic bomb.

4. The Impact of Events upon Ethics

THE NUCLEAR SCIENTISTS brought with them, as they approached the uranium problem, certain unquestioned moral
principles. These commonly shared axioms were quite as much
a part of the ethos of the scientific profession as the experimental method. One of these was the principle that scientists
publish the results of their research freely and fully, without
regard for financial profit or national boundaries. The growth
of science and the pushing back of the frontiers of knowledge
depend upon the cross-fertilization resulting from the unfettered
exchange of ideas. An incident in the life of Madame Curie
illustrates the principle to which all who call themselves
scientists would adhere. When the therapeutic effects of radium
became known, the Curies received letters from American manu-
facturers requesting detailed directions for treating pitchblende
for the obtaining of radium. Pierre discussed the possibilities
with his wife:

> "Well, then, we have a choice between two solutions. We
> can describe the results of our research without reserve, includ-
> ing the processes of purification . . ."
> Marie made a mechanical gesture of approval and mur-
> mured:
> "Yes, naturally."
> "Or else," Pierre went on, "we can consider ourselves to be
> the proprietors, the 'inventors' of radium. In this case it would
> be necessary, before publishing exactly how you worked to
> treat pitchblende, to patent the technique and assure ourselves
> in this way of rights over the manufacture of radium through-
> out the world."

* *

Marie reflected a few seconds. Then she said:

"It is impossible. It would be contrary to the scientific spirit. . . . Physicists always publish their researches completely. If our discovery has a commercial future, that is an accident by which we must not profit. And radium is going to be of use in treating disease . . . It seems to me impossible to take advantage of that." [1]

A second principle assumed by the scientists was that the results of scientific investigation should be used to benefit mankind, not to destroy. The best scientists are often not consciously interested in the practical applications of their "pure research," but devote themselves to their work out of sheer curiosity about the way nature works, or a passionate desire to uncover the orderly laws of the universe. Nevertheless, their implicit assumption is that knowledge of the world is good, and that discovery of the truth will benefit — not harm — their fellow men. A corollary of this assumption is that to use the results of science with the specific intent of harming or destroying persons is a perversion of the scientific spirit itself. A statement of Lise Meitner, made with specific reference to the atomic bomb, states the general principle with which most of her colleagues would heartily agree: "The scientist is ever awe-struck at the discovery of the laws of nature, and to use these laws for construction of weapons which might lead to the annihilation of mankind, must seem blasphemy to him." [2] When in 1940 Arthur Compton asked a young physicist, Dr. Volney Wilson, to prepare a report on whether a chain reaction could be produced using ordinary uranium, Wilson worked intensely for two months and finally submitted a favorable report. In handing his report to Compton he used words that reveal the natural and instinctive moral sense of the scientists during the 1930's: "I believe it can be done, and if so it will be of great importance. But please take me off this job. It is going to be too terribly destructive. I don't want to have anything to do with it." [3]

Such were the moral principles held almost universally by scientists in 1938; yet by 1942 nuclear scientists in America had imposed secrecy upon themselves and their research, and were deeply involved in a full-scale attempt to produce the most destructive and indiscriminate weapon in the history of man. In the presence of the great moral evil represented by aggressive Nazism, the scientists could not hold their moral principles inviolate. They did not abandon their convictions; yet they found that their original ideas about right and wrong were being refracted under the pressure of historical events.

Free publication of research was not given up easily or thoughtlessly. Many Americans less keenly aware than Szilard of the threat posed by Hitler, resisted early attempts to impose restrictions on their right to publish. Fermi, who had just come to America in search of freedom, was in no mood to submit to censorship. In 1940, when all agreed that there must be some sort of restriction in order not to aid the Germans in presenting Hitler with an atomic bomb, the right of censorship was not abjectly surrendered into the hands of military authorities; research scientists voluntarily submitted their papers to the judgment of a board chosen from among their own colleagues.[4]

Neither did the scientists abandon the idea that science ought to serve the welfare of mankind. This very principle, which in normal times would make voluntary development of an instrument of mass destruction reprehensible, was still being followed: in the new historical situation scientists were forced to the view that the benefit of mankind could best be served by taking action — even the construction of an atomic bomb — that would prevent Hitler's achievement of a monopoly of atomic weapons. The scientists did not give themselves up with abandon to the goal of making a bomb *in order to* kill thousands of persons; their avowed purpose was precisely to *prevent* the use of the bomb.

Despite the caution and restraint with which the scientists accommodated their cherished moral principles in response to what appeared to them to be the threat of terrible evil, their action resulted in the establishment of social institutions that developed a power of their own, overwhelmed the conscientious concerns of the scientists, and went much further than they themselves desired. After the end of the war the scientists found themselves fighting a defensive battle against overstringent military security measures and loyalty oaths which threatened to stifle free scientific inquiry and publication.

Moreover, those who had started down the twisting trail of uranium research with the avowed intent of preventing use of the atomic bomb by an unscrupulous dictator began to realize that they had become part of a huge and complex organization directed by men who thought of the (prospective) atomic bomb merely as a bigger and better bomb, "as legitimate as any other of the deadly explosive weapons of modern war." [5] The transformation that took place as a small group of prophetic scientists were incorporated into a massive military organization* is nicely illustrated by a casual conversation that took place shortly after the capture of Weizsacker's papers at Strasbourg. As the full significance of this discovery dawned upon him, Professor Goudsmit remarked to one of his Army colleagues, "Isn't it wonderful that the Germans have no atom bomb? Now we won't have to use ours." Goudsmit was startled by the officer's reply: "Of course you understand, Sam, if we have such a weapon, we are going to use it." [7] The sub-

* From 1939 until mid-1942 government oversight of the uranium project was in civilian hands, successively under the Advisory Committee on Uranium, the National Defense Research Committee, and the Office of Scientific Research and Development. In August 1942 the Manhattan District was created within the Corps of Engineers, to be responsible for all Army activities in the atomic energy field; through April 1943 joint control of the project was exercised by OSRD and the Army. Thereafter the Army, in the person of General Leslie R. Groves, commander of the Manhattan District, was in complete charge of the atomic bomb program. [6]

sequent events proving the accuracy of this remark troubled many scientists. Their departure from the traditional moral principles of science, begun under the threat of danger that turned out to be only a phantom, led eventually to vast destruction of human life — including women and children — which they found difficult to square with their consciences. Albert Einstein spoke for many when he said with deep regret: "If I had known that the Germans would not succeed in constructing the atom bomb, I would never have lifted a finger." [8]

II

The Decision to Drop
the Atomic Bomb

1945

5. The Scientists Think Ahead

THE DREAMS, the calculations, the labors of the scientists bore fruit. The entire atomic energy project was vastly enlarged and reorganized as the Manhattan District within the Army Corps of Engineers. Huge industrial plants were built at Oak Ridge, Tennessee, and Hanford, Washington, to produce U-235 and plutonium; a top-secret laboratory was established on an isolated New Mexico plateau to design and build the bomb itself. On July 16, 1945, the first atomic bomb was successfully tested. Three weeks later an atomic bomb was dropped on Hiroshima; after an interval of two days another fell on Nagasaki. More than 100,000 men, women, and children were killed by the bombs, and as many more were injured.* Within a week Japan surrendered, and the war came to an end.

The dropping of the atomic bomb upon Japan was an action of the American people, yet the American people did not know anything about this act of theirs until after it had transpired. The vast majority even of those whose labor produced the bombs literally did not know what they were making, or how the product of their efforts would be used. Who, then, did make the decision that led to this action? What considera-

---

* The number of casualties at Hiroshima and Nagasaki will never be known precisely. For Hiroshima the Japanese authorities originally listed 71,379 dead and missing, 68,023 injured; the United States Strategic Bombing Survey estimated between 70,000 and 80,000 dead, and an equal number wounded. A Japanese official notice stated in 1959 that the total number of deaths caused by the atomic bombing of Hiroshima was 60,175. For Nagasaki, Japanese authorities listed 25,680 dead and missing (verified cases only); USSBS rejected this figure as too low, and estimated a minimum of 40,000 killed and missing, and 60,000 injured. For the purposes of this study the figures will be taken to be 70,000 killed at Hiroshima, 40,000 at Nagasaki, and an equal number of injured.[1]

tions — technical, military, moral — molded the decision into the form it finally took? What were the conflicting obligations, the limitations upon action, and the opportunities for creative action that faced those who made the decision? Within what larger frame of reference did they interpret the alternatives before them?

The answers to such questions are to be found in the story related in this chapter and the four that follow it. Although our ultimate concern in this book is an ethical one, we may not indulge in ethics before dealing seriously with history. We may not take refuge in some impregnable ethical position from which we can pronounce at the outset a moral judgment upon the decision that led to Hiroshima. Rather, we must confront the actual event in all its complexity and depth of concrete detail, seeking to understand the decision and its context as fully, accurately, and impartially as the available evidence will permit. What is presented in these chapters, therefore, is in a real sense history. Yet our purpose is not to present a purely objective history of the decision — if such a thing were possible — merely recounting the interesting details for their own sake. All history involves selection and interpretation, and our purpose here is so to describe and interpret the events (with respect for their complexity and uniqueness) as to reveal the influence of moral principles and claims in the making of a crucial decision.

In order not to complicate unduly an already inherently complex story, comments on the ethical implications of various events will be kept to a minimum in this review of the deliberations and actions that led to the dropping of the atomic bomb. The chapters in Part III attack the ethical question head-on; many of the story's details will then be seen to have important ethical ramifications.

Our account begins with the searchings and questionings of the scientists as they saw that their efforts were soon to be crowned with success; it continues with the deliberations of

government officials charged with the responsibility of ending
the war quickly and victoriously; it concludes with the rush of
events springing from the decision to use the bomb and resulting in the surrender of Japan.

II

We have seen that America's atomic bomb program was
launched by a group of scientists whose opposition to Hitler
provided them with a strong sense of urgency, a clarity as to
what they must do, and the moral conviction that their action
was demanded by the call of duty. As the hour of their success
approached, their clarity and their unanimity melted away. The
scientists found themselves perplexed by the imponderable implications of atomic energy for postwar international relations,
and divided on the specific issue of whether and how to use the
new weapon against the enemy.

During the first years of the atomic energy project little
thought was given to the questions of the use and ethical
significance of the sought-after bomb. No one could predict the
circumstances that would prevail when the bomb was ready for
use. Furthermore, all thought and energy had to be concentrated upon getting the program organized, and upon the difficult technical problems of producing fissionable material and
constructing a bomb that would work.

The amount of thought given to the moral aspects of the
atomic bomb apparently varied inversely with the intensity and
difficulty of the scientists' work. Hans Bethe later described
the situation at the Los Alamos Scientific Laboratory, where
work intensity increased steadily and reached its peak in the
weeks leading up to the testing of the bomb:

> I am unhappy to admit that during the war — at least — I
> did not pay much attention to this [i.e., the "moral or humane"
> problems of the atomic bomb]. We had a job to do and a very
> hard one. The first thing we wanted to do was to get the job

done. . . . Only when our labors were finally completed when the bomb dropped on Japan, only then or a little bit before then, maybe, did we start thinking about the moral implications.[2]

The situation was different at the Metallurgical Laboratory in Chicago. Although the engineering problems involved in producing plutonium were at their most difficult stage in mid-1944, the basic theoretical difficulties had by then been overcome. Thereafter scientists who had been concentrating on these began to think more seriously about the significance and future of atomic energy. One scientist recalls:

It was then still too early to foresee the outcome of the atomic race with Germany. . . . Everyone took for granted that the new bombs would be used in Europe if they were ready in time. We were concerned rather with postwar developments. What should be done to make sure that the possibilities of atomic weapons in the hand of a future Napoleon or Hitler would not bring world disaster? How could the usefulness of atomic energy in industry and medicine best be developed? What steps should be taken to insure its full application to the advance of science? [3]

At first these questions were discussed informally among the scientists. One result of this questioning was an August 1944 visit to President Roosevelt by Niels Bohr, the beloved "father of nuclear physics," who had been smuggled out of occupied Denmark in a fishing boat in 1943. Bohr, who foresaw the possibility of a postwar breakdown of harmony between Russia and the West, suggested to F.D.R. that a dangerous nuclear arms race might be avoided if the United States, even before reaching the atomic bomb, would share her atomic secrets with the Soviets. Such action, Bohr felt, would allay suspicion and lay a sure foundation for trust and cooperation in the postwar development of atomic energy.[4]

Later in 1944 Dr. Arthur Compton, head of the atomic bomb

work in Chicago, appointed a committee, headed by Dr. Zay Jeffries, to look more thoroughly into the question of the future of atomic energy. The committee's report, entitled "Prospectus on Nucleonics" and submitted November 18, 1944, surveyed the future development of atomic energy and made suggestions that prefigured much of the postwar debate. The Jeffries Report observed that a central international authority would be needed to control the use of nuclear power, and that until such an authority could be set up, the United States could have only the fragile hope that fear of atomic retaliation by us would act as a deterrent against attack from without. The report urged "the necessity for all nations to make every effort to cooperate now in setting up an international administration with police powers which can effectively control at least the means of nucleonic warfare." [5]

Later that year General Leslie R. Groves, head of the Manhattan project, appointed an official committee to look into the future possibilities of atomic energy in a more systematic way. This committee, under the chairmanship of Dr. R. C. Tolman, received a multitude of suggestions from the men on the various atomic projects. Their report, completed on December 28, 1944, dealt not only with the future military development of the bomb but also with the peaceful uses of atomic energy, such as the development of nuclear power and the use of radioactive by-products for scientific, medical, and industrial purposes. [6]

By March 1945 the informal discussions at Chicago had evolved into regularly scheduled seminars in which the scientists debated the necessity of international control of atomic energy following the war. In the same month, Leo Szilard drew up a memorandum in which he discussed the relations between Russia and the United States in the light of atomic energy. Szilard tried to present his memorandum directly to President Roosevelt, but was thwarted by the President's death. He then tried to see President Truman, but was referred to James F. Byrnes, to whom he finally managed to talk on May 28, three days before Mr. Byrnes and other top officials met in Washington to make a crucial decision about the future of atomic energy. Dr. Szilard's memorandum stressed the urgency of avoiding a nuclear arms race against Russia, and the rush toward preventive war which might result. Although Szilard's general demeanor and desire to influence the making of policy made an "unfavorable impression" upon Byrnes, he agreed to give serious consideration to the issues raised by the scientist. However, Byrnes soon discovered that there was no unanimity among the "experts." As he heard other scientists express viewpoints differing from Szilard's, he is said to have remarked, "In this age it appears every man must have his own physicist." [7]

Dr. James Franck, widely respected and beloved among the scientists, also drew up a memorandum dealing with the postwar controls of atomic energy, which he discussed at some length with Vice-President Henry A. Wallace in April.[8]

III

Up to this point the scientists had been concerned with the *postwar* problems of development and control of atomic energy — not with the question of the use of the atomic bomb in World War II. It was still assumed that it was necessary to beat Hitler to the bomb, and that our bomb would be used against Hitler once we had it. The ethical problems involved in dropping an atomic bomb in war had not seriously been considered at this stage.

Now, in the spring of 1945, three developments converged to shift the focus of the scientists' attention to the immediate problem of wartime use of the new weapon. In the first place, the bomb was nearing completion. Whereas until now the path to the atomic bomb had been strewn with many obstacles, any one of which might have meant the failure of the entire project, all the major hurdles had now been passed, and success appeared certain within a few months. The question shifted, therefore, from whether we would have a bomb, to whether and how we ought to use the one we would almost certainly have.

In the second place, as the completion of the bomb became more certain, our use of it against Hitler became more doubtful. The German war machine began to disintegrate, and early in May the war in Europe ended. The nuclear race against Hitler had been won; yet Hitler had been defeated without the use of the bomb. Now the premise upon which the whole project had been based was done away with, and new questions suddenly loomed up.

> In the early days, when success was less certain and timing unsure, and the war with Germany and Japan in a desperate phase, it was enough for us to think that we had a job to do. Now, with Germany defeated, the war in the Pacific approaching a crisis, and the success of our undertaking almost assured, there was a sense both of hope and of anxiety as to what this spectacular development might portend for the future.[9]

Finally, rumors began to circulate about the formation in Washington of a top-level committee to decide how the yet-to-be-tested bomb should be used in the war against Japan. The scientists realized that if their opinions were to be of any influence in the formation of policy, they would have to gather their thoughts and state them effectively.[10]

6. "Shall We Drop the Bomb?"

THE RUMORS reaching the laboratories were correct: a committee was being organized to advise the Secretary of War and the President on the long-range development of atomic energy, and to make specific recommendations on the use of the bomb against Japan.

The need for formation of policy with regard to the atomic bomb was brought to the attention of President Roosevelt by Secretary of War Stimson. On March 15, 1945, Henry L. Stimson reported to the President that recent progress insured the completion of the bomb within a few months, and told him "how important it was to get ready." He described the various views about control of atomic energy and urged that our policy be worked out before the weapon was used. Roosevelt agreed.[1]

This proved to be Stimson's last meeting with the President. Whatever thoughts Roosevelt had on the subject of the atomic bomb apparently died with him. The problem passed into the hands of a new President.

Harry S. Truman was sworn in at the White House on the evening of April 12; immediately following the ceremony he called a Cabinet meeting. Mr. Truman said that he would try to continue the policies, both domestic and foreign, of Mr. Roosevelt's administration. He asked that the Cabinet members stay in their present posts, although he himself, as the new President, would have to assume final responsibility for whatever major decisions had to be made.

The meeting was brief, and in a few minutes the Cabinet filed solemnly from the room; but one man, the oldest of them all, lingered behind. Mr. Stimson said there was something he wished to tell the President without delay. Mr. Truman describes the occasion:

That first meeting of the Cabinet was short, and when it adjourned, the members rose and silently made their way from the room — except for Secretary Stimson.

He asked to speak to me about a most urgent matter. Stimson told me that he wanted me to know about an immense project that was under way — a project looking to the development of a new explosive of almost unbelievable destructive power. That was all he felt free to say at the time, and his statement left me puzzled. It was the first bit of information that had come to me about the atomic bomb, but he gave me no details. It was not until the next day that I was told enough to give me some understanding of the almost incredible developments that were under way and the awful power that might soon be placed in our hands.[2]

It was James F. Byrnes, recently retired from Roosevelt's Office of War Mobilization, and soon to become Truman's Secretary of State, who the next day gave Mr. Truman a little more knowledge about the atomic bomb project. Although the topic was only touched upon briefly, Mr. Byrnes did tell Mr. Truman "with great solemnity" that "we were perfecting an explosive great enough to destroy the whole world." Mr. Byrnes pointed out that this new weapon might vastly strengthen the bargaining position of the United States at the end of the war.[3]

The new President's first days in office were filled with matters of great urgency, including the coming United Nations Conference in San Francisco and the problems the Allies were having with the Russians. He had little opportunity to follow up Mr. Stimson's "urgent matter," but on April 24 Mr. Truman received a reminder from Mr. Stimson:

Dear Mr. President, I think it very important that I should have a talk with you as soon as possible on a highly secret matter. I mentioned it to you shortly after you took office but have not urged it since on account of the pressures you have been under. It, however, has such a bearing on our present Foreign Relations and has such an effect upon all my thinking in this field, that I think you ought to know about it without much further delay.[4]

Mr. Truman arranged to see the Secretary the next day, when Mr. Stimson presented to the President a memorandum dealing with the problems of atomic energy in considerable detail. It said in part:

1. Within four months we shall in all probability have completed the most terrible weapon ever known in human history, one bomb of which could destroy a whole city.
2. Although we have shared its development with the U.K., physically the U.S. is at present in the position of controlling the resources with which to construct and use it and no other nation could reach this position for some years.
3. Nevertheless it is practically certain that we could not remain in this position indefinitely. . . .
4. As a result, it is indicated that the future may see a time when such a weapon may be constructed in secret and used suddenly and effectively with devastating power by a willful nation or group against an unsuspecting nation or group of much greater size and material power. With its aid even a very powerful unsuspecting nation might be conquered within a very few days by a very much smaller one. . . .
5. The world in its present state of moral advancement compared with its technical development would be eventually at the mercy of such a weapon. In other words, modern civilization might be completely destroyed.

The Secretary's memorandum dealt not so much with the immediate military use of the impending weapon as with its long-range political implications. Mr. Stimson raised the question of the control of this new power by international organization, and the question of whether the secret of this new weapon should be shared with other nations. He was acutely aware that "the development of this weapon has placed a certain moral responsibility upon us which we cannot shirk without very serious responsibility for any disaster to civilization which it would further." On the other hand he saw "the opportunity to bring the world into a pattern in which the peace of the world and our civilization can be saved." [5]

Mr. Stimson urged the President to appoint a committee of leading citizens to consider these and other pressing problems which the development of atomic energy was raising. The President agreed, and appointed a highly secret group known as the Interim Committee. Mr. Stimson was its chairman, and Mr. Byrnes acted as the President's personal representative. Mr. George L. Harrison, President of the New York Life Insurance Company, who was a special consultant to Secretary Stimson, served as chairman in Stimson's absence. The other members of the committee were Ralph Bard, Under-Secretary of the Navy; William L. Clayton, Assistant Secretary of State; Vannevar Bush, Director of the Office of Scientific Research and Development; Karl T. Compton, President of the Massachusetts Institute of Technology; and James B. Conant, President of Harvard. Assisting this committee was a Scientific Panel whose members were Enrico Fermi, Ernest O. Lawrence, J. Robert Oppenheimer, and Arthur H. Compton — all of whom had been actively engaged in the development of the atomic weapon. A panel of industrialists was also appointed to inform the Interim Committee on the engineering and manufacturing aspects of the atomic bomb project.

The Interim Committee's assignment was to advise the President regarding the various questions raised about the conduct of the war by the imminent readiness of an atomic bomb, and also to suggest plans for the longer-term development and control of atomic energy. As part of its work, the committee drafted the statements that were published by the President and

the Secretary of War immediately following the first use of the
bomb at Hiroshima, and prepared a bill for Congress concerning postwar domestic control of atomic energy.[6]

II

The Interim Committee held its first meeting on May 9, 1945.
Secretary Stimson reviewed the "basic facts" of the nature and
progress of the atomic bomb program; General Leslie R.
Groves, head of the Manhattan project, supplied further details. The committee's discussion ranged in a general way "over
the whole subject" of atomic energy and the issues it raised.[7]

Three weeks later the Interim Committee gathered for two
days on May 31 and June 1, and plunged into the crucial
question of the military use of the atomic bomb: should it be
used in the war against Japan, and if so, how? In addition to
the Scientific Panel, General Groves and Army Chief of Staff
George Marshall were present for the opening session. Mr.
Stimson began with an impressive statement:

> Gentlemen, it is our responsibility to recommend action that
> may turn the course of civilization. In our hands we expect
> soon to have a weapon of wholly unprecedented destructive
> power. Today's prime fact is war. Our great task is to bring
> this war to a prompt and successful conclusion. We may as-
> sume that our new weapon puts in our hands overwhelming
> power. It is our obligation to use this power with the best
> wisdom we can command. To us now the matter of first im-
> portance is how our use of this new weapon will appear in the
> long view of history.[8]

The committee had many questions to ask its Scientific
Panel. The answers by Dr. Oppenheimer indicated the revolutionary nature of the new weapon. The bomb, although small
enough to be delivered by a B-29 airplane, would explode with
a blast equivalent to about 10,000 tons of TNT, or hundreds

of blockbusters. Blast damage would be maximized if the bomb were exploded in the air above the target; this could be accomplished by using the new proximity fuse. The overwhelming power of the bomb would be most clearly demonstrated upon a target consisting of a large concentration of buildings of varying types of construction. The blast would destroy buildings within a half-mile radius; the intense heat of the explosion would start many fires. Dr. Oppenheimer estimated that if the bomb were exploded over a city, about 20,000 persons would be killed; flash burns and radiation from the explosion would injure many survivors.*

Mr. Stimson responded as one who had visited Japan and thought of it not as an abstract military target but as a land of living people. He pointed out that although the city of Kyoto, lying in the form of a cup surrounded by hills, would on purely technical grounds make an ideal target, it would have to be rejected by him as a target for the atomic bomb because of the city's religious, artistic, and historical treasures. The objective of using the bomb was to be military damage rather than civilian lives.[10]

The committee had other questions: when would the bomb be ready, and how certain was it that it would really work as predicted? Oppenheimer reported that the first bomb would be ready to test in about seven weeks. Although no one could guarantee that "the thing would go off," the scientists had every hope that the bomb would work. The critical problem was one of timing: the principle of the new bomb was to bring

---

* The scientists' best predictions as of May 1945 proved to be low. Actually, the first atomic bombs exploded with a force equivalent to 20,000 tons of TNT, and the resulting deaths totaled about 70,000 at Hiroshima and 40,000 at Nagasaki. Considering the unknowns being pondered, to underestimate the blast by a factor of 2 constituted only a small error. The prediction of casualties was thrown further off by the fact that Oppenheimer, who had based his estimate upon casualty rates for bombing raids with conventional explosives, assumed that Japanese cities would have effective air-raid warning systems, and that people would have taken shelter before the bomb exploded. This assumption proved to be erroneous.[9]

together two subcritical pieces of fissionable material to form a supercritical mass; but this had to be done extremely rapidly, since the chain reaction, once it began, would be completed in a matter of some thousandths of a second. If the chain reaction progressed too far before the two pieces could become fully united, the heat might vaporize the whole bomb before a substantial amount of the uranium actually fissioned — and produce a "fizzle." [11] As one physicist put it, "It might be a mess. It might be a disaster. But it still would not be a bomb." Nevertheless, the scientists were confident that the problem had been overcome and that the test would be successful. One or two additional bombs would be ready for use shortly after the test; thereafter subsequent bombs would follow at the rate of one every few weeks.[12]

General Marshall suggested that, other things being equal, the United States might be in a stronger military position after the war if it did not use the bomb against Japan, but rather kept its existence secret. Thus other nations, not knowing of its existence, would not be stimulated to join an atomic armaments race to produce their own bombs. In this way the superiority of American military power would be guaranteed for some years in advance. This raised the question of whether it was possible to keep the bomb a secret. The scientists present were unanimous in the opinion that the general outlines of the new atomic science were already widely known throughout the world, and would become common knowledge after the war. The crucial secrets of the atomic bomb project were engineering techniques rather than basic scientific knowledge. These secrets would certainly give the United States an initial advantage over other nations — but one that could be maintained only for a limited number of years.[13]

Although many different positions and proposals were brought forth during the Interim Committee's discussion, at least for the sake of argument, it was Arthur Compton's impression that "throughout the morning's discussions it seemed to be a foregone conclusion that the bomb would be used. It was regarding only the details of strategy and tactics that differing views were expressed." [14]

When the committee recessed for luncheon following its morning session, Dr. Compton found himself seated next to Secretary Stimson. In the course of conversation Compton raised with the Secretary a question that several of the Chicago scientists had recently been discussing: might it not be possible to arrange for a nonmilitary demonstration of the bomb in such a manner that the Japanese would be so impressed that they would be clearly convinced of the futility of continuing the war? Could not the bomb be announced and then exploded over a deserted portion of Japanese territory, and the Japanese be warned to surrender before the bomb was dropped on their cities and military installations? Mr. Stimson asked that the general conversation at the table be stopped, and he posed this question to the whole group for its consideration. Various possibilities were brought forward, but one after another it seemed that they must be discarded. It was evident that the Japanese would suspect trickery. Their Air Force still had considerable strength and (if the time and place were announced in advance) might be expected to make every attempt to shoot down the demonstration plane. While the scientists were confident that their test on the New Mexico desert would succeed, it was a very different thing to be certain in advance that the bomb could be delivered and successfully exploded under combat conditions. The atomic bomb was an intricate device, still in the developmental stage. Its operation would be far from routine. If, during the final adjustments of the bomb, the Japanese defenders should attack, a faulty move easily might result in some kind of failure. Furthermore, weather conditions over the Japanese islands were so uncertain that no one could with confidence announce a date and place in advance and be certain that he could deliver a bomb without fail. Even if the plane delivered the bomb safely and on schedule, the possibility of a fizzle or a dud could not entirely be discounted. The committee feared that if we advertised a demonstration and then failed to produce, the psychological effect upon the Japanese would be much worse for the peace of the world than if we had not tried such a demonstration at all. Mr. Byrnes sums up some of the feelings of the committee:

> We feared that, if the Japanese were told that the bomb would be used on a given locality, they might bring our boys who were prisoners of war to that area. Also, the experts had warned us that the static test which was to take place in New Mexico, even if successful, would not be conclusive proof that a bomb would explode when dropped from an airplane. If we were to warn the Japanese of the new highly destructive weapon in the hope of impressing them and if the bomb then failed to explode, certainly we would have given aid and comfort to the Japanese militarists. Thereafter, the Japanese people probably would not be impressed by any statement we might make in the hope of inducing them to surrender.[15]

Would a test over neutral territory be the answer? Even if Japan could be persuaded to send observers, it seemed unlikely that a mere report about a distant explosion could persuade the determined and fanatical military leaders in Tokyo to admit defeat. Furthermore, if an open test were made and failed to bring surrender, we would then have lost forever the chance to deliver a surprising and stunning shock which in itself might be the all-important element in bringing Japan to surrender. Although "the possibility of a demonstration that would not destroy human lives was attractive, no one could suggest a way in which it could be made so convincing that it would be likely to stop the war." [16]

Following lunch, the Scientific Panel was asked to wait outside while the Interim Committee met in closed session.

Then the panel members were invited in again, and the scientists were asked to prepare a report as to whether they "could devise any kind of demonstration that would seem likely to bring the war to an end without using the bomb against a live target." [17]

The next day, June 1, 1945, the Interim Committee submitted its threefold recommendation: (a) that the bomb should be used against Japan as soon as possible; (b) against a dual target (a military or industrial establishment surrounded by adjacent, more lightly constructed buildings) so as to make clear its devastating strength; and (c) without specific warning.[18]

The recommendation of the Interim Committee was not binding, but merely advisory; the Secretary of War alone bore final responsibility for advising the President on the use of the new weapon. The decision of the Interim Committee gave formal and official approval to preparations for military use of the bomb. However, the committee also had directed its Scientific Panel to exhaust every possibility of finding a way in which the atomic bomb might be used to compel the Japanese to recognize the futility of further resistance, and to surrender, without taking the lives of many thousands of Japanese citizens. If the panel had been able to find such a way, Mr. Stimson would have been free to modify the recommendation made by the Interim Committee in the light of such further findings.

III

A footnote to the story of the Interim Committee's deliberations is provided by the action of Ralph Bard, one of the committee members. The possibility of giving Japan specific warning before we dropped the atomic bomb was discussed by the committee, but rejected on the ground "that the Japanese would consider that this was just another threat or another

bluff, and that it wouldn't be effective." Yet during the en-
suing weeks, as developing events made Japan's position increasingly desperate, Bard became more and more convinced
that a warning might be effective in providing Japan's leaders
with an opportunity to surrender. Even if a warning did not
produce surrender, it would cost us nothing — and our reputation as a humanitarian nation would be protected by the
fact that we gave prior warning. On June 27 Bard drafted a
memorandum embodying his ideas, and sent it to Stimson's
deputy, George Harrison:

> Ever since I have been in touch with this program, I have
> had a feeling that before the bomb is actually used against
> Japan that Japan should have some preliminary warning for
> say two or three days in advance of use. The position of the
> United States as a great humanitarian nation and the fair play
> attitude of our people generally is responsible in the main for
> this feeling.
>
> During recent weeks I have also had the feeling very defi-
> nitely that the Japanese government may be searching for some
> opportunity which they could use as a medium for surrender.
> Following the three-power conference [at Potsdam] emissaries
> from this country could contact representatives from Japan
> somewhere on the China coast and make representations with
> regard to Russia's position and at the same time give them some
> information regarding the proposed use of atomic power, to-
> gether with whatever assurances the President might care to
> make with regard to the Emperor of Japan and the treatment
> of the Japanese nation following unconditional surrender. It
> seems quite possible to me that this presents the opportunity
> which the Japanese are looking for.
>
> I don't see that we have anything in particular to lose in
> following such a program. The stakes are so tremendous that
> it is my opinion very real consideration should be given to some
> plan of this kind. I do not believe under present circumstances
> existing that there is anyone in this country whose evaluation
> of the chances of success of such a program is worth a great
> deal. The only way to find out is to try it out.[19]

Bard was not opposed to using the atomic bomb against Japan, if such use was necessary to bring prompt surrender. He was opposed to using the bomb *without warning*, for he felt that there was a good chance that the warning itself would be sufficient to produce surrender.

IV

In the meanwhile Secretary Stimson was receiving other advice regarding the atomic bomb. Reports that Washington would soon be deciding about use of the bomb against Japan caused a vigorous debate to spring up among the atomic scientists over the wisdom and morality of such use. Leo Szilard recalls that "when Germany was defeated, many of us became uneasy about the proposed use of the bomb in the war with Japan." [20] Szilard became a central figure in the debate, circulating petitions urging that the bomb should not be used against Japan. With his social vision and sensitive conscience, Szilard had often been far in advance of his fellows in awareness of the social and political implications of nuclear physics. He had taken the lead in arousing his colleagues and the government in 1939, and had helped to draft the Einstein letter. He then had been willing to approve, and even to urge, the use of the bomb against Hitler; the human destruction involved would be only a small evil compared with what would follow a victory by the Nazis. Now, however, Szilard felt the proposed use of the bomb against Japan was an entirely different question. He sensed the shock that would be felt throughout the world if the atomic bomb killed large numbers of civilians in a nation already essentially defeated.

Szilard's efforts in opposition to using the bomb against Japan stimulated the circulation of counterpetitions which urged just that. One counterpetition signed by some scientists went so far as to say, in part:

In short, are we to go on shedding American blood when we have available a means to speedy victory? No! If we can save even a handful of American lives, then let us use this weapon — now!

Supporters of this petition were deeply aware that thousands of men were being killed on both sides of the battle line, and that those who would withhold the bomb, and thereby extend the length of the war, would be guilty of condoning the continuation of the slaughter. More moderate petitions were also circulated; sixty-odd scientists at Chicago signed a petition recommending that the atomic bomb should not be used, particularly against cities, unless Japan first be given convincing and specific warning and a chance to surrender on terms assuring her opportunity for peaceful development in the future.[21]

v

Dr. Arthur Compton, head of the atomic bomb work at Chicago, appointed a Committee on Social and Political Implications to consider these problems more systematically and to present a report that would give officials in Washington the benefit of the scientists' thinking. Dr. James Franck, Nobel Prize winning chemist and a refugee from Hitler, was chairman of the committee, which also included Leo Szilard and Eugene Rabinowitch (later to become editor of the *Bulletin of the Atomic Scientists*). The committee rushed to complete its report in time to have some influence upon the course of events.[22]

The main burden of the Franck Committee's report was that the use of the bomb against Japan should not be decided solely on short-run military grounds, but that long-term political and social implications should be taken seriously into account. The committee opposed the direct and unannounced use of an atomic weapon against Japanese cities. Such use would in-

evitably entail the death and maiming of tens of thousands of
Japanese civilians, something which, in itself, is morally reprehensible. Such an attack would shock the entire civilized
world, and would develop an attitude of fear, suspicion, and
hatred toward the United States. It would lead to the United
States' being morally isolated, and would jeopardize any future
attempt on her part to negotiate an international agreement
controlling or abolishing the use of atomic weapons, since
she herself already would have used such weapons in war. The
committee suggested, instead, that

> a demonstration of the new weapon might best be made, be-
> fore the eyes of representatives of all the United Nations, on a
> desert or a barren island. The best possible atmosphere for the
> achievement of an international agreement could be achieved
> if America could say to the world, "You see what sort of a
> weapon we had but did not use. We are ready to renounce its
> use in the future if other nations join us in this renunciation
> and agree to the establishment of an efficient international con-
> trol."
>
> After such a demonstration the weapon might perhaps be
> used against Japan if the sanction of the United Nations (and
> of public opinion at home) were obtained, perhaps after a pre-
> liminary ultimatum to Japan to surrender or at least to evacuate
> certain regions as an alternative to their total destruction.

The committee emphasized that, even if we tried to keep
the details of the bomb secret, America could not expect to
keep a monopoly on nuclear weapons "for more than a few
years." After discussing the dangers of an atomic armaments
race and the possibilities of establishing effective international
control over nuclear weapons, the committee concluded:

> We believe that these considerations make the use of nuclear
> bombs for an early unannounced attack against Japan inadvisa-
> ble. If the United States were to be the first to release this new
> means of indiscriminate destruction upon mankind, she would

sacrifice public support throughout the world, precipitate the race for armaments, and prejudice the possibility of reaching an international agreement on the future control of such weapons.

Much more favorable conditions for the eventual achievement of such an agreement could be created if nuclear bombs were first revealed to the world by a demonstration in an appropriately selected uninhabited area.

In case chances for the establishment of an effective international control of nuclear weapons should have to be considered slight at the present time, then not only the use of these weapons against Japan, but even their early demonstration, may be contrary to the interests of this country. A postponement of such a demonstration will have in this case the advantage of delaying the beginning of the nuclear armaments race as long as possible.[23]

In its report, the Franck Committee did not oppose the proposed use of the bomb against Japan on the grounds that it would be inherently immoral to use so massive and indiscriminate a weapon, although individually the members of the committee were acutely and painfully aware of the human destruction that would be involved. Neither did they argue whether the bomb would take or save more lives in World War II; they insisted that the decision about use of the bomb must not be made on the basis of short-run "considerations of military tactics alone." They viewed the problem in a much larger frame of reference, in which the primary danger to be avoided was a postwar nuclear arms race that would threaten not only the security of the United States but of the whole world. Therefore, for the sake of "saving American lives in the future," they urgently recommended that the United States give overriding priority to the establishment of a reliable system of international control over nuclear weapons; this was the all-important goal toward which all present policy and action ought to be directed. Thus, if a technical demonstration of the new bomb would aid in reaching this goal, we should put one on; on the other hand, if a demonstration would merely precipitate an atomic arms race, then we should not.

Dr. Franck was urged by his colleagues to take the report to Washington and to present it personally to Secretary Stimson. Dr. Arthur Compton met him in Washington, and endeavored to make an appointment for Franck to present his paper to the Secretary. It happened that Mr. Stimson was out of town, but his Special Assistant, Mr. Harrison, assured the scientists he would see that the report came to the Secretary's attention.[24]

VI

The report of the Franck Committee did not arrive in Washington in time to be considered by the Interim Committee. Although it was not submitted to the Secretary of War until June 11, its contents were clearly in the minds of the members of the Scientific Panel as they met on the weekend of June 9–10 to search for alternatives to direct military use of the atomic bomb, in accordance with their instructions from the Interim Committee. Arthur Compton describes the mood in which they met:

> We were determined to find, if we could, some effective way of demonstrating the power of an atomic bomb without loss of life that would impress Japan's warlords. If only this could be done! [25]

Despite their determination, the difficulties of devising a demonstration that would be convincing were formidable. One possibility after another was considered, and then rejected as unlikely to break through the fanatical will-not-to-believe of Japan's military clique, and make unmistakably clear the futility of further resistance.* Dr. Oppenheimer described (several years later) the deliberations of the panel:

* As a matter of fact, Japanese Army leaders *did* try to hide the seriousness of the Hiroshima attack from the Japanese Cabinet.[26]

We were asked to comment on whether the bomb should be used. . . .

We said that we didn't think that being scientists especially qualified us as to how to answer this question of how the bombs should be used or not [sic]; opinion was divided among us as it would be among other people if they knew about it. We thought the two overriding considerations were the saving of lives in the war and the effect of our actions . . . on our strength and the stability of the postwar world. We did say that we did not think exploding one of these things as a fire-cracker over a desert was likely to be very impressive. This was before we had actually done that. The destruction on the desert is zero. . . .[27]

In their report submitted on June 16 to the Interim Committee, the Scientific Panel indicated the range of differences of opinion among their scientific colleagues on the question. But speaking for themselves, they concluded:

We can propose no technical demonstration likely to bring an end to the war; we see no acceptable alternative to direct military use.[28]

Dr. Compton commented later:

Our hearts were heavy as on 16 June we turned in this re-port to the Interim Committee. . . . What a tragedy it was that this power should become available first in time of war and that it must first be used for human destruction. If, how-ever, it would result in the shortening of the war and the saving of lives — if it would mean bringing us closer to the time when war would be abandoned as a means of settling international disputes — here must be our hope and our basis for courage.[29]

Dr. Compton felt in later years that the Scientific Panel may have been somewhat remiss in fulfilling its assignment. In-stead of simply reporting the negative conclusion that "we see no acceptable alternative to direct military use," the panel perhaps should have listed the various alternatives they had considered, together with the reasons for the rejection of each. This would have provided the members of the Interim Committee, upon whom responsibility for making a recommendation rested, a better idea of the range of possibilities that were open, and information with which to evaluate the panel's conclusion.[30]

VII

The Franck Committee and the Scientific Panel, each composed of eminent and thoughtful scientists, had reached diametrically opposing conclusions. The petitions and counter-petitions only added to the confusion of those in Washington who were trying to understand the thinking of the scientists. In order to get a more comprehensive and balanced view of the scientists' opinions, General Groves suggested that a poll be taken among those who knew enough to make a judgment on whether the bomb ought to be used against Japan. Accordingly, in July Dr. Arthur H. Compton ordered a poll conducted among the scientists of the Metallurgical Laboratory in Chicago. Each respondent was asked to indicate which of several alternatives was closest to his preference for using the new bomb. The results were as follows:[31]

Alternatives for Using the New Bombs	Number Responding	Per Cent Responding
1. Use them in the manner that is from the military point of view most effective in bringing about prompt Japanese surrender at minimum human cost to our armed forces.	23	15
2. Give a military demonstration in Japan to be followed by a renewed opportunity for surrender before full use of the weapons is employed.	69	46

Alternatives for Using the New Bombs	Number Responding	Per Cent Responding
3. Give an experimental demonstration in this country, with representatives of Japan present; followed by a new opportunity for surrender before full use of the weapons is employed.	39	26
4. Withhold military use of the weapons, but make public experimental demonstration of their effectiveness.	16	11
5. Maintain as secret as possible all developments of our new weapons and refrain from using them in this war.	3	2
Totals	150	100

It is an interesting commentary on Compton's own leanings that in his book *Atomic Quest*, published in 1956, he interprets these figures as follows: "There were a few who preferred not to use the bomb at all, but 87 per cent voted for its military use, at least if after other means were tried this was found necessary to bring surrender." [32] From another point of view, these same results may be interpreted in almost the opposite manner. That is: only 15 per cent favored *unrestrained* use of the bomb "in the manner that is from the military point of view most effective"; 83 per cent felt that restraint was necessary in our use of the bomb, and that full military use of the weapon should be employed (if at all) only after giving the Japanese sufficient warning and opportunity to surrender.

On July 23 General Groves's deputy, Colonel K. D. Nichols, came up to Dr. Compton at Oak Ridge with the word, "Washington wants at once the results of the opinion polls on the use of the bomb." Compton wrote out a message summarizing the results as "objectively" as he could (presumably substantially as he summarized them in his book) and gave it to

Colonel Nichols. An hour later Nichols returned: "Washington wants to know what you think."

What a question to answer! Having been in the very midst of these discussions, it seemed to me that a firm negative stand on my part might still prevent an atomic attack on Japan. Thoughts of my pacifist Mennonite ancestors flashed through my mind. I knew all too well the destruction and human agony the bombs would cause. I knew the danger they held in the hands of some future tyrant. These facts I had been living with for four years. But I wanted the war to end. I wanted life to become normal again. I saw a chance for an enduring peace that would be demanded by the very destructiveness of these weapons. I hoped that by the use of the bombs many fine young men I knew might be released from the demands of war and thus be given a chance to live and not to die.

"My vote is with the majority. It seems to me that as the war stands the bomb should be used, but no more drastically than needed to bring surrender." [33]

VIII

The recommendations of the Interim Committee and the Scientific Panel, the Franck Committee's report, the petitions, and the polls — all this advice was funneled into the office of one man, Henry L. Stimson, the Secretary of War. Stimson has pointed out that the Interim Committee's function was entirely advisory. "The ultimate responsibility for the recommendation to the President rested upon me, and I have no desire to veil it. The conclusions of the committee were similar to my own, although I reached mine independently." [34]

Secretary Stimson, from the very inception of the atomic bomb program, had seen the new weapon as one that should be produced and used as a means of shortening the war and minimizing its destructiveness. Indeed, the only possible justification for the investment of so much money and badly needed scientific talent in this project was that it involved the production of a military weapon that would be of use in shortening the war.

> At no time, from 1941 to 1945, did I ever hear it suggested by the President, or by any other responsible member of the government, that atomic energy should not be used in the war. All of us of course understood the terrible responsibility involved in our attempt to unlock the doors to such a devastating weapon; President Roosevelt particularly spoke to me many times of his own awareness of the catastrophic potentialities of our work. But we were at war, and the work must be done. I therefore emphasize that it was our common objective, throughout the war, to be the first to produce an atomic weapon and use it. The possible atomic weapon was considered to be a new and tremendously powerful explosive, as legitimate as any other of the deadly explosive weapons of modern war. The entire purpose was the production of a military weapon; on no other ground could the wartime expenditure of so much time and money have been justified. The exact circumstances in which that weapon might be used were unknown to any of us until the middle of 1945, and when that time came . . . the military use of atomic energy was connected with larger questions of national policy.

Now that the time for the use of the weapon was at hand, Secretary Stimson was convinced "that to extract a genuine surrender from the Emperor and his military advisers, there must be administered a tremendous shock which would carry convincing proof of our power to destroy the Empire. Such an effective shock would save many times the number of lives, both American and Japanese, that it would cost."

The Secretary of War understood his primary goal to be the achievement of speedy victory with minimum loss of American lives. The question of the use of the bomb was clearly subordinated to the achieving of victory:

. . . the dominant fact of 1945 was war, and . . . therefore, necessarily, the dominant objective was victory. If victory could be speeded by using the bomb, it should be used; if victory must be delayed in order to use the bomb, it should *not* be used.

Stimson felt very keenly his high responsibility to defend and preserve the lives of the men in the armies he had helped to raise — particularly so after his visit in March 1945 to an Air Forces redistribution center, where he had opportunity to talk with soldiers who were being transferred from the European theater to the Pacific. He was profoundly impressed by their war-weariness. To withhold or fail to use effectively any weapon that might spare these men further sacrifice would be flagrant irresponsibility.

In the light of the alternatives which, on a fair estimate, were open to us I believe that no man, in our position and subject to our responsibilities, holding in his hands a weapon of such possibilities for accomplishing this purpose [i.e., victory] and saving those lives, could have failed to use it and afterwards looked his countrymen in the face.

Therefore, in the Secretary's mind, the bomb was

. . . not treated as a separate subject, except to determine whether it should be used at all; once that decision had been made, the timing and method of the use of the bomb were wholly subordinated to the objective of victory; no effort was made, and none was seriously considered, to achieve surrender merely in order not to have to use the bomb. Surrender was a goal sufficient in itself, wholly transcending the use or nonuse of the bomb.[35]

7. Conflicting Plans for Ending the War

THE DELIBERATIONS of the Interim Committee and Secretary Stimson did not take place in an ethics classroom but in the Pentagon. The Scientific Panel could not plan for a demonstration of the second atomic bomb over Japan in the same way that Dr. Oppenheimer could plan for the test of the first bomb over the desert in New Mexico — for the hazards of flying under combat conditions, the psychology of Japanese military leaders, and the possibility of a million casualties in a massive invasion of Japan should the demonstration fail, all these were factors injected into the problem by the war, making the proposed second demonstration a very different thing from the first. Even though the Scientific Panel had in a sense been asked for a technical answer to a technical question, they could not escape from making certain assumptions about the future course of the war — which made their answer *political* as well as technical. That this was so is indicated in Oppenheimer's account of the panel's meeting on June 9 and 10:

> We didn't know beans about the military situation in Japan. We didn't know whether they could be caused to surrender by other means or whether the invasion was really inevitable. But in the back of our minds was the notion that the invasion was inevitable because we had been told that. . . .[1]

Mr. Byrnes confirms that throughout the deliberations of the Interim Committee they "relied on the estimates of the military situation presented by the Joint Chiefs of Staff." [2]

Thus the question of whether to use the bomb against Japan was not settled as an abstract moral, or even military, exercise — but in the context of the wartime situation in mid-1945, and as an inextricable part of the larger problem of how to bring the war to an early end with the least possible loss of life. Expectations as to the future course of the war and alternative ways to end it were as much a part of the moral choice as ethical principles. In fact they helped to determine which ethical principles were relevant. We turn therefore to a description of the war situation as it was developing in mid-1945 and the various alternatives proposed for bringing Japan to surrender.

II

During the first half of 1945 Japan suffered defeat on every front. General Douglas MacArthur recaptured Manila in February; the Marines secured Iwo Jima in March; on April 1 American troops went ashore on Okinawa, the gateway to Japan's home islands. The enemy's resistance intensified as the Americans moved closer to the heart of the Empire. Virtually the entire Japanese garrison of 120,000 men on Okinawa had to be wiped out; thousands of Japanese soldiers lined up and destroyed themselves with hand grenades rather than surrender.[3] The conquest of the 67-mile-long island took nearly three months and cost almost 80,000 American casualties, making it the most costly single engagement in the Pacific war. Air bases within easy reach of the Japanese home islands were quickly constructed.

Meanwhile B-29 bombing raids on Japanese cities, begun in November 1944 from the Marianas Islands, had built up to devastating proportions. A massive incendiary raid on Tokyo on the night of March 9/10 started an uncontrollable holocaust that burned out more than fifteen square miles in the heart of the city's residential and commercial districts, killed an estimated 100,000, destroyed one fourth of the buildings in

Tokyo, and rendered a million persons homeless. A Japanese official described the effects of the B-29 raids as they were extended to city after city:

> Meanwhile, air raids on Japan proper by Allied aircraft were steadily intensified. Medium and small cities, let alone great cities, were [one by one] destroyed in rapid succession with calamitous consequences. Two million, two hundred thousand houses were burned and hundreds of thousands of persons were killed and wounded while the number of war sufferers approximate ten millions.[4]

Moreover, by the spring of 1945 the Imperial Navy had been reduced to a collection of remnants incapable of mounting offensive action. Shortly after the start of the battle for Okinawa, American planes sank Japan's last surviving capital ship, the battleship *Yamato*, as she steamed south toward the invasion fleet. Thereafter the Japanese Navy was unable to muster a fighting force in her own home waters; the Americans maneuvered at will, shelling shore installations and factories, and sending carrier-borne aircraft to raid cities far inland.

The American sea and air blockade squeezed tighter and tighter, reducing the flow of vital oil and foodstuffs into Japan to a trickle. Production in many factories was crippled twice over: first by the cutting off of supplies, then by the bombing of factory buildings. An official Japanese report prepared in early June recognized the impending collapse of the entire wartime economy.[5]

By June 1945 Japan had been decisively defeated on land, sea, and in the air; yet her army still had 2,000,000 undefeated men in her home islands, her *kamikaze* aircraft were capable of inflicting considerable damage upon the American fleet, and her leaders showed no signs of weakening in their determination to fight on rather than accept unconditional surrender. Defeated in fact, Japan was not yet ready to surrender. She clearly could not hope to hold out against the ever-increasing might of her enemy; her situation could only grow worse. All that remained for America to do was to press home the attack until Japan's leaders recognized the reality of her defeat and the futility of further resistance.

III

The Joint Chiefs of Staff met in Washington on June 14, at the request of President Truman, to prepare a plan for completing the final defeat of Japan. There were certain differences of opinion among the Joint Chiefs as to the best method of bringing Japan to the earliest possible surrender with minimum United States casualties. These differences would have to be ironed out before a unified plan could be presented to the President.

The Navy and the Air Force were convinced that, just as Japan had thus far been brought to her knees by sea and air power, so a more intense application of this same power would force her to surrender. No invasion of Japan's home islands would be necessary. However the Army was not convinced. General Marshall agreed with General MacArthur that although bombing and blockade would be very helpful, "in the final analysis, the doughboys would have to march into Tokyo." The Army's view prevailed, and the Joint Chiefs agreed that plans and preparations for an invasion of Japan's home islands must be made. Admiral Ernest J. King (Commander-in-Chief of the United States Fleet) and Admiral William D. Leahy (Chief of Staff to the President) "did not like the idea" but they "reluctantly acquiesced" to making plans and preparations, as precautionary measures, without sharing the Army's conviction of the *necessity* of the invasion. General H. H. Arnold, commanding general of the Army Air Forces, shared the Navy's skepticism about the necessity of marching to Tokyo — although he favored occupying the southern Japanese island of Kyushu in order to establish more air bases for an all-out bombing campaign against the rest of Japan.[6]

Despite their differences in basic philosophy, the Joint Chiefs were able to agree on a three-stage plan for ending the war, which they presented to President Truman on June 18. First, the sea blockade and air bombardment of Japan should be steadily intensified. Then about November 1, 1945, General MacArthur would lead an invasion of Kyushu. The island would be secured after a tough fight, and air bases would be established for the support of operations farther north. Finally, about March 1, 1946, the main Japanese island of Honshu would be invaded in the area of the Tokyo plain. The Joint Chiefs expected that the entire plan would take about one year, victory coming by the end of 1946. Allied casualties would be figured in the hundreds of thousands, and (if past experience were any guide) Japanese casualties would be several times as heavy. President Truman approved these plans, but ordered the Joint Chiefs to report back to him before the plans had advanced so far that he would have no choice left in the matter.[7]

The invasion of the Japanese homeland in accordance with these plans was not something to look forward to with pleasure. The Japanese had, at that time, an army whose total strength was about 5,000,000 men, of whom about 2,000,000 were in the home islands. These soldiers were fresh and well trained. They were capable, as we had learned by bitter experience, of skilled and desperate resistance even in the face of certain defeat. The prospect of having to kill the better part of 2,000,000 men on the Japanese home islands was a grim one. Although the Japanese Navy had practically ceased to exist, except as a harrying force against an invasion fleet, the Japanese Air Force was a much larger threat. It had been reduced mainly to reliance upon *kamikaze* suicide attacks, but these attacks had already inflicted serious damage on our sea-going

forces at Okinawa, and the prospect of facing thousands of
suicide aircraft massed for a last-ditch defense of Kyushu and
Honshu filled our naval leaders with deep concern. However,
Army leaders, in whose view the Joint Chiefs acquiesced, saw
no alternative but to go through with forcible invasion and
seizure of Japanese home territory.

The record of the Joint Chiefs' discussions reveals that their
agreement upon plans for invasion was permeated by hopes that
a successful operation on Kyushu might suffice, and that we
would not have to force our way into the Tokyo plain. It was
clearly understood that plans for undertaking this second step
would be kept under constant review.[8]

The atomic bomb was of course still untested, and hence
only a possibility, at the time that these plans were crystallized.
The scientists, and indeed Secretary Stimson, were confident of
the successful outcome of the test. Still, no one could estimate
what the effect of two or three bombs might be on the outcome of the war. There was no alternative but to proceed with
plans using conventional weapons. "Planning went on virtually
as if the atomic bomb did not exist." [9]

IV

At the last minute, and almost accidentally, an alternative
course of action was suggested. Secretary Stimson's deputy,
John J. McCloy, who was present at the June 18 meeting at
which the President approved the Joint Chiefs' plan, describes
what happened:

> After the President's decision had been made and the con-
> ference was breaking up, an official, not theretofore participat-
> ing, suggested that serious attention should be given to a politi-
> cal attempt to end the war. The meeting fell into a tailspin,
> but after control was recovered, the idea appealed to several
> present. It appealed particularly to the President. . . .

It was also at this meeting that the suggestion was first broached that warning be given the Japanese of our possession of the bomb before we dropped it. Although all present were "cleared," the uninhibited mention of "the best-kept secret of the war" caused a sense of shock, even among that select group.

Now this incident indicates that at the time everyone was so intent on winning the war by military means that the introduction of political considerations was almost accidental. . . .

As a result of the meeting, a rather hastily composed paper was drawn up. It embodied the idea which later formed the basis of the appeal to the Japanese to surrender. That proposal, it will be recalled, was refused brusquely by the Japanese Government. . . .[10]

As a consequence of this discussion, Secretary Stimson was asked to draw up a memorandum on a possible warning that might persuade the Japanese to surrender without a fight to the bitter end. His assignment, he later recalled, "was originally prompted not by the problem of atomic energy but by the American desire to achieve a Japanese surrender without invading the home islands." After discussing the matter with Secretary of the Navy James V. Forrestal and Acting Secretary of State Joseph C. Grew (who had also been advocating a political approach to Japan), Stimson had drafted a memorandum which he submitted to the President on July 2. In it Stimson pointed out that the Japanese are highly patriotic and would be susceptible to calls for fanatical resistance to repel an invasion of their sacred homeland. Once we had actually landed on Japanese soil, we should "probably have cast the die of last ditch resistance." He therefore suggested that before the invasion, and before the expected Russian declaration of war, Japan should be warned and given a chance to surrender. The warning should include a strong threat and an explicit warning of the destruction that would come to Japan if she should continue to resist; but it should also include commitments on our part which would give her hope for a better life in the future if she surrendered. Stimson said in addition that he personally thought it would substantially add to the chances of Japan's accepting the ultimatum if we stated that we would not exclude a constitutional monarchy under her present dynasty.[11]

President Truman approved of the Secretary's memorandum in principle, and decided that such an ultimatum should be solemnly issued by the United States and the United Kingdom, with the concurrence of China, at the forthcoming Potsdam Conference, thus demonstrating to Japan that all her enemies were in complete unity.[12]

V

What to do about the Japanese Emperor was a critical problem. Acting Secretary of State Grew, who had served as United States Ambassador to Japan from 1932 until 1941 and knew the Japanese people and their psychology better than anyone else in the top ranks of our government, strongly advocated retaining the Emperor. Staunch Japanese loyalty to the Emperor made our talk of abolishing the Emperor system a major obstacle to Japanese surrender, Grew argued. A clear and authoritative statement that the United States was willing to retain the Emperor as head of state would greatly increase the chances of an early Japanese surrender. Stimson's memorandum of July 2 supported this position.[13]

Grew and Stimson were opposed by those who viewed the Emperor system as the root from which sprang Japan's fanatical militarism. This group insisted that the whole system must be eradicated before Japan could become a peace-loving nation, and some went so far as to accuse Grew of advocating appeasement. A further factor made it tactically difficult to follow Grew's advice. Many high U.S. officials had throughout the war ridiculed and denounced the Japanese Emperor, and so contributed to an American public opinion tending to identify the Emperor with the Japanese military clique as instigator of the war. It would not be easy suddenly to reverse positions and offer to retain the figure we had so recently been denouncing.[14]

This problem passed into the hands of James F. Byrnes when he became Secretary of State on July 3, 1945, three days before he was scheduled to depart with the President's party for the Potsdam Conference. Byrnes was not acquainted with the discussions about the proposed ultimatum to Japan; he discovered that opinion within the State Department was still split on the question of giving assurances regarding the Emperor. Shortly before boarding the train for the first leg of the journey, Byrnes telephoned former Secretary of State Cordell Hull, gave him the gist of the proposed ultimatum to Japan as drafted in Stimson's memorandum of July 2, and asked his opinion on the Emperor question. Hull replied that our offering to retain the Emperor

> seemed too much like appeasement of Japan, especially after the resolute stand we had maintained on unconditional surrender. I pointed out that, as it was worded, it seemed to guarantee continuance not only of the Emperor but also of the feudal privileges of a ruling caste under the Emperor. I said that the Emperor and the ruling caste must be stripped of all extraordinary privileges and placed on a level before the law with everybody else.

Hull sent a follow-up cable to Byrnes recommending a wait-and-see policy: at the moment the United States should not commit itself one way or the other regarding the Emperor, but should wait until our intensified bombing and the Russian entry into the conflict brought the war to a point of climax. For whatever reasons, Hull's advice was taken. It was decided at Potsdam that the forthcoming ultimatum to Japan would make no mention of the Emperor.[15]

VI

And so to the American leaders, mulling over the problem aboard the cruiser *Augusta* en route to Potsdam, there appeared to be four alternative ways to complete the defeat of Japan and bring her to surrender.

1. The most obvious, and also the most time-consuming and bloody of the alternatives, was the direct invasion and seizure of the Japanese home islands. All were agreed that this method would, in the end, produce surrender. However, the price seemed extremely high.

2. The Air Force and the Navy were convinced that they could bring about surrender for a much lower price by continuing the sea and air blockade of Japan and intensifying the strategic air bombing of her cities and industries. Indeed, General Arnold predicted in July that air bombardment would bring surrender by October 1945.[16] However, the Army was not convinced that the Air Force and Navy plan could be relied upon to bring surrender. Official Army doctrine has been (and still is) that a nation has not been really defeated until the lowly infantryman has trod upon its soil and holds it with his presence. To buttress this conviction, the Army could point to the European theater, where, despite three years of terrific pounding by American and English bombers, Germany was conquered only by an invading army that defeated her armies on the ground, and seized her territory in person. It appeared to the Army that only a repetition of this process could bring about the surrender of Japan.

3. Again, the scientists were confident that the atomic bomb would provide the shock and the overwhelming power which would lead Japan to recognize the folly of further resistance and thus bring her to surrender quickly. However, early in July the bomb was still only a possibility. The scientists had not yet produced conclusive evidence proving that "the thing would go off." The tactical military application of a brand-new weapon

under fire was something else again. Even if the weapon proved successful in action, no one could predict precisely what its effect would be upon the enemy's will to resist. Besides, the number of bombs available before the end of the year appeared to be strictly limited.

4. The last alternative was the political approach, represented by the proposed Potsdam ultimatum. Certain of our leaders had high hopes that this method would indeed bring the Japanese to surrender. Others had serious doubts about the likelihood of Japan's accepting the ultimatum, but felt that nothing could be lost by such an attempt; besides, giving the Japanese a chance to surrender would be a good propaganda stunt and would present the Allied position in a favorable light. The Army planners, who were working on the invasion of Japan, had apparently no doubt that the Potsdam Declaration would fail to bring surrender; it was considered to be in the same class with the stepped-up strategic bombing and intensified blockade: all were preliminaries that paved the way for the invasion of Japan by weakening the Japanese will to resist.*

There were, then, three short-run and easier plans for bringing Japan to surrender: bombing and blockade, the atomic bomb, and the political approach. Each of these had certain advocates who, of course, could be accused of bias because of their special interests. None of the advocates of these three approaches could convince all of the planners that their approach was sure to bring victory. Consequently, no one in a responsible position could recommend reliance upon any one of these three alternatives to the extent that planning for the actual invasion of Japan could be given up. Therefore plans for the invasion had to proceed in case the other three alternatives

---

* The official Army history goes so far as to describe the Army planners' attitude toward the Potsdam Declaration thus: "The Potsdam Ultimatum was issued on 26 July 1945 as a calculated effort to lower Japanese will to resist while military pressures were building up." [17]

failed to produce surrender. In Australia the American divisions scheduled to make the first assaults on the beaches of Kyushu began reorganization in anticipation of the kind of fanatical resistance the Japanese were expected to provide; soldiers with wives and children were replaced, in so far as possible, with men who had no dependents. The whole massive and complex machinery of invasion — ships, men, weapons, supplies — was under way and moving inexorably toward the hostile beaches of Japan.

8. The Decision Is Made

ALTHOUGH the main purpose of the Potsdam Conference was to settle many urgent political and economic matters arising out of the termination of the war with Germany (its code name was TERMINAL), President Truman and his advisers traveled to Potsdam preoccupied with the war still going on against Japan. In his report to the nation on the conference, Mr. Truman described this concern:

> The Conference was concerned with many political and economic questions. But there was one strictly military matter uppermost in the minds of the American delegates. It was winning the war against Japan. On our program, that was the most important item.[1]

Yet the Far Eastern questions — urgent and imminent as they were — did not find a place on the official agenda of the conference, nor were they discussed in the scheduled conference sessions. There were good reasons for this: the fact that the U.S.S.R. was not at war with Japan; and the reluctance of the United States to submit to negotiation her plans for implementing surrender and occupying Japan. Furthermore, some of the main issues were of vital concern to China, who had no representative at the conference. The result was that such crucial questions as issuing to Japan a last call to surrender and plans for the use of the atomic bomb were settled informally at the margins of the conference as leading figures arranged for occasional tête-à-têtes to talk over specific issues. The only formal three-power consultations on Far Eastern matters took place among the military chiefs.[2]

During the week before the conference began two events occurred, both of which bore directly on the problem of ending the war against Japan: an official Japanese "peace feeler" and the successful test of the first atomic bomb.

II

While the President and his party were en route to Potsdam, intelligence officers in Washington were decoding an intercepted Japanese message. The message, dated July 12, was from Foreign Minister Shigenori Togo in Tokyo to Ambassador Naotake Sato in Moscow; it contained these words:

> See [Foreign Commissar] Molotov before his departure for Potsdam. . . . Convey His Majesty's strong desire to secure a termination of the war. . . . Unconditional surrender is the only obstacle to peace. . . .

Sato was instructed to inform Molotov that the Emperor wished to send Prince Fumimaro Konoye as a special envoy to Moscow. The Prince would carry a personal letter from the Emperor setting forth the Imperial views, and would be empowered to enter into direct negotiations as a personal representative of the Emperor. Although emphasizing His Majesty's "strong desire to secure a termination of the war," the message did not state that the main purpose of the proposed visit would be to seek Russia's good offices in securing a negotiated peace (which was in fact the case); it merely stated in general terms that the envoy would be authorized to discuss all issues involving Soviet-Japanese relations, including the question of Manchuria. The message stressed that so long as Britain and America insisted upon the unconditional surrender formula, Japan — despite the Emperor's peaceful intentions — would have no alternative but to fight on. Sato was instructed to secure permission for Konoye's party to enter the

U.S.S.R., to secure Soviet aid in facilitating air travel, and obtain an appointment for Konoye to see Molotov immediately upon the latter's return from the Potsdam Conference.[3]

Top Washington officials who read copies of this cable on July 13 recognized that it constituted "the first real evidence of a Japanese desire to get out of the war."[4] Prior to the interception of this cable, there had been no indication that the Japanese government had any other intention than to continue to pursue the war with the utmost vigor. In May and June there had been two unofficial peace feelers: Japanese naval and military attachés had independently approached the American OSS organization in Switzerland in unauthorized attempts to establish negotiations to end the war. In each case, however, the Japanese officer acted on his own initiative, without authority, and, after having established contact with the Americans, found his efforts squelched by his superiors in Tokyo. That these abortive efforts were correctly understood by the United States government not to represent official Japanese willingness to end the war is indicated by a press release of July 10, 1945, in which Acting Secretary of State Joseph Grew stated:

> We have received no peace offer from the Japanese Government, either through official or unofficial channels. Conversations relating to peace have been reported to the Department from various parts of the world, but in no case has an approach been made to this Government, directly or indirectly, by a person who could establish his authority to speak for the Japanese Government, and in no case has an offer to surrender been made. In no case has this Government been presented with a statement purporting to define the basis upon which the Japanese Government would be prepared to conclude peace. . . .[5]

The intercepted series of cables beginning with the one dated July 12, however, was an entirely different matter.

Through their ability to decipher Japanese code, American officials were able to probe the enemy's most secret thoughts, and were intimate observers of a dramatic internal struggle over Japan's war policy. Sato, with his blunt realism bordering on insubordination, pointing out how fantastic were his superior's hopes that Russia could be induced to take the initiative in a negotiated peace; Foreign Minister Togo, insisting that Sato carry out instructions, and finally making clear that Japan was ready to accept almost any surrender short of unconditional surrender — it was all there, clear as crystal, as the exchange of cables progressed:

> *Sato to Togo:* . . . There is no chance whatever of winning the Soviet Union to our side and of obtaining her support on the basis set forth in your cables. . . . Japan is defeated. . . . We must face that fact and act accordingly. . . .
> *Togo to Sato:* . . . In spite of your views, you are to carry out your instructions. . . . Endeavor to obtain the good offices of the Soviet Union in ending the war short of unconditional surrender. . . .[6]

Here was intelligence of unimpeachable authenticity showing that the Japanese government, while determined to fight to a suicidal end rather than accept unconditional surrender, was most urgently seeking to end the war on almost any other terms — provided only that the Emperor be preserved. The contents of the first exchange of cables were in the hands of Truman and Byrnes a day or two before the Potsdam Conference opened; details concerning further messages continued to arrive as the conference progressed.[7]

What influence did this vital information have upon American plans and efforts to bring the war to an early halt? Apparently it had none whatever. America's top officials, gathering in Potsdam, accepted at face value Togo's brave words about fighting to the end rather than accepting unconditional surrender, but did not read the between-the-lines willingness to capitulate barely short of unconditional surrender. Hence Togo's fighting words merely confirmed General Marshall's previous estimate of Japanese military fanaticism:

> From these messages, specifically those from the Japanese Prime Minister [sic], it was evident to us that the army was still largely in control and they were preparing to fight to the bitter end just as they had done on all the islands up to and including Okinawa where I think we had to kill 120,000 of them.

Marshall later admitted that " . . . with all of this information of these messages we had deciphered and all we were not conscious of such an immediate prospect of a surrender." [8]

Secretary of State Byrnes concurred in Marshall's skepticism; he felt that Togo's threat to fight on meant that "we could not rely on Japan's inquiries to the Soviet Union about a negotiated peace as proof that Japan would surrender unconditionally . . . . Under those circumstances, agreement to negotiate could only arouse false hopes. Instead, we relied upon the Potsdam Declaration." [9]

Secretary of War Stimson also knew of the cables in which Japan "had gone so far as to make tentative proposals to the Soviet Government, hoping to use the Russians as mediators in a negotiated peace." Yet, felt Stimson, the Japanese overture could not be considered seriously by the United States, because "these vague proposals contemplated the retention by Japan of important conquered areas . . . There was as yet no indication of any weakening in the Japanese determination to fight rather than accept unconditional surrender." In Stimson's view the quickest way to produce Japan's surrender was not to attempt by diplomatic means to persuade her leaders that they ought to give up, but rather to step up our military pressure until all her leaders were convinced of the hopelessness of their cause.

In war, as in a boxing match, it is seldom sound for the stronger combatant to moderate his blows whenever his opponent shows signs of weakening. To Stimson, at least, the only road to early victory was to exert maximum force with maximum speed. It was not the American responsibility to throw in the sponge for the Japanese; that was one thing they must do for themselves. . . .[10]

Whether due to shortness of time and press of other urgent business, or the inability or unwillingness to subject the series of deciphered messages to sensitive and painstaking analysis, the result is indisputable: during the two weeks between the first cable and the promulgation of the Potsdam Declaration, the United States "failed to turn this newly won and unquestionably vital intelligence data to active and good account." [11]

III

As the delegates of the Big Three were gathering at Potsdam on the eve of their conference, another group of men converged upon an isolated rendezvous point in the wild desolation of the New Mexico desert. High upon a steel tower, silhouetted against the stormy sky by streaks of lightning, waited the first atomic bomb. Anxious scientists under the leadership of Dr. Robert Oppenheimer prepared the instruments and wiring for the final test, which climaxed six years of secret labor. The test had to be postponed for two hours because of stormy weather. As the minutes to zero were counted off, tension heightened to the breaking point. Then, at 5:30 A.M. on July 16, 1945, the desert was suddenly bathed in a tremendous burst of light.

The whole country was lighted by a searching light with the intensity many times that of the midday sun. It was golden, purple, violet, gray and blue. It lighted every peak, crevasse and ridge of the near-by mountain range with a clarity and beauty that cannot be described . . . Thirty seconds after the explosion, came . . . the strong, sustained, awesome roar which warned of doomsday and made us feel that we puny things were blasphemous to dare tamper with the forces heretofore reserved to the Almighty. . . .[12]

The awestruck scientists realized that the explosion had surpassed their most optimistic hopes: the atomic bomb was a spectacular success. Washington was immediately informed, and the news was relayed to Potsdam. There President Truman, upon returning from a day's tour of the ruins of Berlin, found an excited Stimson waiting to give him a message couched in medical terms:

Operated on this morning. Diagnosis not yet complete but results seem satisfactory and already exceed expectations. . . . Dr. Groves pleased.[13]

IV

The first report of the successful test of the new bomb reached President Truman on the evening of July 16. A second brief but enthusiastic message from Harrison arrived the next day — the opening day of the Potsdam Conference. It was not until the 21st that a special messenger aircraft arrived with a full report by General Groves describing the test and its results. Secretary Stimson found it to be "an immensely powerful document, clearly and well written, and with supporting documents of the highest importance . . . It gave a pretty full and eloquent report of the tremendous success of the test and revealed far greater destructive power than we expected . . ."[14]

The time for decision had come. President Truman called an urgent meeting with his top advisers — Stimson, Byrnes, Admiral Leahy, General Marshall, General Arnold, and Admiral King — to review military strategy in the light of this revolutionary development. The attitude of skepticism with regard to the atomic bomb, which had been widespread prior to the New Mexico test, gave way to enthusiasm as Truman and his advisers discussed the possible use of the bomb against Japan. It appeared that the overwhelming power and revolutionary nature of the bomb might have important psychological effects upon the Japanese will to resist. General Marshall felt that the shock value of the bomb would be even more important than its physical destructiveness, and Secretary Byrnes hoped that the bomb might be the deciding factor required to knock a wavering Japan out of the war.[15]

Truman also consulted with Churchill, who "unhesitatingly told me that he favored the use of the atomic bomb if it might aid to end the war." For Churchill, the brilliant light of the atomic bomb banished the dark prospect of having to conquer Japan by a bloody yard-by-yard invasion of her home islands, and replaced this "nightmare picture" with a "vision — fair and bright indeed it seemed — of the end of the whole war in one or two violent shocks."

I thought immediately myself of how the Japanese people, whose courage I had always admired, might find in the apparition of this almost supernatural weapon an excuse which would save their honour and release them from their obligation of being killed to the last fighting man.

. . . To avert a vast, indefinite butchery, to bring the war to an end, to give peace to the world, to lay healing hands upon its tortured peoples by a manifestation of overwhelming power at the cost of a few explosions, seemed, after all our toils and perils, a miracle of deliverance.[16]

The advice received by President Truman was unanimous. The Interim Committee had recommended that the bomb be used against Japan as soon as possible; Prime Minister Churchill was enthusiastic about its use; now the President's highest military and civilian advisers recommended that the atomic bomb be dropped on Japan. The President was ready to make his decision:

> I then agreed to the use of the atomic bomb if Japan did not yield.
> I had reached a decision after long and careful thought. It was not an easy decision to make. I did not like the weapon. But I had no qualms if in the long run millions of lives could be saved.[17]

Thus the decision was made. Japan would be warned to surrender — but the atomic bomb would be used against her unless she accepted surrender in accordance with the forthcoming Potsdam Declaration.

The basic decision — to drop the bomb on Japan — had been made. But an important secondary question remained: how and where should the bomb be used? The question of target selection was crucial. Truman directed Stimson to have the bomb dropped upon a "military target," by which he meant not merely a specific military installation but an urban center of first importance to Japan's war production effort.[18]

A key role in choosing targets in accordance with these instructions was played by General H. H. Arnold, commanding general of the Army Air Forces. Arnold reports that he sat down at Potsdam with Secretary Stimson, Mr. McCloy, and General Marshall to discuss "the big question: how soon would we be ready to use the bomb against Japan, and what should the targets be?" Choosing among those Japanese cities that had deliberately been left unscathed by the regular B-29 bombing operations, Arnold presented the names of five cities "of great importance to the Japanese production effort . . . because of their size and manufacturing or industrial significance": Hiroshima, Niigata, Nagasaki, Kokura, and Kyoto. When the names of the cities were submitted to Mr. Stimson, he "struck off the list of suggested targets the city of Kyoto. Although it was a target of considerable military importance, it had been the ancient capital of Japan and was a shrine of Japanese art and culture. We determined that it should be spared." The four remaining cities were approved as targets.[19]

On July 25 the orders were sent from Washington to General Carl A. Spaatz, commanding general of the Strategic Air Forces in the Pacific:

> The 509 Composite Group, 20th Air Force will deliver its first special bomb as soon as weather will permit visual bombing after about 3 August 1945 on one of the targets: Hiroshima, Kokura, Niigata and Nagasaki. . . .[20]

The fact that definite orders to use the bomb were issued the day before the Potsdam Declaration was published did not mean that American leaders discounted the Declaration as a mere propaganda stunt, or assumed in advance that it would be rejected by the Japanese. As President Truman later explained: "It was, of course, necessary to set the military wheels in motion, as these orders did, but the final decision was in my hands, and was not made until we were returning from Potsdam." Truman instructed Stimson that "the order would stand unless I notified him that the Japanese reply to our ultimatum was acceptable." [21]

Meanwhile the American and British delegates had been reaching agreement upon the text of the proposed warning to Japan. According to Mr. Byrnes, the attempt was made so to phrase the ultimatum that "the threat of utter destruction if Japan resisted was offset with hope of a just though stern peace if she surrendered." (It may be noted that the *threat* of "utter destruction" did not hint at the existence of a new and overwhelmingly powerful weapon; neither did the *hope* extended to Japan include any mention of the retention of the Emperor.)[22]

The agreed text was cabled to Chungking for the approval of Chiang Kai-shek. When his favorable reply was received on July 26, the Potsdam Declaration was immediately dispatched to Japan through diplomatic channels, and simultaneously released to the press:[23]

PROCLAMATION BY HEADS OF GOVERNMENTS, UNITED STATES, UNITED KINGDOM, AND CHINA

We, the President of the United States, the President of the National Government of the Republic of China, and the Prime Minister of Great Britain, representing the hundreds of millions of our countrymen, have conferred and agree that Japan shall be given an opportunity to end the war.

2. The prodigious land, sea, and air forces of the United States, the British Empire, and China, many times reinforced by their armies and air fleets from the West, are poised to strike the final blows upon Japan. This military power is sustained and inspired by the determination of all the Allied nations to prosecute the war against Japan until she ceases to resist.

3. The result of the futile and senseless German resistance to the might of the aroused free peoples of the world stands forth in awful clarity as an example to the people of Japan. The might that now converges on Japan is immeasurably greater than that which, when applied to the resisting Nazis, necessarily laid waste the lands, the industry, and the method of life of the whole German people. The full application of our military power, backed by our resolve, will mean the inevitable and complete destruction of the Japanese forces, and just as inevitably the utter devastation of the Japanese homeland.

4. The time has come for Japan to decide whether she will continue to be controlled by those self-willed militaristic advisers, whose unintelligent calculations have brought the Empire of Japan to the threshold of annihilation, or whether she will follow the path of reason.

5. Following are our terms. We shall not deviate from them. There are no alternatives. We shall brook no delay.

After specifying the Allied terms regarding an end to militaristic government, temporary occupation of the Japanese home islands, disarmament and return home of her soldiers, establishment of democratic government and basic human freedoms, the rebuilding of industry, and access to raw materials and world trade, the Potsdam Declaration concluded:

12. The occupying forces of the Allies shall be withdrawn from Japan as soon as these objectives have been accomplished, and there has been established, in accordance with the freely expressed will of the Japanese people, a peacefully inclined and responsible Government.

13. We call upon the Government of Japan to proclaim now the unconditional surrender of all the Japanese armed forces, and to provide proper and adequate assurances of their good faith in such action. The alternative for Japan is complete and utter destruction.

The point of decisive action had been reached: we had issued a stern warning calling upon Japan to surrender — and we were committed to use the atomic bomb against her if she refused. The key to the future now lay with Japan: it was her moment to decide and to act.

v

The proclamation of the Potsdam Declaration precipitated a major crisis within the Japanese Cabinet. How should Japan react to this attempt by the Allies to end the war short of invasion? Japan herself had been attempting to bring the war to an end by arranging negotiations with the Allies through the good offices of Russia — yet this Declaration was by no means an invitation to negotiate. It was a barefaced command to surrender: "Following are our terms. We shall not deviate from them. There are no alternatives. We shall brook no delay."

There was a sharp division of opinion in the Cabinet. The military leaders, led by the Minister of War, General Korechika Anami, favored a strong answer to the Declaration that would positively reject it with contempt. In contrast, the Foreign Minister, Mr. Togo, was convinced that there was no alternative for his country save to accept the Allies' ultimatum (with the sole condition that the Emperor should be retained); he felt that a deliberate and public rejection of the Potsdam Declaration would be disastrous. Yet he recognized the strength and passion with which the military leaders held to their position, and saw that it would be impossible at that time for the Cabinet to bring itself publicly to accept the Declaration. The rather ticklish strategy of the "peace party" was to stall for time, while forestalling the militarists' moves toward outright rejection of the Allied terms. Mr. Togo's eloquence caused rejection of a motion to the effect that the Cabinet "issue a statement that the Government regarded the Declaration as absurd and . . . could not consider it." After lengthy discussion the Cabinet settled on a wait-and-see policy: ". . . it was agreed that for the time being we should wait to see what the response of the U.S.S.R. would be to our approach to her, planning to decide our course thereafter." It was decided that the newspapers should be authorized to print the Potsdam Declaration (with the deletion of certain phrases expressing Allied good-will and magnanimity) without official government comment thereon. The press should be allowed to make editorial comment, but "the Board of Information should lead the press to minimize publicity." [24]

Having achieved Cabinet agreement on this position on Friday, Mr. Togo was shocked to discover that "the newspapers of the following morning reported that the government had decided to ignore the Potsdam Declaration." [25] The Saturday papers reported that the government's attitude toward the proclamation was *mokusatsu* — literally "to kill it with silence," and therefore, more idiomatically, "to ignore it," "to treat it as unworthy of notice," or "to treat it with silent contempt." * Thus the actual policy adopted by the government on Friday

* The ordinary Japanese word for "no comment" would be *mokushi* (to keep or observe silence).[26]

("wait-and-see," and in the meanwhile "no comment") was by Saturday transformed by the use of the word *mokusatsu* into a policy of contemptuous rejection of the Potsdam Declaration. How the word *mokusatsu* got into Saturday morning's headlines is a mystery no one has yet been able to explain. Mr. Togo protested vigorously when the Cabinet met on Saturday, "pointing out that the newspaper report was at variance with our decision of the preceding day." [27] But the damage had already been done, and was irrevocable. By now the extremists within the military, taking their cue from the newspaper reports of the government's "rejection" of the Declaration, were clamoring for unrestrained denunciation of the Allied proposal; Premier Kantaro Suzuki could hold this tide in check only by reiterating in his Saturday afternoon press conference the position as stated in the papers of that morning:

> I consider the joint proclamation of the three powers to be a rehash of the Cairo Declaration. The government does not regard it as a thing of any great value; the government will just ignore [*mokusatsu*] it. We will press forward resolutely to carry the war to a successful conclusion.[28]

The end result of this confusion was that the anxiously awaiting Allies heard broadcasts from the Tokyo radio announcing that Japan would "take no notice of" the Potsdam Declaration; the understanding both of broadcaster and listeners was that the Imperial Government had rejected the Allied ultimatum with a gesture of contempt. Secretary Stimson understood that Suzuki had "rejected the Potsdam ultimatum by announcing that it was 'unworthy of public notice.' In the face of this rejection we could only proceed to demonstrate that the ultimatum had meant exactly what it said . . ." [29]

The Japanese response was a blow to those who had hoped for a political settlement of the war. Secretary of State Byrnes commented: "That was disheartening. There was nothing left to do but use the bomb." Even after his initial disappointment, Byrnes kept hoping against hope:

> Despite the Japanese Premier's statement, I continued to hope the Japanese Government would change its mind. I was greatly disappointed when August 2, the day of our departure from Potsdam, arrived and no further word had been received. I recognized then that our hope of avoiding use of the bomb was virtually gone.[30]

The final deadline was August 3. On that day — in the absence of any positive word from Japan — President Truman, aboard the cruiser *Augusta* in the middle of the Atlantic Ocean, made the decision irrevocable by refraining from rescinding the orders of July 25 to General Spaatz. The die was cast.[31]

VI

It has been suggested by some that the error in the *mokusatsu* episode was not a slip of the tongue in Tokyo but, rather, an error in translation on the part of inept U. S. monitors. The word *mokusatsu*, which can carry various shades of meaning, was used by Prime Minister Suzuki to mean "no comment," but was rendered "reject with contempt" by a translator unfamiliar with the subtleties of the Japanese language. This theory will not bear the weight of the evidence. Foreign Minister Togo's angry protest to the Cabinet indicates that he understood the use of the word *mokusatsu* to commit his government to rejection of the Potsdam Declaration — the very policy he was striving to avoid.

This theory does, nevertheless, raise a tantalizing question: would the outcome of the war have been different had the Japanese government's intended "no comment" come through clearly to the Allies? Probably not. Official silence regarding the Potsdam Declaration would undoubtedly have been taken by the Allies to mean that their ultimatum was receiving serious consideration in Tokyo. Continued silence, however, in the absence of any other action, would almost certainly have been interpreted as stalling — and the Japanese were contemplating no other concrete action. They were waiting to see how their overture to Russia turned out; yet orders had already been issued insuring that the bomb would drop unless Japan accepted the Potsdam Declaration by August 3. The Japanese were still waiting for word from Moscow when the atomic bomb fell on Hiroshima.

9. Attack and Surrender

THE DIRECTIVE to General Spaatz of July 25, which "set the military wheels in motion," actually only increased the velocity of wheels that had been set moving long before. Once the decision had been made to use the atomic bomb against Japan, there would be no time to train crews, set up bases, transport the bomb material, or establish laboratories to assemble the bomb. All this had to be prepared in advance on the assumption that these preparations would come to fruition in a final positive decision. As early as 1943, plans were made for modifications to a small number of B-29 aircraft which would enable them to deliver a single large-sized bomb.

In the fall of 1944, Colonel Paul W. Tibbets, Jr., was chosen to organize and to train the Air Force unit that would be responsible for the actual delivery of the bomb. The 509th Composite Group, consisting of about 1800 Air Force officers and men, plus a detachment of scientific and technical personnel, was established at Wendover Field in Utah, and underwent months of specialized training in precision, high-altitude bombing.[1]

A base for the 509th had to be constructed on the island of Tinian in the Marianas, complete with laboratory facilities for the final assembly of the bombs. By April 1945 the 509th had completed its training, and its base was finished. On May 6 the first contingent of ground maintenance crews left Seattle by troopship for the Marianas. The 509th transferred from the United States and set up shop on Tinian, still not knowing what their mission would be, except that it was "something special." While hundreds of B-29's from the 313th Wing, also based on Tinian, took off day after day for the bombing of Japan, the 509th confined its activities to training flights in groups of three B-29's each. Each bomber carried a single large bomb, the same shape and size as the atomic bomb, but loaded with TNT. At first they flew to neighboring Japanese bases, such as Marcus Island, Truk, and Rota, and practiced dropping their "pumpkins," as the bombs were called. On July 20 they began training flights over Japan itself, always flying in isolated groups of three planes, and dropping a single bomb on a Japanese city. This training was to familiarize the men of the 509th with flying over Japan itself and also to accustom the Japanese to the sight of a small group of B-29's flying over their territory and doing practically no damage. It was thereby hoped that the aircraft carrying the actual atomic bomb might be exempt from fighter and antiaircraft opposition.[2]

Immediately after the successful New Mexico test of the atomic bomb, the remaining fissionable material then available was rushed to Tinian, where final assembly of the bomb was to take place. By August 3 all was in readiness. Weather was unfavorable on August 4 and 5; however, good weather was predicted for the 6th. On Sunday, August 5, the bomb was made ready and loaded into Colonel Tibbets' flagship, the *Enola Gay*. Briefings were held, and the crew for the first time were told of the extraordinary power of the bomb they were about to carry.

The orders had been given, the weather was good, the bomb was loaded into the plane; but the delivery of this bomb to Japan was still not a simple or routine matter. The evening before, scientists attached to the 509th had watched four consecutive B-29's crash in flames at the far end of the runway, as they failed to gain sufficient speed for take-off. Captain William S. Parsons, Navy ordnance expert responsible for technical control of the bomb, decided that should this happen to the *Enola Gay* there would be danger of an atomic explosion that might wipe out the entire Air Force population on Tinian. He therefore decided to go along with the flight, leaving the bomb deactivated until after the plane was safely in the air, and then to make final assembly in flight. Captain Parsons was the only man on the flight who had full knowledge of the nature and workings of the bomb; he therefore borrowed a pistol to be used (upon himself) if there should be any danger of his falling into enemy hands.[3]

At 2:45 on Monday morning, August 6, 1945, the *Enola Gay* and two accompanying B-29's took off from the island of Tinian, bound for Japan. The weather planes, which had preceded them by an hour, reported that the weather was clear over the primary target of Hiroshima. This report sealed the fate of the city. At 8:15 the planes reached Hiroshima. Weather was clear; there was no enemy opposition; the bombing run was routine. The bombardier aimed his missile at a spot near the center of the city, touched the release switch — and the bomb fell. As smoke and cloud boiled upward from Hiroshima, the anxiously awaiting officers at Tinian received a message by radio: "Mission successful."[4]

Since the prime objective of the atomic bombing was to convince the Japanese that further resistance was useless and could only result in needless destruction, the attack on Hiroshima was followed by a propaganda effort directed to the Japanese people. Radio broadcasts played up the revolutionary nature of the new bomb, but also laid emphasis upon the fact that surrender was possible on honorable terms. Millions of leaflets were dropped bearing the following message:

TO THE JAPANESE PEOPLE

America asks that you take immediate heed of what we say on this leaflet.

We are in possession of the most destructive explosive ever devised by man. A single one of our newly developed atomic bombs is actually the equivalent in explosive power to what 2,000 of our giant B-29's can carry on a single mission. This awful fact is one for you to ponder and we solemnly assure you it is grimly accurate.

We have just begun to use this weapon against your homeland. If you still have any doubt, make inquiry as to what happened to Hiroshima when just one atomic bomb fell on that city.

Before using this bomb to destroy every resource of the military by which they are prolonging this useless war, we ask that you now petition the Emperor to end the war. Our President has outlined for you the thirteen consequences of an honorable surrender. We urge that you accept these consequences and begin the work of building a new, better, and peace-loving Japan.

You should take steps now to cease military resistance. Otherwise, we shall resolutely employ this bomb and all our other superior weapons to promptly and forcefully end the war.[5]

II

The dropping of the second bomb shortly after the first was an integral part of the American plan to knock Japan out of the war with a sudden strong blow. Japan had scientists who were well aware of the difficulties involved in obtaining enough fissionable materials for an atomic bomb. After long concentrated effort, one bomb might be built, they knew. But they might also suppose that it would take a similar lengthy time to gather enough fissionable material to make a second bomb, and then a third. If they reasoned that the United States had used its one-and-only atomic bomb, and that future atomic attacks would come only singly and after long intervals, the Japanese militarists might be convinced that they could weather the destruction of these atomic blows long enough to enable their army to reach a favorable decision on the invasion beaches. Therefore our leaders planned to drop a second bomb shortly after the first in a deliberate attempt to create the impression that we had an unlimited supply of bombs and would not hesitate to use them. (As a matter of fact, we were in possession at that time of only two bombs; following the Nagasaki attack, we could not have dropped another atomic bomb on Japan for some weeks.) Our strategy was to make Japan aware that she was being subjected to an overwhelmingly destructive military force, so overpowering that any future resistance would indeed be folly. We wanted to dispel any illusion that Japan might be able to hold out against our atomic might. One involved in the decision of the United States describes the thinking of our leaders:

> The second bomb was ready for use on August 9th. Its prompt use would emphasize our ability and determination to carry through if necessary. . . . We would let the Japanese know that great industrial plants were turning out such bombs as rapidly as possible. Our hope was that quick surrender would make their further use unnecessary.[6]

No sign or word came from Japan that the Hiroshima bomb had influenced her in the direction of surrender. Consequently, there was nothing to stop the motion of the wheels of war which had been gaining momentum for months. The President had an order issued to General Spaatz directing him to "continue operations as planned unless otherwise instructed." [7]

The use of our second bomb was originally scheduled for August 11. However, a weather report predicted a long period of bad weather beginning on that day, which would prevent visual bombing over Japan. Since the 509th was committed to visual bombing, which was more accurate than bombing by radar, the second sortie was moved up two days to August 9.[8]

Three of the scientists who were responsible for the assembling of the second bomb at Tinian took steps to insure that the Japanese scientific community realized the nature of these bombs and the seriousness of their threat to Japan. Luis Alvarez, Robert Serber, and Philip Morrison wrote a note addressed to Dr. Ryokichi Sagane, a Japanese physicist, with whom they had worked some years before at the University of California:

> We are sending this as a personal message, to urge that you use your influence, as a reputable nuclear physicist, to convince the Japanese General Staff of the terrible consequences which will be suffered by your people if you continue in this war.
>
> You have known for several years that an atomic bomb could be built if a nation were willing to pay the enormous cost of preparing the necessary material. Now that you have seen that we have constructed the production plants, there can be no doubt in your mind that all the output of these factories, working 24 hours a day, will be exploded on your homeland.
>
> Within the space of three weeks we have proof-fired one bomb in the American desert, exploded one in Hiroshima, and fired the third this morning.
>
> We implore you to confirm these facts to your leaders, and to do your utmost to stop the destruction and waste of life which can only result in the total annihilation of all your cities, if continued. As scientists, we deplore the use to which a beautiful discovery has been put, but we can assure you that unless Japan surrenders at once this rain of atomic bombs will increase manyfold in fury.[9]

Alvarez taped copies of this note to three instrument boxes that were to be parachuted to the ground from the second plane as the bomb fell from the first. (One of the messages was found at Nagasaki, and turned over to Japanese Naval Intelligence; whether it aided in bringing Japan to surrender is doubtful. Long after the surrender, Dr. Sagane finally received a copy of the note addressed to him.)[10]

The second atomic sortie proceeded less smoothly than the first. The lead plane was to rendezvous with the two instrument

planes over a small island just off the coast of Japan. The first
two planes circled for forty-five minutes over the island, waiting
for the second instrument plane. Finally, with gasoline and
time running out, they decided to go on alone. Weather planes,
which had preceded the strike group by an hour, radioed that
weather was favorable and visibility good over both targets,
Kokura and Nagasaki. However, by the time the two bombers
reached Kokura almost an hour later, the weather had changed.
For more than an hour the B-29's circled over the city — the
pilots cursing the dense clouds that obscured their target. They
kept circling, waiting, but there was no opening in the clouds.
At about 10:30 they noticed puffs of black smoke, which indicated antiaircraft fire from Japanese batteries below. The puffs
of smoke came closer. Fighter planes were then seen rising to
the attack. The fliers turned and proceeded southward toward
Nagasaki, their second target. Clouds by now obscured this city
also. Those in charge of the bomb in the lead plane were faced
with an agonizing decision. Their orders were to bomb visually
and visually only. Should they continue to circle, endlessly,
waiting for the clouds to break, and thus run out of fuel and
be forced to crash-land in the ocean, losing their bomb? Or
should they bomb by radar, thus going directly against their
orders? Or should they try to get back to Okinawa and land
with their bomb intact? Fuel was now so low that the additional weight of carrying the bomb back to Okinawa made it
questionable whether they could reach the island safely. The
decision was finally made by the officer in charge of the bomb
that they should violate orders and bomb by radar. Moments
later a rift in the clouds was seen. Quickly the plane flew over
its target, the bombardier pulled the release, and the bomb was
dropped directly over the industrial valley of Nagasaki at
11:01 A.M.

The planes left the coast of Japan, after having flown over
the Empire for three hours and seventeen minutes, longer by far

than any other mission of the war. When the lead plane landed on Okinawa, two of its motors stopped dead halfway down the runway for lack of fuel. As the fliers waited while their planes were refueled, they heard the radio news that Russia had just entered the war against Japan.[11]

Now our atomic bolt had been shot. "We believed that our attacks had struck cities which must certainly be important to the Japanese military leaders, both Army and Navy, and we waited for a result," commented Secretary Stimson. "We waited one day." [12]

III

On August 10, 1945, one day after the bombing of Nagasaki, the government of Japan announced that it was willing to surrender to the Allies in accordance with the Potsdam Declaration, "with the understanding that the said declaration does not comprise any demand which prejudices the prerogatives of His Majesty as a Sovereign Ruler." [13]

This message put squarely before the Allied statesmen the question of the future of the Emperor, upon which they had up to this point been unable to agree. The President summoned Stimson, Forrestal, Byrnes, and Leahy to the White House to decide what our reply to the Japanese offer should be. Stimson urged a reply that would make it clear that Japan could retain the Emperor. The Secretary of State remained hesitant. The "understanding" in the Japanese message might be interpreted to mean that the defeated enemy was setting a condition which we must accept before she would surrender. "I do not see why we should retreat from our demand for unconditional surrender," said Byrnes. "That demand was presented to Japan before the use of the bomb and before the Soviet Union was a belligerent. If any conditions are to be accepted, I want the United States and not Japan to state the conditions." The

President agreed with this way of thinking, and asked Mr. Byrnes to draft a reply.[14]

Mr. Byrnes's task was a delicate one. Simply to accept the Japanese note as it stood would be equivalent to acceding to a demand voiced by a vanquished foe. On the other hand, a flat rejection of the Japanese condition might produce outraged determination on the part of Japan to continue the war to the bitter end regardless of the cost. He drafted a carefully worded reply that avoided the appearance of recognizing a condition set by Japan but at the same time implied that the Emperor would retain his supreme position within the Empire — subject only to the authority of the Supreme Allied Commander.

> From the moment of surrender the authority of the Emperor and the Japanese Government to rule the state shall be subject to the Supreme Commander of the Allied powers who will take such steps as he deems proper to effectuate the surrender terms.
>
> The Emperor will be required to authorize and ensure the signature by the Government of Japan and the Japanese Imperial General Headquarters of the surrender terms . . . and to issue such other orders as the Supreme Commander may require to give effect to the surrender terms.
> . . . .
> The ultimate form of government of Japan shall, in accordance with the Potsdam Declaration, be established by the freely expressed will of the Japanese people.[15]

This message was quickly cleared with our allies, and forwarded to the Japanese government on August 11. Then followed three anxious days of waiting. "Never," Secretary Byrnes recalled, "have I known time to pass so slowly!" [16] At last came the reply: Japan accepted. The war was over.

IV

As soon as the existence of the atomic bomb and the destruction of Hiroshima were announced, it was clear to all that the new weapon, by its very nature, raised problems not involved in the use of other weapons. Even before the war ended, a vigorous debate began over the ethical implications of the atomic bomb. To the issues of that debate we now turn.

III

Dropping the Atomic
Bomb: Right or Wrong?

10. Immediate Reactions

WAS IT RIGHT or wrong to drop the atomic bombs on Japan? The questions that scientists, soldiers, and statesmen had debated in whispered secrecy were shouted from the housetops after Hiroshima. The spectacular advent of the atomic bomb, and its apparent bringing of the war to a prompt close, aroused widespread public interest throughout America in atomic energy and in the ethical problems it raised. The atomic bomb became a public issue — and, inevitably, a subject for public opinion polls. In December 1945 *Fortune* Magazine published the results of a public-opinion survey in which people were asked to describe their feelings about America's use of the bomb against Japan. The alternatives posed and the results were as follows:[1]

	Alternatives	*Per Cent Responding*
1.	We should not have used any atomic bombs at all.	4.5
2.	We should have dropped one first on some unpopulated region, to show the Japanese its power, and dropped the second one on a city only if they hadn't surrendered after the first one.	13.8
3.	We should have used the two bombs on cities just as we did.	53.5
4.	We should have quickly used many more of them before Japan had a chance to surrender.	22.7
5.	Don't know.	5.5

So it was that only a few months after Hiroshima, fully three quarters of the American public felt our use of the bomb was morally justifiable, and nearly a third of these harbored the vindictive feeling that the Japanese should have been punished even further before they had a chance to surrender. Only one person in five showed any uneasiness of conscience about our use of the atomic bomb.

The existence of a general attitude of complacency about the atomic bomb, indicated by the *Fortune* poll, was also noted by the Catholic journal *Commonweal,* which editorially decried the lack of public condemnation of the bomb's use. This was confirmed by a survey sponsored by the Social Science Research Council, which reported that within the first year of the atomic age the American public had reached a state where it "does not seem emotionally disturbed about the bomb. . . . The majority have found a way to push the bomb into the back of their minds," thus making it "possible for them to be free of active personal concern." [2]

Thus, those who were disturbed about the use of the atomic bomb — in the main, the most outspoken were churchmen and scientists — found themselves to be a small minority of the American people. Even within their own groups opinion was by no means unanimous. Many atomic scientists supported the use of the bomb against Japan and brushed aside their colleagues' conscientious scruples: "After all," retorted Enrico Fermi, "the thing's superb physics!" Yet even those who supported use of the bomb against Japan for the sake of ending the war quickly were appalled at the massive destruction of life caused by their new weapon. Fermi's wife reports that among the Los Alamos scientists a "sense of guilt" was felt "more or less deeply, more or less consciously. It was there, undeniably." J. Robert Oppenheimer, director of the Los Alamos Scientific Laboratory and the man who, more than any other, deserves credit for creation of the atomic bomb, could say, "In some sort of crude sense which no vulgarity, no humor, no overstatement can quite extinguish, the physicists have known sin; and this is a knowledge which they cannot lose." [3]

The scientists' feeling of guilt did not cause them to brood over the events of the past, but rather to muster their efforts to influence the events of the future so that atomic energy would never again be used to destroy human life. Associations were quickly organized at Los Alamos, Chicago, and Oak Ridge to "urge and in every way sponsor the initiation of international discussion leading to a world authority in which would be vested the control of nuclear energy." [4] The scientists hoped that the achievement of such international control might lead to the establishment of mutual trust and peace among nations; thus their labors would result in a double benefit for mankind — not only a new source of unlimited energy, but the abolition of war itself.

Opinion was not unanimous within the churches. A few church spokesmen approved the use of the atomic bomb against Japan on the grounds that it "saved countless lives." [5] The official journal of the United Lutheran Church in America was content to leave the question of the morality of the bomb in the hands of the military, going so far as to say:

> If, as is proven, they [the atomic bombs] aided in depriving Japan of plants for the replacement of munitions destroyed in battle, or of sustenance for the population, or of such morale as is essential to a nation's continuance in combat, then adequate military reasons for employing the bomb are furnished.[6]

Others implicitly condoned the bomb's use merely by keeping silence — or by passing over the immediate moral issue to urge a return to faith so that this newest gift of science (capable of being used for good or evil) might be used in the future for the benefit of man, rather than for his destruction.

However the most vocal and influential spokesmen for the American churches, both Protestant and Catholic, either questioned the use of the bomb or condemned it outright. Although grounds for the moral judgment varied, there was a substantial consensus among leading churchmen that our use of the bomb against Japan was morally indefensible.

The first immediate reactions that came from Protestant church leaders following the announcement of the bombing of Hiroshima, although not clearly condemnatory, gave an indication of a certain uneasiness of conscience. On August 9, 1945, John Foster Dulles and Bishop G. Bromley Oxnam issued a statement (prepared before the bombing of Nagasaki) on behalf of the Federal Council of Churches of Christ in America:

> If we, a professedly Christian nation, feel morally free to use atomic energy in that way [i.e., to obliterate Japanese cities], men elsewhere will accept that verdict. Atomic weapons will be looked upon as a normal part of the arsenal of war and the stage will be set for the sudden and final destruction of mankind. . . .[7]

The statement recommended that we "seek to show quickly and dramatically how our new power can be used to stop war — not merely to prosecute it," and urged that the United States suspend any further use of the new weapon until the Japanese had time to react to the bomb and to accept our surrender terms.* The statement did not condemn explicitly either the atomic bomb itself or our use of it. Yet the concern lest the dropping of atomic bombs be considered as acceptable as conventional methods of warfare, and the fact that a statement was issued at all — something the churches had not done following the March incendiary raid on Tokyo in which an estimated 100,000 persons were killed — clearly indicated that the churchmen had serious questions about the morality of using the atomic bomb.

* This recommendation could have brought no pressure to bear upon Truman and his advisers, since in their eyes this was precisely what they were attempting to do. No more atomic bombs were dropped after the Federal Council's statement was published, so the churchmen took comfort in the thought that their statement might have had some influence in staying the use of further atomic bombs — until they later learned that the United States had no other bombs to drop. (April 1959 interview with Richard M. Fagley, Secretary of the Federal Council's Commission on a Just and Durable Peace, who in 1945 participated in drawing up the statement.)

The immediate reaction of Roman Catholic leadership was also negative. The semiofficial Vatican newspaper *Osservatore Romano*, in its first comment on the use of the bomb, stated: "This incredible destructive instrument remains a temptation, if not for horrified contemporaries, then for posterity." The editorial commended Leonardo da Vinci for destroying his plans for a submarine lest men use it to destroy civilization; but, unfortunately, those who used the atomic bomb "did not think as did Leonardo." The official Vatican Press Office allowed itself to be quoted: "The use of atomic bombs in Japan has created an unfavorable impression on the Vatican." However, the next day the Vatican denied any official papal condemnation of the bombing of Hiroshima.[8]

Many church periodicals were more outspoken. The influential *Christian Century* denounced what it called "America's Atomic Atrocity," and condemned the use of the bomb as "impetuous, indeliberate, and wanton." The Catholic journal *Commonweal* cried "Horror and Shame!" while the *Catholic World* branded the bombing of Hiroshima "atrocious and abominable."[9]

Pacifists were unanimous in decrying the use of the bomb. Forty-nine Protestant pacifist leaders issued a statement charging that our "reckless and irresponsible employment" of the bomb had "dragged the war and all of us with it, to a new low of inhumanity." The pacifist *Catholic Worker* denounced the bombing as "the most terrible crime ever committed by a 'Christian' nation against the Mystical Body of Christ."[10]

A commission of twenty-six distinguished Protestant theologians (including both pacifists and nonpacifists), appointed by the Federal Council of Churches to study "the relation of the Church to the war in the light of the Christian faith," reported their feelings of deep penitence for the "morally indefensible" bombing of Hiroshima and Nagasaki, and stated that they felt "compelled to judge our chosen course inexcusable."[11]

What were the moral grounds on which churchmen (and others) condemned the use of the atomic bomb against Japan? On what grounds did those responsible for the decision defend their act? In the following chapters we shall examine the major arguments and ethical principles set forth on both sides of this debate, beginning with the justification offered by those who made the decision and then considering in systematic order the main criticisms raised against this justification.

11. Motives for Using the Bomb

PART OF the moral judgment on any action must include a judgment upon the motives of the agent. What were the motives of United States officials who made the decision to drop the atomic bomb upon Japan? What was their purpose in using the bomb?

The primary purpose of those who planned the bomb's use was, as Secretary Stimson put it, "to end the war in victory with the least possible cost in the lives of the men" in the American armed services.[1] The end was victory, and this could only be achieved when the Japanese surrendered. But how could the Japanese government be persuaded to surrender? Vivid in the memory of our military leaders was the defeat of Germany. She had finally been brought to surrender only after invading armies had forcibly seized her territory, smashed her capital city block by block to rubble, reduced her economy to chaos and her people to starvation, and hounded her fugitive leader to suicide in a cellar. Would it be necessary to go through the same process to wrest a surrender from Japan?

Japan, despite her many defeats up to mid-1945, was in some ways in a better position to defend her homeland than was Germany. Her main armies never had been defeated: 2,000,000 fresh and well-trained troops were prepared to offer stubborn and even fanatical resistance in defense of their home islands. Although the Allies held air superiority, they could not prevent hundreds of *kamikaze* suicide aircraft from inflicting heavy losses on their invasion fleet. Japan's mountainous terrain was ideal for bitter-end guerrilla resistance, and ill suited for the highly mechanized type of warfare in which America's equipment gave her superiority. These factors persuaded Secretary Stimson that, if we had to invade Japan in order to bring her to surrender, "we shall in my opinion have to go through with an even more bitter finish fight than in Germany . . . and we shall have to leave the Japanese islands even more thoroughly destroyed. . . ." Moreover, if surrender in Japan were achieved only after the disintegration of her legitimate central government (as was the case in Germany), the bloody rooting out of stubborn Japanese defenders would have to be repeated in large areas of China, Southeast Asia, and on many islands from the Marshalls to the East Indies.[2]

On the other hand, if the Japanese government could be persuaded to surrender — before an actual invasion of Japanese soil galvanized a united population into suicidal desperation — the Japanese traditions of reverence to the Emperor and obedience to authority could be counted upon to insure a rapid return to peace, not only in Japan proper but in the far-flung territories occupied by her 3,000,000 overseas troops. Such was the thinking that went into the preparation of the Potsdam Declaration. Should this ultimatum fail to bring Japanese surrender, then the atomic bomb, by its dramatic and massive destructive power, might convince the Japanese leaders that further resistance was utterly futile and could lead only to the certain and useless destruction of the Japanese nation. The atomic bomb, by providing a tremendous shock and bringing Japan to a speedy surrender, "would save many times the number of lives, both American and Japanese, that it would cost." [3]

II

In formulating these plans, Stimson and his associates proceeded on the basis of two assumptions about the future course of events — assumptions that it will be helpful to analyze further. The first was that if the atomic bomb were not used to

produce an early surrender, invasion of the Japanese home islands would be necessary. This assumption, of course, represented the Army point of view and was opposed by Navy and
Air Force leaders, who believed that sea and air power could
bring Japan to surrender without invasion. Despite the fact that
only one of the four members of the Joint Chiefs of Staff believed an invasion would be necessary to defeat Japan, King,
Leahy, and Arnold aquiesced in the decision to proceed with
planning for such an invasion, and this tended to create the impression that the Joint Chiefs were agreed unanimously on invasion of Japan as the only way to end the war. This impression, at least for the members of the Interim Committee, was
no doubt reinforced by the fact that the whole atomic bomb
project, including the Interim Committee's deliberations, was
carried on under Army auspices and control. For example,
when the Interim Committee met to consider recommendations
for the use of the atomic bomb, General Groves and Army
Chief of Staff Marshall were present, and could describe the
prospects of the war from the Army point of view, but no Navy
or Air Force officers were present to state the alternative position. The result, as Robert Oppenheimer describes it, was that
"in the back of our minds was the notion that the invasion was
inevitable because we had been told that." James Byrnes confirms in his account that in the deliberations of the Interim
Committee "we relied on the estimates of the military situation
presented by the Joint Chiefs of Staff" — which Byrnes specifies as involving the two-stage invasion of the Japanese home
islands.[4]

In actual fact an invasion — the necessity for which was
taken for granted by Truman, Stimson, and Marshall — probably would not have been necessary to produce a Japanese surrender. Japan, despite the fanatical determination of her military leaders to fight on, was on the verge of collapse. This fact
was plain to those in Japan who had eyes to see. A brutally
frank report on the state of the nation's economy was presented

in June 1945 to the highest levels of the Japanese government. After the middle of the year, the report stated, transportation would be "faced with insurmountable difficulties"; communication with the Chinese mainland and Southeast Asia would be impossible if Okinawa were lost (which it was); railroad transportation would be "confined to local areas"; steel production, at about one fourth of the 1944 level, would not permit construction of ships; various industries would have to suspend operations for lack of coal; production of chemicals was "falling off at an alarming rate" that would shortly influence the production of oil and explosives; food shortages had already resulted in the "appearance of starvation conditions" in certain sections of the country; and rapid inflation had begun which would "seriously undermine" the whole wartime economy.[5]

Japan had lost the power to recuperate from increasingly severe air and sea attack. Under such conditions, the Japanese armed forces could hardly have continued major resistance for very long. The United States Strategic Bombing Survey, following its detailed investigation of the impact of American bombing on the state of the Japanese nation, and interviews with high Japanese officials, concluded:

> . . . it is the Survey's opinion that certainly prior to 31 December 1945, and in all probability prior to 1 November 1945, Japan would have surrendered even if the atomic bombs had not been dropped, even if Russia had not entered the war, and even if no invasion had been planned or contemplated.[6]

It seems clear that America's leaders, lacking the benefits of adequate wartime intelligence (and hindsight), made the decision to drop the atomic bomb on the basis of an overestimation of Japan's ability to resist. This estimate was doubtless reinforced by the public statements of Japanese leaders vowing that Japan would fight to the bitter end — which we took at face value.

III

The second expectation about the future, which also proved to be faulty, involved the number of casualties caused by the bomb. The Interim Committee — on the basis of Oppenheimer's estimate — was thinking in terms of 20,000 persons killed by each bomb, or a total of 40,000 by the proposed one-two atomic attack. Yet the actual attack killed about three times that number of persons.[7]

Oppenheimer's estimate assumed that the population of the attacked cities would have taken shelter, yet no one in Hiroshima had done so when the bomb exploded in the air over the center of the city. Earlier in the morning an air raid alert had been sounded (presumably because of the weather plane that preceded the atomic bomb mission by an hour), but the "all clear" signal came about 7:30, forty-five minutes before the *Enola Gay* and her two escorts flew over. No warning was sounded at the approach of these planes; presumably the Japanese assumed that they were reconnaissance craft presenting no danger to the civilian population. Thus at the time of the explosion, many workers were still en route to their jobs, and nearly all the schoolchildren were at work in the open on a project of dismantling buildings to create fire-breaks as a precaution against incendiary raids. "Because of the lack of warning and the populace's indifference to small groups of planes, the explosion came as almost a complete surprise, and the people had not taken shelter. Many were caught in the open, and most of the rest in flimsily constructed homes or commercial establishments."[8]

Failure of the population to take shelter increased the casualty rates substantially. An estimated 25 per cent of the deaths at Hiroshima were caused by flash burns, all of which could have been prevented by the flimsiest of shelter. Even one layer of cloth will ordinarily provide protection, since flash burns (analogous to sunburn) affect only those portions of the body directly exposed to the fireball of an atomic explosion. Another 20 per cent were killed by gamma rays from the bomb, from which ordinary housing and clothing does not afford protection; however, use of basement or underground air raid shelters would have reduced this figure considerably. Many additional casualties were due to falling debris and the conflagration which burned people unable to extricate themselves from wrecked buildings; proper air raid shelters would have reduced deaths from these causes substantially.[9]

Of course, the massive power of the atomic bomb, which destroyed simultaneously and totally almost all of the city's medical and relief facilities, accounted for casualties that even the most alert Japanese defense could not have prevented. The commanding Army general and his entire staff — who might have organized rescue work — were wiped out. Only three of the city's forty-seven hospitals could be used — and even these did not keep out the rain. Of the city's 300 physicians, 90 per cent were killed or injured; of 2400 nurses and orderlies, more than 1800 were instant casualties. Of thirty-three modern fire stations, twenty-six were rendered useless; with three quarters of the firemen dead or injured, fires burned unchecked throughout the city. And so many wounded, who in an ordinary air raid might have been rescued, died either in the burning wreckage or from lack of adequate medical attention.[10]

Much the same story can be told of Nagasaki, which was scarcely better prepared than Hiroshima, despite the fact that some news of the Hiroshima disaster had appeared in the local newspaper on August 8. The official report of the Nagasaki Prefecture indicates the lack of proper air raid precautions:

> The day was clear with not very much wind — an ordinary midsummer's day. The strain of continuous air attack on the city's population and the severity of the summer had vitiated enthusiastic air raid precautions. Previously, a general alert had

been sounded at 0748, with a raid alert at 0750; this was can-
celled at 0830, and the alertness of the people was dissipated
by a great feeling of relief.

Although air raid officials sighted the two B-29's approaching
the city, the alert was not sounded until 11:09 A.M., eight
minutes *after* the bomb fell. Only about 400 people had taken
refuge in the city's underground tunnel shelters, which were
adequate for 30 per cent of the population. Those who did take
shelter were uninjured, although the tunnels were very close to
ground zero.[11]

Thus it may clearly be stated, without underestimating
the power of the atomic bomb, that casualties from the two
atomic raids could have been greatly reduced if the Japanese
had used their air raid alert system and had taken adequate
shelter. What caused this failure in Japanese civil defense?

In part, the failure may be explained by weariness (in the
case of Nagasaki) and the complacency of a city (Hiroshima)
which had so far escaped serious air attack. But the tendency
to ignore the small flights of B-29's as harmless was the result
not only of Japanese carelessness but of a deliberate policy of
our Army Air Force. For weeks Colonel Tibbets of the 509th
had been sending isolated groups of three B-29's on training
flights over Japan — hoping (as we have noted) that the small
damage inflicted by their practice bombs would induce the
Japanese to consider such groups of planes not worth attacking.
So well did Colonel Tibbets' tactic succeed that his flights became an object of derision in the propaganda broadcasts of
Tokyo Rose, who informed her GI listeners: "You are now
reduced to small missions of three planes, and the bombs they
drop are just duds." [12]

Although Tibbets' tactic was undertaken for the purpose of
protecting his men from Japanese fighters and antiaircraft
attack, it also had the unintended result of lulling the Japanese
into carelessness in regard to air raid precautions. While the

Interim Committee, in one compartment of the atomic bomb project, was reaching its decision on the assumption of adequate Japanese civil defense measures, Colonel Tibbets, in his compartment, was taking action that inadvertently led to the absence of such measures, and thereby vastly increased the number of casualties.

The complexity and compartmentalization of the huge and highly secret atomic bomb project reinforced the limitations imposed upon men's knowledge by the uncertainties and the breakdown of communications inherent in modern war. Truman and Stimson acted in good faith upon the basis of the best information and predictions available to them; it must be said that their motives were far less bloodthirsty than the actual results of using the bomb may have led their critics to infer. Yet the inaccuracies in their advisers' predictions about the course of future events combined (in this case) to make the choice before America's leaders appear more simple than it actually was. As it appeared to Truman and his advisers, the only alternative to sacrificing 40,000 lives with the atomic bomb was to allow the loss of hundreds of thousands of lives in a prolonged invasion of Japan; viewed in this light, "the decision was not difficult." [13] Had the massive evil of the invasion not loomed so certain, had the choice presented itself as the sacrifice of 110,000 lives as over against a surrender brought about within three months by blockade and conventional bombing (involving a minimum loss of *American* lives), the decision, perhaps still in favor of using the bomb, would not have appeared so clear-cut.

IV

The prompt termination of the Pacific war, a few days after the atomic attack, seemed to vindicate the hopes of those who had argued in favor of using the bomb against Japan. Despite the fact that casualties were three times higher than anticipated, America's leaders publicly claimed that the results justified their action: the bomb stopped the war and resulted in the (net) saving of many thousands of lives.

President Truman, in his report to the nation upon his return from the Potsdam Conference, stated on August 9:

> Having found the bomb we have used it. We have used it against those who attacked us without warning at Pearl Harbor, against those who have starved and beaten and executed American prisoners of war, against those who have abandoned all pretense of obeying international laws of warfare. We have used it in order to shorten the agony of war, in order to save the lives of thousands and thousands of young Americans.
>
> We shall continue to use it until we completely destroy Japan's power to make war. Only a Japanese surrender will stop us.

Two months later Mr. Truman, in a message to Congress, claimed that "the atomic bomb did not win the war, but it certainly shortened the war. We know that it saved the lives of untold thousands of American and Allied soldiers who would otherwise have been killed in battle." [14]

Other key members of the government repeated Truman's theme. Secretary of State Byrnes admitted that the two atomic bombs had caused "many casualties, but not nearly so many as there would have been had our air force continued to drop incendiary bombs on Japan's cities. Certainly, by bringing the war to an end, the atomic bomb saved the lives of thousands of American boys." Arthur H. Compton claimed that the use of the atomic bomb resulted in "the net saving of many lives, probably millions of lives," and commented that "when the boys who had been poised for the invasion of Japan began to come home, I could not help feeling that our choice was justified." Vannevar Bush summed up the government's position thus:

The ships and troops were moving, the first waves of troops had been told off for the sacrifice on the beaches, and all the juggernaut of massive land war was under way. Into this acute situation came the atomic bomb, with a maximum of surprise and dramatic effect . . . Two bombs went off, and the war ended. It is useless to argue how much they advanced the end. Certainly enough to save more lives than they snuffed out, and more treasure than their use cost.[15]

V

Many critics accepted the government's *criteria* for judging the use of the atomic bomb (i.e., immediate consequences) but denied that the *results* produced were sufficient to support the government's claims. Was not Japan already essentially defeated? Was she not already desperately seeking to end the war by negotiation? The bomb did not appreciably shorten the war — and the agony at Hiroshima was the more reprehensible because it was unnecessary.

How is one to judge these claims and counterclaims? Since the debate turns upon the consequences resulting from the use of the bomb, it is necessary at this point to examine in considerable detail the sequence of events produced in Japan by the impact of the bombing of Hiroshima and Nagasaki. Fortunately, these events are now known with sufficient certainty to allow a reliable judgment to be made as to whether the use of the atomic bomb really shortened the war and saved lives.

12. Did the Bomb Shorten the War?

IN HIS IMPERIAL RESCRIPT of August 15, 1945, the Emperor Hirohito announced to the "one hundred million" people of Japan the surrender of their nation. After noting that the general war situation had "developed not necessarily to Japan's advantage," His Imperial Majesty went on to attribute the decision to surrender to the atomic bomb:

> Moreover, the enemy has begun to employ a new and most cruel bomb, the power of which to do damage is indeed incalculable, taking the toll of many innocent lives. Should We continue to fight, it would not only result in an ultimate collapse and obliteration of the Japanese nation, but also it would lead to the total extinction of human civilization. Such being the case, how are We to save the millions of Our subjects; or to atone Ourselves before the hallowed spirits of Our Imperial Ancestors? This is the reason why We have ordered the acceptance of the provisions of the Joint Declaration of the Powers.[1]

The record of events within the Japanese government during July and August 1945 confirms the Emperor's statement in the imperial rescript: the atomic bomb, while playing an insignificant role in the *defeat* of Japan, was the decisive factor in the *surrender* of Japan.[2]

Defeat in war is a military event; recognition of the fact of defeat and acceptance of surrender on the basis of such recognition are political acts. A prolonged and complex political struggle took place within the Japanese government during the summer of 1945, which finally led to the official recognition of Japan's defeat and her acceptance of "unconditional surrender."

127

The atomic bomb played a vital role in the outcome of that struggle.

II

The unfolding of events in Tokyo in the summer of 1945 centered in the contest between the powerful *gumbatsu* (military clique) and those who had come to the conclusion that Japan's only hope of avoiding national destruction lay in the immediate cessation of the war, even if this meant accepting the Allied demand for unconditional surrender. The military clique had gained control of the Japanese government in the 1930's, initiated Japan's expansionist moves in Manchuria, China, and Indochina, and, under the premiership of General Hideki Tojo, initiated what was to have been a short and decisive war in the Pacific by a crippling attack on Pearl Harbor. Although Tojo's government had fallen in July 1944, shortly after the loss of Saipan, and a few sympathizers with the peace party had been introduced into the two succeeding Cabinets, the militarists had remained in a dominant position and still were able to direct government policy toward their desired end, namely, the continued and vigorous prosecution of the war.[3]

General Kuniaki Koiso's government, which had replaced Tojo's, fell on April 5, 1945, following the American invasion of Okinawa. Through the maneuvering of Marquis Koichi Kido, the Lord Keeper of the Privy Seal, and others of the peace party, the aged Baron Kantaro Suzuki, a retired admiral, was appointed Premier. Suzuki later recalled that, although as Premier-designate he "did not receive any direct order from the Emperor" with regard to ending the war, he clearly saw His Majesty's deep concern over the sufferings of his people, and was tacitly "given to understand" that the Emperor wished him to exert every effort to make peace as quickly as possible. In testimony given after the war, Suzuki affirmed that this was his purpose from the very beginning of his premiership.[4]

To this end Suzuki chose Admiral Mitsumasa Yonai, known to be a moderate, as Minister of the Navy, and persuaded Shigenori Togo to become Foreign Minister. Togo had openly opposed the initiation of the war in 1941, had later resigned from Tojo's cabinet in protest against the latter's militaristic policies, and was known in 1945 to be strongly in favor of promptly ending the war. It would therefore appear that by April 1945 the Emperor, the Lord Privy Seal, the Premier, the Foreign Minister, and the Minister of the Navy all favored termination of the war. Nevertheless, their desire for peace did not determine the official policy of the government, but thus far was only the *inward* hope of certain key individuals. The extremists were still in control of the Army and had exacted, as a condition of their support of the new Cabinet, a commitment from Suzuki to prosecute the war to the bitter end. Assassination, which had been used by the *gumbatsu* as a tool for gaining control of the government during the 1930's, was an ever-present threat to anyone who openly challenged its continued direction of government policy.[5]

Certainly Suzuki's early statements in office do not give the impression of a man striving to find a way to end a war. In his opening address to the Diet, Suzuki stated that unconditional surrender was out of the question; there was only one path for Japan to follow, and that was "to fight to the very end." In his first statement to the press, the new Premier pledged that he would give his whole strength to defend the state; should death in the line of duty be his lot, he urged Japan's "one hundred million people" to surge forward over his prostrate body to defend the Emperor and the homeland![6]

Attempts to plumb the depths of Suzuki's true "intentions" are doubtless by this time futile. One possible explanation of his behavior is that he accepted the Army's condition of support in good faith, fully hoping to "terminate the war" as soon as possible — in victory. Only as he assumed the responsibility of office and learned how desperate Japan's position was did he come to realize that it was necessary to "terminate the war" in surrender. Another theory is that his later claim to peaceful intentions was merely self-justification, aided by a faulty memory. Still another theory ascribes the contradictions of his period in office to the vacillation of an old man. Suzuki's own explanation was that the Emperor's strong desire for an end to the hostilities put him in a "very difficult position," since an open and aboveboard effort on his part to carry out His Majesty's wishes probably would have invited assassination (Suzuki had been near death in 1936 after having been shot by a *gumbatsu* would-be assassin) and seizure of power by the militarists, thereby ending any hope of stopping the war short of national destruction. Therefore, explained Suzuki, he had been forced to play a deceptive and inconsistent role — on the one hand promoting an increased war effort and a determination to fight on, while on the other hand simultaneously working behind the scenes with "invisible technique" toward negotiations for ending the war. "Had we laid bare our hearts and revealed our firm beliefs, we would never have been able to achieve our goal." [7]

III

Whatever one may conclude with regard to Suzuki's personal motives, it is clear that the peace party faced a formidable and delicate task in moving toward peace despite the stubborn opposition of entrenched militarists who were determined not to surrender. The contradictions and vacillations in government policy during the summer of 1945 reflected the closeness and complexity of the struggle between the two opposing factions. For example, on June 8 the government formally adopted a "Fundamental Policy to Be Followed Henceforth in the Conduct of the War," which committed the nation to muster its entire strength to strike dead the invaders of their homeland and to end the war in victory. Within two weeks the government, reversing itself, decided to initiate overtures to Moscow with a view to obtaining a negotiated peace. (This decision did not represent a softening of the militarists' opposition to surrender: they could agree to the *technique* of ending the war by diplomatic means without giving up their insistence upon favorable terms for Japan in any negotiated peace settlement. On the other hand, the peace party was prepared to negotiate a settlement barely short of unconditional surrender.) [8]

After an abortive attempt to approach the Kremlin through Jacob Malik, Russia's ambassador to Japan, Foreign Minister Togo decided upon a more drastic step. After consultations involving the Emperor, the Premier, and the former Premier, Prince Fumimaro Konoye, it was decided that Konoye would be sent to Moscow as a special envoy of the Emperor to seek Moscow's good offices in negotiating an end to the war. It was understood between Togo and Konoye that the latter would go to Moscow with a free hand, and that the sole purpose of his mission would be to get Japan out of the war on any basis whatsoever — short of unconditional surrender. On July 12 Togo dispatched a message to the Japanese ambassador in Moscow, Naotake Sato, instructing him to inform Foreign Commissar Molotov of the Emperor's desire for peace and to arrange for Konoye's visit. (It was this secret message that within a few hours appeared on the desks of top officials in Washington.) In Moscow, Sato was first put off by a request that the purpose of Konoye's proposed visit be specified more clearly, then by the absence of Molotov at Potsdam. It was not until August 8, four weeks after his receipt of the original urgent message, that Sato managed to see Molotov — and Molotov's response was very different from what Sato had hoped. [9]

In the meantime, while Sato was waiting to see Molotov, news reached Japan of the proclamation by her enemies of the Potsdam Declaration. On the morning of July 27, 1945, Japan's response to the Allied ultimatum was debated by the Supreme

Council for the Direction of the War (Japan's "inner war cabinet" charged with the initiation and direction of national war policy, consisting of the Premier, the Foreign Minister, the Minister of War, the Minister of the Navy, and the Chiefs of the Army and Navy general staffs — and known as the "Big Six"). War Minister Anami and the two service chiefs insisted that the terms were dishonorable and strongly urged rejection and public denunciation of the Declaration. Suzuki, Togo, and Navy Minister Yonai felt that there was no way out for Japan but to accept the Allied terms. Realizing the impossibility of persuading his opponents to accept the Declaration, Togo managed to get the Supreme Council and the full Cabinet, which met that afternoon, to agree to postpone final action on the Potsdam Declaration until Moscow's response to Japan's overture could be ascertained. The government would neither accept nor reject the Declaration for the present, but the newspapers would be allowed to print, without official comment, an expurgated version of the text.[10]

The *mokusatsu* fiasco destroyed whatever hopes Togo may have had of achieving acceptance of the Potsdam Declaration; there was nothing left to do but to await a favorable response from Moscow. Tokyo was still waiting when the atomic bomb fell on Hiroshima.

IV

The first notice that Tokyo had of the atomic catastrophe was that the Hiroshima radio suddenly went off the air. A Domei News Agency telegram dispatched from the vicinity of Hiroshima about noon gave some indication of the seriousness of the disaster, but it was not until the following morning, August 7, that the truth reached Tokyo in one terrifying clipped sentence: "The whole city of Hiroshima was destroyed instantly by a single bomb." [11]

The revolutionary nature of the new bomb was quickly picked up from news broadcasts from Washington reporting President Truman's statement. The Army imposed censorship, and hastily sent an investigation team to the site of the disaster.

When Foreign Minister Togo attempted to get information about the attack from War Minister Anami, he could get no satisfaction; Togo suspected that Anami was trying to conceal the full impact of the truth. The Army, felt Togo, "obviously intended not to admit the nature of the atomic attack, but to minimize the effect of the bombing." On August 8 Togo had an audience with the Emperor, whom he informed about the atomic attack. Then

> . . . I said that it was now all the more imperative that we end the war, which we could seize this opportunity to do. The Emperor approved of my view, and warned that since we could no longer continue the struggle, now that a weapon of this devastating power was used against us, we should not let slip the opportunity by engaging in attempts to gain more favorable conditions. Since bargaining for terms had little prospect of success at this stage, he said, measures should be concerted to insure a prompt ending of hostilities. . . .[12]

After this audience, Togo urgently requested Premier Suzuki to call an immediate meeting of the Big Six; however the Premier replied that it would be impossible to gather the group before the next morning.

That evening in Moscow, Ambassador Sato had his long awaited appointment with Mr. Molotov. Sato began the interview with a polite greeting, but Molotov interrupted and began to read from a piece of paper a statement that included these words:

> . . . the Soviet Government declares that from tomorrow, that is from August 9, the Soviet Union will consider herself in a state of war against Japan.

Two hours later (1:00 A.M., August 9 Tokyo time) the armies
of the Soviet Union struck across the border into Japanese-held
Manchuria. Thus ended Japan's attempt to halt the war
through Russia's good offices.[13]

V

The Big Six met at 11:00 A.M. on August 9 in an atmosphere of
immediacy created by the early morning news that Russia had
invaded Manchuria — made yet more terrible by the rapidly
spreading rumor that Tokyo would soon be the next atomic
bomb victim. By this time, no one present was any longer opposed, in principle, to an acceptance of the Potsdam Declaration. Yet there was sharp disagreement on the *conditions* of
accepting "unconditional" surrender. Suzuki, Togo, and Yonai
agreed with the others that if the Allies excluded preservation of
the Emperor system — Japan's "national polity" — there would
be no alternative but to fight on. But they insisted that Japan
must accept the Potsdam Declaration immediately with the
single proviso that the Emperor be retained. War Minister
Anami and the two service chiefs strongly favored continuing
the war. Although they no longer promised ultimate victory,
they urged fighting on until the enemy could be engaged in a
decisive battle on the invasion beaches of Kyushu, where they
felt confident that Japan's armies could inflict "extremely heavy
damage on the enemy." While the repulsed Americans were
licking their wounds, peace terms more favorable to Japan could
be negotiated. If, however, their colleagues on the Council
desired immediate peace, Anami's party insisted upon additional conditions that would: (1) prevent an occupation of the
country by American troops, or at least exclude them from the
Tokyo area and restrict the number of troops and their locations
to a minimum; (2) allow Japan to try her own war criminals;
and (3) permit Japan's officers to disarm and demobilize their

own troops without surrender to American officers. Army Chief of Staff General Yoshijiro Umezu felt particularly strongly about the last condition; he emphasized that Japan's armies had not yet been defeated, that her soldiers and sailors were "not permitted" to surrender, and that the word "capitulation" could not be found in the Japanese military dictionary.[14]

The Foreign Minister replied that any attempt to bargain with the Allies about these three conditions would provoke the Allies into breaking off negotiations and renewing the war with full fury. Togo ridiculed the Army's hopes of throwing back the invaders; prolonging the war would only leave Japan in a more disadvantageous position. Although he personally desired better terms, Togo argued that unless the present opportunity to end the war were to be lost, the Potsdam Declaration must be accepted promptly — with the sole reservation about preserving the Emperor's status. This was the most, not the least, that Japan could ask.[15]

While this debate was proceeding, news was brought into the council chamber that Nagasaki had suffered the same fate as Hiroshima. This news gave little comfort to those who were wistfully speculating that the United States perhaps had only one atomic bomb, and lent added credence to the rumors that another bomb was scheduled to fall on Tokyo within two or three days. The news of the second bomb added a further dimension of urgency to the debate, but did nothing to reconcile the clash of the opposing groups. The Supreme Council adjourned after two hours, still split three against three.[16]

The debate was resumed in the meeting of the full Cabinet that afternoon, where the leading protagonists — as during the morning — were Foreign Minister Togo and War Minister Anami. Hour after hour the arguments were repeated, each side striving to win the support of as many ministers as possible. Finally at 10:00 P.M., after more than six hours of wrangling, Premier Suzuki called for a vote: six supported surrender with the sole reservation about preserving the imperial system, three favored Anami's three further conditions, and five were undecided. The Cabinet, the ultimate arbiter of the state's will, was in stalemate. Suzuki declared a recess, and the ministers bowed themselves out of the room.[17]

VI

Suzuki and Togo went immediately to the imperial palace, where they were at once received by the Emperor. They gave the Emperor a detailed account of the events of the day, and made it clear that a decision favorable to the termination of the war could not be expected from either the Big Six or the Cabinet. The Premier solemnly proposed that an imperial conference be convened that night, and His Majesty gave his sanction.[18]

To call an imperial conference under such circumstances was completely unprecedented. Although all major governmental policies in Japan were ascribed to the Emperor, the Cabinet was the ultimate constitutional policy-making body. When the Cabinet reached a decision on a major issue, an "imperial conference" was held, during which the already fixed policy was rehearsed by the Cabinet in the presence of the Emperor — who often spoke not a word. This formality completed, the policy of the government was declared to be the will of the Emperor. The Emperor was carefully insulated from the controversy that preceded crystallization of a policy; since he represented the *whole* nation, it would be unthinkable for His Majesty to take sides, or even to be asked to express his opinion, while an issue was being decided. The figure of the Emperor was maintained as the symbol of national unity by sparing the "August Mind" the details of debate; only after an issue was settled was it brought to the Emperor for his "approval." The Cabinet's decision was, by definition, the Emperor's will; faced with a unanimous decision by his "advisers," the Emperor had no choice but to acquiesce — regardless of his personal opinion in the matter.*

Long tradition required that the Cabinet have reached unanimity (not merely a majority) before its decision could be brought before the Emperor in an imperial conference. If a Cabinet could not reach unanimity on a major issue, the government fell, and a new Cabinet was formed. Normal procedure would have required that the Suzuki Cabinet, having failed to reach unanimity on an issue of life and death to the nation, should resign — but these were not normal times. With Tokyo threatened by atomic attack and Manchuria being overrun by the Red Army, resignation of the government would have been completely irresponsible, and easily might have led to panic and disintegration throughout the country. Unprecedented and undesirable as it might be to come before the Emperor without an agreed recommendation, there was no alternative but to press on in the hope of somehow reaching a decision. The Cabinet members were summoned.[20]

It was ten minutes before midnight on August 9 when the Emperor entered an underground air raid shelter in the palace grounds to listen to the arguments and pleas of the Empire's top political and military leaders. Premier Suzuki took the floor and reported to the Emperor what he had told him privately little more than an hour before: neither the Supreme Council nor the Cabinet, both of whom had met that day, were able to reach any conclusion about the action to be taken with regard to the Potsdam Declaration. Since the decision could not be postponed any longer, it was necessary to submit the decision to His Majesty and to request an imperial opinion, even though it was unthinkable indeed to take such a step without being

---

* Thus in 1941 Emperor Hirohito was personally opposed to war against the United States. Nevertheless, the Tojo government was unanimously agreed upon war. This became the Emperor's "will"; there was nothing, constitutionally or practically, that the Emperor could have done to prevent hostilities.[19]

able to present an accompanying unanimous recommendation. After his apology, Suzuki called upon various members of the Cabinet to present their opinions, and during the next two hours the opposing sides stated once again the same arguments they had repeated endlessly throughout the day. After this recital Suzuki took the floor. He stated what was all too obvious — the fact that the Cabinet had reached an impasse — and declared that the gravity of the situation left him no other course than to seek a decision from His Majesty himself. Turning toward the Emperor, the Premier respectfully announced, "Your Imperial Majesty's decision is requested as to which proposal should be adopted — the one stated by the Foreign Minister or the one containing the four conditions." [21]

When the Emperor, who had been taught to equate his own will with the will of his "advisers," was suddenly asked to resolve an otherwise irreconcilable conflict, there was no precedent for such an action; he could do nothing else but express his own personal opinion — an opinion which up to this moment had been completely irrelevant to the policies of the state. "Without the slightest hesitation," but with emotion visibly welling up within him, the Emperor rose from his chair. As the others quickly rose and bowed toward their ruler, the Emperor had already begun to speak:

> . . . I have given serious thought to the situation prevailing at home and abroad and have concluded that continuing the war can only mean destruction for the nation and a prolongation of bloodshed and cruelty in the world. I cannot bear to see my innocent people suffer any longer. Ending the war is the only way to restore world peace and to relieve the nation from the terrible distress with which it is burdened.
>
> . . . .
>
> I cannot help feeling sad when I think of the people who have served me so faithfully, the soldiers and sailors who have been killed or wounded in far off battles . . . Nevertheless, the time has come when we must bear the unbearable.

> . . . I swallow my own tears and give my sanction to the
> proposal to accept the Allied proclamation on the basis outlined
> by the Foreign Minister.[22]

As the Emperor turned from the conference table and slowly
left the room, Premier Suzuki declared, "His Majesty's decision
should be made the decision of this conference as well." Legally, the Emperor's "decision" was no decision at all; it was as
though he had merely said, "If it were up to me to decide, this
is what I would do." The Emperor's admonitions had no legal
authority to bind the will of the state, unless the Cabinet, as the
constitutional authority, confirmed the Emperor's "decision." [23]

What it lacked in legal authority, the Emperor's judgment
made up in overawing *influence*. The imperial conference adjourned, and the Cabinet met immediately afterwards in
the home of the Premier. There, between three and four in the
morning, the assembled ministers unanimously approved the
"imperial decision," thus making legal the decision made by
the Emperor an hour before. The Foreign Office rushed to draft
a document that would embody the Cabinet's decision, and in
the early morning hours of Friday, August 10, cables announcing
Japan's acceptance of the Potsdam Declaration, "with the understanding that the said declaration does not comprise any
demand which prejudices the prerogatives of His Majesty as a
Sovereign Ruler," were on their way through diplomatic channels to Washington, London, Chungking, and Moscow. The
decision was made. The fate of the nation rested in the hands
of its enemies.[24]

VII

Climactic as the day had been, the final climax was not yet.
For all depended upon the nature of the Allies' reply. If it
hedged about the preservation of the Emperor, or rejected it
outright, the position of the end-the-war party would collapse;
they would have no alternative but to acquiesce in the con-

tinuance of the war, even though it meant national suicide. In this case the power and position of Togo and his group would be undermined, and their lives doubtless endangered by the resurgence of military fanatics to control. On the other hand a clear assurance from the Allies guaranteeing the status of the Emperor would quash the military's objections. Throughout the long hours of August 10 and 11 tension and anxiety built up as the men in Tokyo waited for a reply.

Secretary Byrnes's reply contained two main provisions: (1) "From the moment of surrender the authority of the Emperor and the Japanese Government to rule the state shall be subject to the Supreme Commander of the Allied powers . . ."; and (2) "The ultimate form of government of Japan shall . . . be established by the freely expressed will of the Japanese people." Byrnes had carefully drafted his reply so that the retention of the Emperor (who was indispensable to the Allies if the transition from war to peaceful occupation were to be accomplished smoothly) was clearly implied, but not stated so clearly that it would appear that the victorious Allies had agreed to a condition set by their defeated enemy. By means of deliberate ambiguity Japan's condition of surrender was in fact to be accepted — but the fiction of "unconditional surrender" was to be maintained.[25]

The reply, neither rejecting the Emperor nor clearly committing the Allies to guarantee his retention, was received in Togo's Foreign Ministry with dismay. Both its parts would surely provoke the opposition of the militarists. Was it not an affront that not only the government, but also the Emperor himself would be "subject to" a foreign Supreme Commander? And the re-emphasis of the Potsdam provision about the "freely expressed will" of the people raised questions: did this mean that the imperial institution and His Majesty's prerogatives as a sovereign ruler were to be subject to a vote of the people — unthinkable! — or only that the people would determine by their vote the nature of the administrative and legislative organs of the state under the Emperor?

The stubborn and inconclusive debate of August 9 began all over again on a new level, and raged throughout the 12th and the 13th. Both sides agreed that the national polity must be preserved — but one side insisted that surrender on the basis of Byrnes's note would preserve it, while the other argued that it would destroy it. Anami and his followers again urged that the nation fight on until the enemy could be engaged and defeated on the beaches. Togo pointed out that such a course could only lead to needless suffering and the ultimate destruction of the national polity; the only way to preserve the Emperor was immediate acceptance of surrender on the basis of Byrnes's reply. Togo was brought to the verge of resigning in despair when Premier Suzuki was won over to Anami's side; but Kido managed to persuade the wavering Premier that he must follow the desire of the Emperor, which was for immediate peace. Once again the debate progressed from the Big Six to the full Cabinet, where, by the evening of the 13th, irreconcilable disagreement produced the same result as before: stalemate.[26]

Meanwhile the situation in Tokyo was beginning to deteriorate. Posters mysteriously appeared in the tram stations and throughout the city denouncing Marquis Kido and others of the end-the-war party as traitors to be shot on sight: "Kill Lord Keeper of the Privy Seal Kido!" Assassination and a coup by the military fanatics was an ever-increasing possibility.[27]

Early on the morning of August 14 thousands of leaflets came fluttering down from the sky over Tokyo. A palace attendant picked up one and delivered it to Marquis Kido. Glancing at the leaflet, Kido's heart sank. It bore the text of Japan's offer to surrender and a translation of the Allies' reply. No longer could the secret be kept from the people. Kido rushed to take the leaflet to the Emperor. He urged upon His Majesty the necessity for prompt resolution of the Cabinet's impasse: further delay would only provide opportunity for an extremist coup. If a decision to surrender was to be reached at all, it must be reached at once.[28]

The Emperor immediately called another imperial conference for 11:00 A.M. So suddenly were the ministers summoned that there was no time to change to court clothing; some arrived wearing hastily borrowed neckties. Prime Minister Suzuki once again apologized to His Majesty for the inability of the Cabinet to present a unanimous recommendation. The opposing arguments were repeated once more and then the Emperor began to speak:

> I have listened carefully to each of the arguments presented in opposition to the view that Japan should accept the Allied reply as it stands without further clarification or modification, but my own thoughts have not undergone any change. I have surveyed the conditions prevailing in Japan and in the world at large, and it is my belief that a continuation of the war promises nothing but additional destruction. I have studied the terms of the Allied reply and have concluded that they constitute a virtually complete acknowledgment of the position we maintained in the note dispatched several days ago. In short, I consider the reply to be acceptable.
>
> . . . .
>
> It is my desire that you, my Ministers of State, accede to my wishes and forthwith accept the Allied reply. In order that the people may know of my decision, I request you to prepare at once an imperial rescript so that I may broadcast to the nation. Finally, I call upon each and every one of you to exert himself to the utmost so that we may meet the trying days which lie ahead.[29]

This time the Emperor's words were final. The Cabinet met immediately and endorsed His Majesty's decision, authorized the Foreign Office to inform the Allies, and drafted the rescript which — in an unprecedented action — the Emperor would broadcast to the people the following noon.

Traffic ground to a halt, the nation stood hushed, as on August 15 the people of Japan heard the voice of their Emperor announce the end of the war:

To Our Good and Loyal Subjects:

After pondering deeply the general trends of the world and the actual conditions obtaining in Our Empire today, We have decided to effect a settlement of the present situation by resorting to an extraordinary measure.

We have ordered Our Government to communicate to the Governments of the United States, Great Britain, China and the Soviet Union that Our Empire accepts the provisions of their Joint Declaration.

. . . .

We cannot but express the deepest sense of regret . . . However, it is according to the dictate of time and fate that We have resolved to pave the way for a grand peace for all the generations to come by enduring the unendurable and suffering what is insufferable.

. . . Beware most strictly of any outbursts of emotion which may engender needless complications . . . Let the entire nation continue as one family from generation to generation, ever firm in its faith of the imperishableness of its divine land . . . Cultivate the ways of rectitude; foster nobility of spirit; and work with resolution so as ye may enhance the innate glory of the Imperial State and keep pace with the progress of the world.[30]

VIII

It is possible, on the basis of the record of the events above recounted, to answer the question with which this chapter began: did the atomic bomb significantly shorten the war? The evidence is clear. The atomic bomb made possible a surrender which otherwise would not have come for months. The bomb did not defeat Japan; she was already essentially defeated, and the physical damage caused by the bomb advanced her military defeat only insignificantly. Neither did the bomb change any votes in the Supreme Council for the Direction of the War; the Big Six remained divided three against three even after Hiroshima and Nagasaki. The bombing of Hiroshima, the Russian invasion of Manchuria (which was precipitated by the Hiroshima attack), and the bombing of Nagasaki — all making their impact within three days — constituted a cluster of catastrophes that created a situation of extreme emergency in Tokyo. This crisis situation threw off balance the war party, made them less self-confident, less tenacious, their arguments less cogent and convincing to other members of the Cabinet. Most important, the bomb created a situation in which the Emperor could "emerge" from his isolation to play an active and decisive part in Japan's decision to surrender, imposing — in a completely unprecedented and extra-legal way — his own personal will upon a stalemated government. Historian Robert J. C. Butow concludes, in his *Japan's Decision to Surrender*:

> The atomic bombing of Hiroshima and Nagasaki and the Soviet Union's declaration of war did not produce Japan's decision to surrender, for that decision — in embryo — had long been taking shape. What these events did do was to create that unusual atmosphere in which the theretofore static factor of the Emperor could be made active in such an extraordinary way as to work what was virtually a political miracle.[31]

As it worked out, the end-the-war party barely managed to prevail. Without the atomic crisis situation, within which the tremendous influence of the supposedly infallible Emperor could be brought decisively to bear, it is clear that the end-the-war party could not have challenged successfully the military party. (For years the military clique had been deliberately building up the imperial authority and using the symbol of the

Emperor as a means of achieving the unquestioning obedience of the nation to their own extremist policies — but now, ironically, they found this enhanced authority turned against them.) Without the urgency injected into the situation by the atomic bomb, the Army view would have prevailed, or, at any rate, the stalemate would have continued, and the fighting would have gone on for months despite Japan's deteriorating economic situation. The use of the atomic bomb allowed the peace party to achieve surrender and thus substantially shortened the war.

13. Did the Bomb Save Lives?

SHORTENING THE WAR was not an end in itself; the object of stopping the war was to minimize the suffering and loss of life inherent in war. To shorten the war by two months by means of killing 110,000 people, if the natural course of the war would have taken only half that number of lives, would be a contradiction. Therefore it is relevant to ask whether, compared with the other alternatives open to United States leaders, the use of the atomic bomb saved lives.

In the discussion that follows — and, it is fair to say, in the thinking of Truman and Stimson — it must not be supposed that the bare preserving of human biological existence is the sole or overriding criterion. To urge the "saving of lives" is a shorthand way of urging a reduction in the total mass of suffering and evil produced by modern war — killing, maiming, bereavement, orphanhood, disruption of the fabric of civil life, hatred, hopelessness, destruction of homes and goods. The *number* of persons killed may serve as a rough measure of the total amount of evil and suffering produced by a given attack.

In order to judge whether the use of the atomic bomb really "saved lives" we must examine the other alternatives for ending the war which were open to United States leaders in 1945 and estimate in each case the probable number of lives that would have been lost.

II

It is clear that the invasion of the Japanese homeland would have produced more casualties than the bombing of Hiroshima and Nagasaki actually did. United States military leaders were expecting the conquest of Japan to take a year and to cost on the order of 250,000 American lives and a total of a million American casualties. United States generals expected to lose in one year nearly as many casualties as the total sustained on all fronts in the previous four years of war (United States dead from battle causes totaled 311,000 in World War II).[1]

In every campaign from Guadalcanal to Okinawa, Japanese casualties had been several times those of the United States. (For example, in the reconquest of the Philippines, Mac-Arthur's forces killed 317,000 Japanese soldiers, while suffering 61,000 casualties that included killed, wounded, and missing. On Okinawa 107,000 Japanese soldiers were killed out of a total garrison of 120,000; the United States lost about 10,000 killed and missing.)[2] Japanese soldiers fought to the death or deliberately destroyed themselves rather than allow themselves to be captured. The tenacity of Japan's two million soldiers in defending their homeland was expected to be even greater, and promised heavy loss of life both to invader and defender. In short, it is quite clear that the number of Japanese casualties, not to mention American losses, would have been vastly greater in the case of an invasion than the 110,000 killed at Hiroshima and Nagasaki.

III

Yet invasion of the Japanese homeland was not the only available alternative, according to Air Force and Navy strategists. Even if Japan hung on for months, they insisted, we could continue to blockade and bomb her almost at will. The final result could not be in doubt: in the end Japan would be starved and beaten into submission — and with a minimum of American casualties.

The most optimistic Air Force prediction was that made by

General Arnold, who stated (in July) that the B-29 bombing campaign could bring Japan to surrender by the end of October 1945. The United States Strategic Bombing Survey concluded, after its postwar investigation of the effects of bombing, that the Japanese would have surrendered prior to December 31, 1945, and probably prior to November 1, 1945. Assuming, for the sake of argument, that the atomic bomb had not been used, and that the Japanese had held out until December 1, 1945 (three and one-half months longer) before surrendering, it is possible to estimate the number of casualties which would have resulted in the process of bringing Japan to her knees by continued bombing and blockade.[3]

Clearly the concentrated bombing of Japanese cities with incendiaries and high explosives would have been a major cause of casualties. The B-29 raids took a total of 330,000 lives from November 1944 to the close of the war.[4] Apart from the great Tokyo raid of March 9 (100,000 dead) and the two atomic bomb raids (110,000 dead), the B-29's killed 120,000. The great bulk of these fell between mid-March and mid-August — at a rate in excess of 20,000 per month. At this rate, continued bombing would have killed about 75,000 by December 1. Indeed the total would probably have been higher, since B-29's based on Okinawa were just going into action to supplement those based on the Marianas when the war ended.

The Russians were committed to the invasion of Manchuria during the latter half of August. After the bombing of Hiroshima on August 6, the Russians invaded Manchuria on the 9th. The Red Armies did not cease fire upon notice of Japan's surrender on August 14, but continued to sweep through Manchuria until their predetermined objectives were taken. On September 10 they announced the casualties for the campaign: 80,000 Japanese killed; 594,000 Japanese captured; 8000 Russians killed.[5] The striking thing about the Russian figures is that the number of Japanese "captured" is seven times the number killed — whereas in all the previous engagements between the Americans and the Japanese, the ratio had been reversed. (For example, in the Philippines American forces killed 317,000 Japanese and captured only 7236; on Okinawa, 107,000 were killed and 10,600 prisoners were taken.)[6] It seems obvious that the reason for the unusual Manchurian figures is that hundreds of thousands of Japanese "captured" had surrendered voluntarily in obedience to the Emperor's command to lay down their arms. Had the Russians invaded Manchuria later in August, as scheduled, and fought for two or three months against a stubbornly resisting foe (instead of two weeks against a surrendering foe) there can be little doubt that, at the very minimum, casualties on both sides would have been tripled: 240,000 Japanese and 25,000 Russians.

During the summer of 1945 Chinese armies on the mainland were steadily pushing the Japanese north and east toward the coast. Casualty rates are not known, but certainly Japanese and Chinese lives would have continued to be lost in China if fighting had continued until December 1.

Sea blockade was squeezing Japan tighter and tighter, and had by August reduced her imports of food to a mere trickle. A systematic bombardment of her extremely vulnerable railroad system was about to begin in August. This would have disrupted the transporting of food and coal from the northern island of Hokkaido to the large urban areas of Honshu. The areas of "starvation conditions" (see page 120) would no doubt have increased sharply as winter approached.

It seems clear that continuation of conventional bombing by B-29's for three months would have taken twice the number of Japanese lives lost at Nagasaki; the Russian operation in Manchuria would have cost more than double the lives sacrificed at Hiroshima; fighting in China and starvation at home would have added to the number of casualties. It is not unreasonable to estimate that, had the war continued for three months without the use of the atomic bomb and without invasion, more than twice the number of Japanese persons would have been killed as were killed at Hiroshima and Nagasaki — not to mention the Russian, Chinese, and American casualties.

In short, once the Allied attempt to end the Pacific war by political means had foundered on the Japanese "rejection" of the Potsdam Declaration, American leaders saw themselves facing a choice between two alternatives: use the atomic bomb to jolt Japan out of the war, or refrain from using it and prosecute the war with conventional means. To have continued the war, either by invasion or solely by blockade and bombing, would have cost many more Japanese lives than the atomic bombing of Hiroshima and Nagasaki actually took. The evidence indicates with a high degree of probability that using the atomic bomb as we did indeed shortened the war and saved many lives, both American and Japanese.

IV

A nagging question still troubles the conscience: even though the bomb as it was used saved more lives than it took, was not the cost in human suffering and death unnecessarily high? Might not *some other use* of the bomb have accomplished prompt surrender and sacrificed fewer lives?

We must examine the several possibilities open to United States leaders, estimating in each case the probable effect and the number of casualties that would have resulted.

First of all, was the second bomb really necessary? Was adequate time given after Hiroshima for Japanese authorities to comprehend the significance of the new weapon and for the machinery of government to arrive at a decision to surrender?

We have seen that the use of the second bomb was soberly and deliberately planned in order to provide maximum shock and to convince the Japanese that we had ample bombs and were determined to use them. Dr. Karl T. Compton (a member of the Interim Committee) reported after his firsthand investigation in Japan following the war: ". . . it was not one atomic bomb, or two, which brought surrender; it was the experience of what an atomic bomb will actually do to a community, *plus the dread of many more,* that was effective." [7]

There seems to have been a certain ambivalence in the thought of those who recommended use of both available bombs. One theory was that maximum shock could be achieved by dropping two bombs in quick succession so as to make a double impact before Japan had the chance fully to react. Yet there are several indications that American leaders hoped the impact of the first bomb would be sufficient to produce surrender. If Japan, after a brief but reasonable interval, showed no signs of moving toward surrender, then and then only should the second bomb be dropped to show her we meant business. For example, President Truman's announcement of the Hiroshima bombing threatened that if the Japanese leaders "do not now accept our terms they may expect a rain of ruin from the air, the like of which has never been seen on this earth." The President's address to the nation upon his return from Potsdam (August 9) noted that "the first atomic bomb was dropped on Hiroshima, a military base," in order "to avoid, in so far as possible, the killing of civilians. But that attack is only a warning of things to come. If Japan does not surrender, bombs will have to be dropped on her war industries and, unfortunately, thousands of civilian lives will be lost." [8] The leaflets dropped by the million over Japan following Hiroshima urged the Japanese people to take steps to persuade their government to stop the war before atomic bombs were used further. "Otherwise," we would "resolutely employ this bomb" to bring the war to an end by sheer force.[9]

Truman, in his *Memoirs,* implies that an interval was al-

lowed for the Japanese to reach a decision to surrender. After
Hiroshima, he reports, "still no surrender offer came. An order
was issued to General Spaatz to continue operations as planned
unless otherwise instructed." [10]

Despite these various indications that top United States leaders were thinking in terms of a deliberate BOMB-PAUSE-
BOMB sequence, the actual timing of the bombs left only a
two-day interval between Hiroshima (August 6) and Nagasaki
(August 9) — scarcely adequate time for any government, no
matter how monolithic, to reach a major decision completely
reversing its long standing policy. Leaflets were dropped, but no
time was allowed for people to "petition the Emperor" before
we used the bomb again. The implication of the context in
Truman's *Memoirs* account is (although it is not stated explicitly) that the order to continue atomic bombing was sent to
Spaatz prior to the arrival of the *Augusta* in the United States
on August 7. If this is so, Truman allowed the Japanese leaders
less than forty-eight hours from the time of the impact of the
bomb at Hiroshima. Truman's speech threatening the dropping
of atomic bombs on other cities than Hiroshima, if Japan failed
to surrender, came *after* the second bomb had already fallen on
Nagasaki. In short, the actual event of dropping the bomb on
Nagasaki failed to leave the time interval assumed both by con-
temporary documents and by later accounts.

Why was the interval between the two bombs so short? The
second atomic sortie, originally scheduled for August 11, was
advanced to August 9 because a weather forecast predicted
cloudy weather over Japan beginning on the 11th. As Truman
put it, "We gave the Japanese three days in which to make up
their minds to surrender, and the bombing would have been
held off another two days had weather permitted." [11] If it had
been decided clearly to allow Japan a four-day interval before
dropping the second bomb, it would have been understandable
that bad weather could have forced *postponement* of the second

drop — but how could it have forced (as Truman implies) an *advancement* of the schedule? The evidence is clear: despite the tacit assumption that there would be an adequate interval, there was no clear policy decision about the timing of the second bomb. This matter, as well as the selection of the specific target from the list of four cities, was left to the discretion of the military commander, to be determined on purely tactical grounds.

It would seem that determination of the length of time between atomic bombs best calculated to allow the Japanese to surrender without undue delay was a political matter. Yet the scheduling of the second atomic bomb was decided on tactical (not political) grounds by an Air Force commander (not a political leader) in the Pacific (not in Washington). Had the original schedule been followed, the lives of 40,000 people in Nagasaki would have been spared, since Japan indicated on August 10 her desire to surrender, and her leaders were in process of reaching that decision on the 9th.

Apart from the question of timing, was the dropping of the second bomb necessary to convince Japan that we had more bombs and meant business? Granted that the news of the fate of Nagasaki effectively brought to bear upon Japanese leaders "the threat of many more" — was there no way to achieve this desirable end except by the bombing of a second city?

It would seem that with some imaginative thought the Interim Committee — or the State Department — could have devised a more effective warning to Japan than that in Truman's statement released on August 6. That statement identified the new weapon as an atomic bomb, as well as threatening "a rain of ruin from the air." A warning more specifically designed as an instrument to move the Japanese government to a prompt decision to surrender could have: (1) emphasized the potency of the bomb and the destruction produced in Hiroshima; (2) pointed out the reluctance of the United States to use further atomic bombs unless forced to by Japanese stubbornness; (3) declared that we had more bombs and were determined to use them until Japan surrendered; (4) given Japan a specific deadline (say August 12) for accepting the Potsdam Declaration, after which time we would surely use more atomic bombs to force her acceptance; and (5) stated that Japan could treat this warning as a propaganda bluff only at her own peril. The Japanese were intelligent enough to see that the United States would not go on public record committing itself to such action without being able and determined to make good its threat. It is difficult to believe that such a warning would not have gone far toward creating the "threat of many more," producing much the same effect upon the Big Six as did the news of Nagasaki — which changed no votes but increased the sense of urgency. Even had such a warning failed, the attempt would have delayed the second bomb only by four or five days. Essentially the same effect could have been produced by a blunt military method and by a more subtle political method. America chose the military method.

In sum, the evidence seems conclusive that had the will to produce Japanese surrender with a minimum loss of life, and the will to subordinate tactical decisions to political control, been strong enough, a stern warning and adequate time could easily have been provided Japan. It is hard to escape the conclusion that such a course would have produced surrender as promptly as the course actually followed — and that the atomic bombing of Nagasaki was unnecessary.

v

If the bombing of Nagasaki was unnecessary, was the killing of 70,000 persons at Hiroshima also unnecessary? A technical demonstration on a desert island in the presence of United Nations representatives had been urged by the Franck Committee, and many moralists revived the suggestion after Hiroshima. Would such a demonstration, followed by a warning, have produced an impact sufficient to induce Japan to surrender?

Even if the intricate and time-consuming problem of arranging for official Japanese observers had been solved, it is difficult (after studying Butow's account) to imagine that War Minister Anami would have been very much impressed by reports and photographs. One determined not to believe could easily argue that the bomb would not be very effective against buildings, or that improved air defenses could prevent the enemy from dropping the bomb, etc. The urgency deriving from the actual delivery of the bomb upon one's home territory would have been lacking.

Would a demonstration of the bomb on an uninhabited spot in Japan have proved effective? Doubtless the accomplished fact of delivery upon Japanese territory, and the impossibility of hiding the fact of the new bomb from the general population, would have made a much greater impact than a demonstration on a desert island. Most of the objections raised against this type of demonstration during the deliberations of the Interim Committee and its Scientific Panel (the moving of American prisoners to the area, opposition by fighter aircraft, fear of a dud) assumed *prior* announcement of the demonstration. However, the demonstration raid could have been flown unannounced, just as was the Hiroshima raid. After the demonstration, the Japanese authorities could have been instructed by radio to inspect the damage, and to surrender before the bomb was directed against live targets.

The main objection raised against this type of demonstration was that, although an atomic explosion is an awe-inspiring sight, destruction produced upon a bare landscape is negligible. The power of the bomb to flatten buildings and to destroy the entire social fabric of a city would be left to the imagination, not burned into the eyes of the observers. Harold Urey, after much searching of heart, decided on this ground not to sign a petition circulated among the scientists urging President Truman to stage such a technical demonstration. In Urey's opinion, "the difference between abstraction and reality" was crucial. Only the reality of what the bomb actually could do to a city would be certain to shock Japan out of the war.[12]

Would a technical demonstration on Japanese territory have provided sufficient shock to produce surrender? It *might* have. Yet it must be remembered that in the face of the full-blown horror of two destroyed cities, plus the Russian invasion of Manchuria, the war party in Tokyo remained adamant. Whether anything less than the actual use of the bombs could have produced the atmosphere of emergency which permitted the Emperor to use his influence to end the war must remain conjectural. Had such a demonstration been tried and had it failed to produce surrender, use of a second atomic bomb on a city would have caused many fewer casualties than at Hiroshima and Nagasaki, since the Japanese presumably would have taken air raid precautions much more seriously following the demonstration. The shock effect would also have been smaller than was actually the case at Hiroshima, for the edge of surprise would already have been dulled.

VI

Another alternative was possible in August 1945 — a military demonstration. In this case, the sortie would have proceeded precisely as at Hiroshima, except that the target would have been a major military installation, like a supply dump or air base. Such a target would have conformed to the "dual-target" recommendation of the Interim Committee, in that it would have included closely built-up areas, a variety of sturdy and flimsy buildings (probably surrounded by a fringe residential area), aircraft, railroad cars, and motor vehicles. Had the atomic bomb been dropped on such a target, its full power would have been made evident to the Japanese. Steel frame buildings would have been twisted and gutted, aircraft and railroad equipment overturned and smashed, barracks and houses reduced to rubble and set on fire. All military personnel within a mile would have been killed. Doubtless civilians also would have been killed if the target were surrounded by residential areas; but the number of civilian deaths would have been small in comparison with the military, whereas at Hiroshima the number of military deaths was small compared with the civilian. Morally, an attack upon a purely military target would have been preferable to a direct attack upon a civilian center.

Granted that such a military attack might have assuaged American consciences, would it have produced surrender? The power of the bomb to destroy and the quality of its impact upon a built-up area would have been plainly demonstrated. There would have been no need to interpolate what this bomb might do to an industrial city; the implications would have been unmistakably clear. Had the target been a supply dump of equipment essential to the defense of the Kyushu invasion beaches, the impact upon General Anami and his friends might have been even greater than was that of the destruction of Hiroshima. It would seem that most of the elements making Hiroshima an effective force toward surrender would have been present also in the case of a military demonstration.

The advantages of dropping the atomic bomb on a "purely military" target are obvious. Tens of thousands of women and children would have been spared death and agonized suffering. The reputation of the United States would have been enhanced rather than tarnished. The probability of producing a shock sufficient to induce Japan to surrender must be rated much higher for a military demonstration than for a technical demonstration. Had a military demonstration, followed by a stern warning, failed to produce surrender, dropping the second available bomb on a city would probably have produced a cumulative effect upon Japan's leaders as great as the cumulative effect of Hiroshima and Nagasaki.

However, there also were difficulties connected with a military demonstration. If a somewhat isolated installation were attacked, the Japanese military might seal off the area and successfully hide the destruction from the people — and even from the government. (The Army, in fact, attempted to minimize the seriousness of the damage even in the case of Hiroshima.) If this were to happen the atomic bomb would be of little effect in precipitating a surrender. Yet most of the large military installations located near Japan's population centers had already been attacked and damaged to a greater or lesser extent, and an essential part of our plan for using the atomic bomb was that it should be dropped on a virgin target, so that the complete devastation could be unequivocally ascribed to the new weapon.[13]

But the primary reason that demonstration of the atomic bomb on a purely military target was not attempted apparently is that it was never considered. And the reason it was never considered is that the distinction between attack on a military target (in which civilians might incidentally suffer injury and death) and attack on a city (in which military objectives would be damaged as a result of direct attack upon the fabric of civil life) was lost.

It is interesting to note that the *language* of President Truman's speech of August 9 clearly implies a distinction between military target and city. If the single word "Hiroshima" is omitted from Mr. Truman's statement, his words describe perfectly a military demonstration:

> The world will note that the first atomic bomb was dropped on . . . a military base. That was because we wished in the first attack to avoid in so far as possible, the killing of civilians. But that attack is only a warning of things to come. If Japan does not surrender, bombs will have to be dropped on her war

industries and, unfortunately, thousands of civilian lives will be lost.[14]

Yet Truman's use of the name Hiroshima in this context, and its identification as "a military base," suggests that for him it was no longer possible to think of a military target without thinking of a whole city.

The President's own accounts of the selecting of targets bear out this conclusion. In his *Memoirs* he describes his concern that the new weapon be used "in the manner prescribed by the laws of war. That meant that I wanted it dropped on a military target." In other words, the bomb should be dropped on "a war production center of prime military importance." Elsewhere Mr. Truman reports that he inquired of Secretary Stimson which cities in Japan were "devoted exclusively to war production." [15]

This type of thinking was not peculiar to Mr. Truman; he merely reflected the general consensus among American leaders. As an example, when Arthur Compton recommended that the atomic bomb be used militarily, "but no more drastically than needed to bring surrender," he did not have in mind the sort of restraint that would attack air bases but stop short of bombing cities. Rather, he meant that the *number* of cities attacked with the new bomb should be kept to the minimum necessary to induce surrender.[16]

Apparently the Interim Committee also thought solely in terms of a city for a target. In order to demonstrate most clearly the power of the new bomb, the committee recommended a "dual target"— industrial or military installations surrounded by close-packed residential buildings — which inevitably meant an urban center. For the Interim Committee the only real choice was between a technical demonstration and military use. Once the possibility of a demonstration was eliminated, it was assumed that there was no further decision to be made regard-

ing degrees of military use, or targets other than cities. Therefore a military demonstration was never considered as a live
option.[17]

VII

At the bottom of the debate over a demonstration is the question of the proper use of force: shall military power be used in
an all-out and total fashion, or in a graduated and restrained
fashion? Many of those who suggested a demonstration did not
object so much to the indiscriminate quality of the atomic
bombing of Japan as to what seemed to them to be a total and
unrestrained use of force. We had two bombs, and we used
them both within three days to destroy two cities. This was
excessive force, and hence immoral. Implicit in this concept
is the recommendation that power be applied to Japan in
gradually increasing amounts until a force sufficient to induce
surrender had been reached. For example, Japan might first
be given an explicit warning about the new weapon. If she
refused to surrender, a demonstration bomb could then be
dropped on an uninhabited portion of her territory in order to
impress her leaders with the force at our disposal. If that failed,
the bomb should be used to destroy a key military installation.
The bomb should be dropped on a city only as a last resort,
after all other means of inducing Japan to surrender had failed.

Truman and Stimson would doubtless answer this argument
by saying that they didn't have a whole arsenal of bombs with
which to experiment upon Japan, but only two, with others
available only weeks in the future and then one by one. While
admitting the desirability of using just the precise amount of
force necessary to knock Japan out of the war, and no more,
they could point out that obtaining, in advance, knowledge of
even the approximate amount of force required was inherently
impossible during wartime, and that every day's delay in experi-

mentation meant more American and Japanese lives unnecessarily lost. Bearing on their shoulders responsibility for millions of American soldiers and sailors, and faced with the approaching invasion, they were convinced that the most certain — and therefore the most responsible — course was to use the two bombs with maximum force in the hope of ending the war abruptly. Mr. Truman describes the atmosphere within which the decision was made:

> We could hope for a miracle, but the daily tragedy of a bitter war crowded in on us. We labored to construct a weapon of such overpowering force that the enemy could be forced to yield swiftly once we could resort to it. . . .[18]

VIII

We can now answer the question of whether or not the use of the atomic bomb really saved thousands of lives. There can be no doubt that the atomic attack was the decisive factor in inducing Japan's leaders to surrender when they did; the bomb probably shortened the war by a matter of months. Using the bomb saved lives — in the sense that holding back the bomb and continuing the war by conventional means (either with or without invasion of Japan's home islands) would have cost many more lives than were actually sacrificed at Hiroshima and Nagasaki.

Yet it would have been possible to employ the bomb in such a way as to produce surrender at a smaller cost in lives. Although it is doubtful whether a technical demonstration would have effectively jolted Japan out of the war, it is possible that a demonstration of the bomb against a purely military target, followed by a warning, might have done so. At any rate, the 40,000 lives snuffed out at Nagasaki could almost certainly have been spared had a carefully devised warning been issued following the Hiroshima attack.

14. Social and Political Consequences

THOSE RESPONSIBLE for using the atomic bomb against Japan justified their decision in terms of immediate consequences: surrender achieved and lives saved. Certain critics of the decision agreed that the bombing of Hiroshima and Nagasaki should be judged by its consequences — but focused on different consequences. Granted that the short-run consequences for ending World War II were good, were they not outweighed by the production of long-term evil consequences — such as the introduction of fear and suspicion into the postwar world and the initiation of rivalry leading to an atomic arms race that threatens the peace and the very existence of the civilized world? This was the burden of the Franck Report in June 1945, which urged that decisions about the first use of the atomic bomb "should not be left to the considerations of military tactics alone," but should be made by "the highest political leadership of this country" taking into account long-term social and political implications of atomic weapons. For the Franck Committee the question of the death and suffering of thousands of civilians, however deplorable, and the question of the prompt ending of the war, however desirable, paled into insignificance before the likelihood of an atomic arms race which, because of the high premium put on hitting first, would degenerate into a rush toward total war. Achievement of effective international control to prevent this great danger was of prime importance. The use of the atomic bomb against Japan should be subordinated to this end.[1]

Following the war, this general line of thought appeared as

criticism of the decision to use the bomb against Japan: the use of the bomb stirred up moral revulsion against the United States, aroused widespread fear and suspicion of the United States' intentions, made our expressed desire to prevent use of atomic bombs in future wars appear insincere — since we had not hesitated to use them against an almost defeated foe — undermined our efforts to achieve international control of atomic energy, and precipitated an atomic arms race.

II

The difficulty in evaluating such criticism lies in the intangible nature of the consequences involved. There indeed was moral revulsion against the bombing of Hiroshima, and our reputation abroad undoubtedly suffered; but there was also admiration for our scientific achievement and rejoicing that the war was ended. Doubtless our use of the bomb to kill more than a hundred thousand Oriental civilians has contributed to anti-American feeling throughout the world, but it can be argued that such feeling is much more due to our economic abundance, our support of the Western colonial powers, and the behavior of American tourists abroad than to our use of the atomic bomb.

There has been suspicion and bitterness between East and West; it may be argued that these were not caused by the atomic bomb but were the inevitable result of a basic conflict between Communist doctrine and Western democracy which was already manifesting itself early in 1945, before the dawn of the atomic era.

III

At this point it is necessary to digress and grapple with a criticism that lays the entire blame for the whole East-West conflict at the door of those who decided to drop the atomic bomb. A British scientist, P. M. S. Blackett, has charged that the atomic bomb was aimed not so much at Japan as at Russia. The United States used the bomb on August 6 to distract the world's attention from the Russian invasion of Manchuria (scheduled for August 8) and end the war quickly before the Russians could make a significant contribution to the defeat of Japan — and thus to shut Russia out of her rightful share in the occupation and control of the conquered country. According to this theory, Russia's suspicions and belligerent attitude toward the United States stem from her bitterness over this incident. The dropping of the atomic bomb, says Blackett, was not so much the last action of World War II as the first action of the cold war against Russia. Hence the atomic bombing of Japan, although it may be judged successful as a cynical political maneuver, must be judged morally indefensible.[2]

The available evidence does not support Blackett's charges. United States military policy as early as 1943 consistently posited the necessity of Russia's joining the war against Japan. At Yalta in February 1945, Roosevelt and Churchill, in return for certain concessions, obtained Stalin's agreement that "two or three months after Germany has surrendered and the war in Europe has terminated the Soviet Union shall enter into the war against Japan." [3] One of President Truman's primary objectives at Potsdam was to urge Russia to live up to this commitment:

There were many reasons for my going to Potsdam, but the most urgent, to my mind, was to get from Stalin a personal reaffirmation of Russia's entry into the war against Japan, a matter which our military chiefs were most anxious to clinch. This I was able to get from Stalin in the very first days of the conference. . . .[4]

Following the successful test of the atomic bomb in New Mexico, there was no change in the American policy at Potsdam. Truman inquired of General Marshall whether, now that we had the new weapon, we still needed the Russians in the Pacific war. Marshall replied that with the bomb we no longer really needed the Russians; however, their entry into the war would probably bring victory quicker and with smaller loss of American life. Even if we defeated Japan without the Russians' aid, we could not prevent them from marching into Manchuria and seizing virtually whatever they wanted; therefore it was still expedient for us to encourage them to come in soon enough to be of some help in defeating Japan.[5]

On July 24 the combined British and American Chiefs of Staff presented to Churchill and Truman their final report incorporating their agreements on the prosecution of the Pacific war. One of their recommendations was that the Soviet Union be encouraged to enter the war. This recommendation was formally approved by both the Prime Minister and the President. Thereupon the Combined Chiefs adjourned and rode over to the Cecilienhof Palace to confer with their Russian counterparts. Plans for the Soviet invasion of Manchuria, and other aspects of the Far Eastern operations, were discussed in a friendly and cooperative way.[6]

On July 29 Molotov made a request to Truman and Byrnes regarding Russia's entry into the Pacific war. The Soviet government, he said, considered that the proper method would be for the United States and Britain to address a formal request to the Soviet government for its declaration of war against Japan. Molotov's request "disturbed" Byrnes. By this time the Secretary of State would personally have been quite happy to keep the Russians out of Manchuria. However, his own feelings did not keep him from sitting up late at night typing out a letter that would provide Stalin with a ready-made (and legally very shaky) justification for breaking Russia's existing neutrality pact with Japan. Had the United States been engaged in a conspiracy to prevent Russian entry into the war, surely Byrnes could at least have gone to bed early — and no doubt could have found other ways to delay. It is difficult to believe, never-theless, that such delay would have prevented Russia from entering the war against Japan, if she determined that it was in her national interest to do so.[7]

There is no evidence that the atomic bomb caused in Ameri-can policy a last-minute change designed to keep Russia out of the Pacific war. But there is evidence that the atomic bomb did cause the Russians to change *their* policy in order to get into the war earlier. In his first meeting with Stalin, President Tru-man raised the question of Russia's entry into the war. Stalin affirmed his intention to abide by the Yalta agreement, but said that a satisfactory agreement between Russia and China must be signed before military operations could begin. To this end negotiations with China would be resumed upon his return to Moscow from Potsdam. The Soviet position was reaffirmed on July 24 by General Alexei Antonov, Red Army Chief of Staff — who told the Combined Chiefs of Staff that Soviet armies would be ready to commence operations in Manchuria in the last half of August, the precise date to depend upon reaching accord with China — and as late as July 29 by Molotov in a conversation with Truman and Byrnes. Yet the Russian armies plunged across the Manchurian border on August 9, two days after Hiroshima, and while the negotiations with China *were still in progress.*[8]

In short, the evidence indicates that the United States con-sistently urged early Russian entry into the war against Japan, and did so at Potsdam despite the personal misgivings of some of her highest officials. Both this urging and the prompt use of the atomic bomb were motivated by the same desire: namely, to end the war at the earliest possible moment with the least cost in American lives. The evidence suggests not that the U.S. changed her time table for the atomic bomb but rather that Russia changed her schedule and hurried into the war after the bombing of Hiroshima, so as to claim the concessions made at Yalta.

IV

Other critics of America's bombing of Hiroshima and Nagasaki charged that our use of atomic energy to secure short-term wartime objectives jeopardized our long-term hope of security through international control of atomic energy. Efforts to achieve international control have not succeeded; but most observers would probably agree that a basic cause of the failure was the conflict between Russia's antipathy to any control system that would permit foreign inspectors within her borders and the refusal of the United States to give up her atomic monopoly before a reliable control system was established. It is questionable whether using the first atomic bomb in a demonstration, rather than to attack a city, would have made much difference in this fundamental conflict.

Did the United States, by using the atomic bomb in the war against Japan, give sanction to this new weapon and make it likely that atomic weapons will be used in any future war? The importance of the precedent created by the first breach of the barrier between discriminate and inherently indiscriminate weapons must not be underestimated. This importance may be indicated by imagining the converse: had the United States refrained from using the atomic bomb during the war, a powerful moral inhibition would have been brought to bear upon any nation that in the future might consider wartime use of its atomic weapons. Yet some would argue that precisely because of the spectacular destruction of Hiroshima the atomic bomb has become a powerful force for peace: the vision of what a future world war would mean has been so vividly impressed upon the mind of mankind that men have become determined never again to use atomic weapons "in anger." [9] At any rate it is indisputable that Russia and the United States have taken great pains to avoid use of nuclear weapons, and none has been used in the fifteen years since Hiroshima — despite grievous provocations on both sides.

Did the bombing of Hiroshima precipitate the atomic arms race that now daily threatens the world with disaster? Undoubtedly the explosion at Hiroshima started the atomic arms race, but it is not at all obvious (given what we know of Russia's determination to surpass the United States in every field) that introducing the atomic bomb into the world by a technical demonstration rather than by full military use would have prevented the arms race. Had we kept our own development and possession of atomic weapons secret, the sense of urgency might well have been absent from Russian nuclear research, and the arms race thus postponed. But it is interesting (if futile) to speculate upon the possible behavior of the Soviet Union during the years 1945-1948 had she not known that the United States possessed the atomic bomb. With the massive Red Army still intact, and the Western powers nearly completely demobilized, Russia might have been tempted into adventures (in Iran, for example) that would have forced the United States to use or to threaten to use the atomic bomb against her former ally.

v

The primary difficulty in this sort of calculation of long-term political consequences is the very intangible and indefinite nature of the consequences. No matter on which side of the argument one finds himself, such speculations illustrate the virtual impossibility of predicting beforehand, or analyzing afterwards, the social and political consequences deriving from the atomic bombing of Japan. For every argument suggesting bad consequences there seems to be an equally convincing argument suggesting good consequences. Even were one able to determine on which side the heavier weight lay, the balancing of long-term evil against short-term good presents an almost insoluble problem.

Certainly the long-range consequences of using the atomic

bomb should have been considered seriously by Truman and his advisers as they made their decision. One may argue that in the light of such consequences the threshold between "conventional" weapons (which *can* be used discriminately) and atomic weapons (which are inherently indiscriminate) was leaped over much too lightly. Yet, when one sees the difficulty of clearly weighing long-range and intangible consequences, even after the event, it is hard to blame Stimson and Truman for concentrating on the more tangible and predictable short-range consequences. These considerations should give pause to those moralists who insist that the essence of ethics is the calculation of consequences, and who too easily assume that diverse and intangible consequences of major political actions may be accurately predicted and also reduced to numerical quantities that can then be weighed against each other.

15. The Evolution of Mass Bombing

MANY MORALISTS carefully avoided the morass of calculations into which they saw some of their colleagues sinking — calculations about numbers of dead and net lives saved, attempts to compare tangible and intangible, immediate and long-term consequences of the bombing of Hiroshima and Nagasaki. They saw the question of the consequences of the act as basically irrelevant to the rightness or wrongness of the act. What counted was the intrinsic quality of the act itself: if it conformed to an objective standard of rightness, the act was right; if not, it was wrong.

In the case of the atomic bombing of Japan, the ethical principle that applies is the immunity of noncombatants from direct attack, a principle upheld both by centuries of Christian tradition and by international law. Civilians who are not directly participating in war work are immune from direct attack; obliteration bombing constitutes such a direct attack, and so is clearly immoral; the atomic bombing of Hiroshima and Nagasaki was the epitome of obliteration bombing — and hence must be categorically condemned. (Some moralists would go further and condemn the atomic bomb itself as inherently immoral because it is inherently incapable of discrimination between combatant and noncombatant.)

Roman Catholic moralists consistently chose this approach to the question of the morality of using the atomic bomb against Japan, and were nearly unanimous in condemning the bomb's use. Thus, Father James M. Gillis, in commenting on a statement by thirty-four non-Catholic clergy condemning the bomb for various other reasons, brushed these aside and stated the essential point as Catholic moralists saw it: "Why not stick to the essential moral problem — is it or is it not ethically right to bomb civilian populations, directly and intentionally?" [1] Monsignor Fulton J. Sheen preached a sermon condemning the use of the atomic bombs because it violated "the moral distinction that must be made in every war — a distinction between civilians and the military"; as for Truman's contention that the war was shortened and lives were saved, "that was precisely the argument Hitler used in bombing Holland." A commission of Catholic theologians, in their report on "The Ethics of Atomic War," stated: "Deliberate and direct attack on this portion of the enemy's people [civilians], no matter what the end sought, [is] simple murder." [2]

(A surprising exception to the general Catholic approach to the bombing of Hiroshima appeared in the Jesuit journal *America*, which in its editorial seemed to accept a utilitarian standard for judging the morality of the use of the bomb: "The moral issues raised by the discovery and use of the atomic bomb are numerous and extremely grave — so grave, indeed, that moral theologians will hesitate to give a forthright decision as to whether or not its use as a weapon of war can be justified for any reason or on any grounds. . . . It is our earnest prayer that the evil which will come from the atomic bomb will not outweigh the good which our war leaders, rightly or wrongly, hoped to achieve by its use.") [3]

Catholics were more consistent in judging the atomic bomb on these grounds, but many Protestants joined them. A national Baptist journal condemned "this ghastly slaughter of women and children who have not the remotest connection with a military objective . . ." The Federal Council of Churches Commission on the Relation of the Church to the War in the Light of the Christian Faith linked the atomic bombing of Japan with the practice of obliteration bombing and condemned both: the bombing of Hiroshima and Nagasaki "cannot properly be treated in isolation from the whole system of obliteration attacks with explosives and fire-bombs, of which the atomic raids were the stunning climax . . . the policy of obliteration bombing as actually practiced in World War II, culminating in the use of atomic bombs against Japan, is not defensible on Christian premises." [4]

It will help us assess the relevance of these moral judgments to the atomic bombing of Japan if we look briefly at the development of obliteration bombing during World War II, and the parallel development of opinion about such bombing.

II

In 1937 Franco's forces bombed and strafed the Spanish town of Guernica, killing hundreds of unarmed civilians; the civilized world was shocked at what it considered to be a sickening atrocity. The same year, the United States government protested the Japanese bombing of Nanking: "This Government holds the view that any general bombing of an extensive area wherein there resides a large populace engaged in peaceful pursuits is unwarranted and contrary to the principles of law and humanity." (The Japanese replied that they were attacking military targets only.) On the first day of World War II, President Roosevelt addressed "an urgent appeal to every government which may be engaged in hostilities publicly to affirm its determination that its armed forces shall in no event, and in no circumstances, undertake the bombardment from the air of civilian populations or of unfortified cities . . ."; he reaffirmed this stand the following year when he said, "The bombing of helpless and unprotected civilians is a tragedy which has aroused the horror of all mankind. I recall with pride that the United States consistently has taken the lead in urging that this inhuman practice be prohibited." [5]

Hitler's vicious bombing of Warsaw and Rotterdam was widely condemned as a typical outgrowth of his treachery and ruthless militarism. (It must be noted, however, that these bombings, although indiscriminate, were tactical rather than strategic, being undertaken in support of troops about to enter the cities.)[6] In Britain, Winston Churchill (then First Lord of the Admiralty) denounced the bombing of cities as "a new and odious form of attack," and the Foreign Office defined the government's attitude toward bombing: "His Majesty's Government have made it clear that it is no part of their policy to bomb nonmilitary objectives, no matter what the policy of the German Government may be. In spite of the wanton and repeated attacks by the German Air Force on undefended towns in Poland, Norway, France, Holland and Belgium, His Majesty's Government steadily adhere to this policy." [7]

Until well into 1940 civilized opinion was unanimously against the bombing of civilians; this form of attack was considered fit only for totalitarian dictators. Bombing attacks could be and should be restricted to specific military targets. "The RAF started the war with the doctrine that . . . night bombing can be precise enough for attacking specific targets." [8]

During 1940 and 1941, confidence in the doctrine of precision bombing was eroded as the RAF discovered through bitter experience that daylight raids were too costly, and that its night raids could not regularly hit or even locate such large targets as the Ruhr railroad marshaling yards. By late 1941 the British had abandoned the idea of precision bombing and adopted area bombing, "not as a method desirable in itself but as an expedient of necessity to be resorted to until the precision of night attacks could be improved." The primary reason for the shift was the ineffectiveness of so-called "precision" bombing. Such bombing was never really 100 per cent precise in the first place; improved fighter and antiaircraft opposition drove bombers to higher and higher altitudes, where their accuracy grew less and less. In contrast, area bombing could be carried on at night, during inclement weather, and also when smoke obscured the location of key targets. The purpose of area bombing was not to bomb civilians directly, but, as was explained on the floor of the House of Commons, "night bombing of military objectives necessarily involves bombing the area in which they are situated," and the area might consist largely of workers' houses, or even a whole town.[9]

This halfway house was abandoned when Air Marshal Sir Arthur Travers Harris took over the RAF's bomber command on March 3, 1942. Harris regarded area bombing not as a temporary expedient but as the most promising method of aerial attack. He and his staff doubted that the industrial base of Germany's war economy could be crippled by strategic bombing, but were convinced that a direct attack on enemy urban populations could break Germany's morale and thus her will to resist. And so "obliteration bombing" replaced the temporary expedient of "area bombing"; 60 per cent of the RAF's total tonnage in 1942 and 1943 was concentrated on urban obliteration raids.[10] One detects in the justifications given for this form of attack a mixture of revenge for what German bombers had done to British cities and sincere adherence to the theory that the war could be shortened by a direct assault upon the will-to-resist of the German people.[11]

This change in strategy was accompanied by a shift away from the official policy to which His Majesty's government had committed itself to "steadily adhere." In 1943 Prime Minister Churchill praised the obliteration bombing campaign in these terms:

> The almost total systematic destruction of many of the centers of German war effort continues on a greater scale and at a greater pace. The havoc wrought is indescribable and the effect upon the German war production in all its forms . . . is matched by that wrought upon the life and economy of the whole of that guilty organization . . .

Mr. Churchill spoke of the "systematic shattering" of German cities, and of "beating the life out of Germany." He promised the House of Commons that "there are no lengths in violence to which we will not go." Another official spokesman formulated the government's new policy: "Our plans are to bomb, burn, and ruthlessly destroy in every way available to us the people responsible for creating this war." [12]

III

By the first months of 1943 the United States Eighth Air Force had overcome its organizational and logistic problems, and was ready to join the RAF in increasingly large-scale operations over Germany. The AAF's fleet of flying fortresses was built upon the fundamental assumption that long-range daylight precision bombing was not only feasible but was the most effective way of destroying the German wartime economy. It was only with difficulty that the AAF had managed to convince the British, who remembered their painful losses of 1940 and 1941, that this strategy would be effective without involving prohibitive losses. At the Casablanca Conference in January 1943, the two Allies adopted a joint operational plan for the strategic bombardment of Germany, the object of which was "the progressive destruction and dislocation of the German military, industrial, and economic system, and the undermining of the morale of the German people to a point where their capacity for armed resistance is fatally weakened." The plan envisioned both a precision attack by the Americans on specific "military, industrial, and economic" targets, and the "undermining of the morale of the German people" through urban obliteration attacks carried out mainly by the British.[13]

Although there was thus a rough division of labor between British and Americans, both Allies agreed upon the necessity of the over-all attack. Despite AAF commitment to the concept of daylight precision bombing, poor weather and stiff German fighter opposition (which forced a temporary abatement of the daylight raids) meant that the AAF shared to some extent in obliteration attacks. Nevertheless, the Americans remained committed to the superiority (both military and moral) of precision bombing. President Roosevelt assured Congress in 1943 that we were "not bombing tenements for the sadistic pleasure of killing as the Nazis did, but blowing to bits carefully selected targets — factories, shipyards, munitions dumps." [14]

IV

As the war wore on, the distinction between area and precision bombing tended (at least in the public mind) to become lost, and bombing of all types was increasingly regarded as a military necessity. The extent to which obliteration of urban areas came to be accepted in the United States as normal military procedure is illustrated by the public reaction to a strong protest against the bombing of civilians published in 1944. In March of that year the American pacifist journal *Fellowship* printed an article entitled "Massacre by Bombing," by the British pacifist Vera Brittain, which vigorously attacked the existing policy of strategic obliteration bombing of German cities. The article was prefaced with an endorsement by twenty-eight American clergymen.

Miss Brittain carefully distinguished between obliteration bombing of cities and the tactical bombing that "forms part of a military campaign"; she deliberately emphasized in her article the killing of civilians in areas of little military importance. The reaction against her protest, both by President Roosevelt and by most churchmen, ignored the distinction between precision and obliteration attacks. Stephen Early, Roosevelt's secretary, responding to *Fellowship* on behalf of the President, wrote that, although the President was "disturbed and horrified" by the killing of civilians in air raids, "the bombing is shortening the war, in the opinion of an overwhelming percentage of military authorities . . ." No awareness is shown in Early's letter of the distinction between obliteration and precision bombing, which was so obvious in Brittain's article, and which President Roosevelt had so carefully made in his statement to Congress in 1943.[15]

The *New York Times* printed a story about the Brittain article on its front page; it stimulated a heavy reader response. Letters to the *Times* ran fifty to one in opposition to the protest, and tended strongly to assume that to cease *obliteration* bombing was equivalent to giving up bombing altogether. Letters from leading clergymen, both Protestant and Catholic, included such phrases as these:

> What would these twenty-eight do about it? Would they have the Axis win?
>
> Every minute of delay in winning this war is death to yet other men, women and children.
>
> Will you please ask these gentlemen [the twenty-eight endorsing clergymen] what the alternative is? Are we to give up blasting factories and nests of cannon used for the purpose of killing our soldiers?

Among the prominent churchmen who favored the continuation of our bombing policy were Daniel A. Poling, Bishop William T. Manning, and Bishop G. Bromley Oxnam.[16]

Editorials in the Catholic *Commonweal* and the Protestant *Christian Century* voiced support of Miss Brittain's protest.[17] Despite these questionings of our bombing policy, the general impression given by the reaction to "Massacre by Bombing" is that the distinction between obliteration and precision bombing by 1944 had been lost in the minds of most Americans. Whatever bombing was militarily necessary to win the war must be done. To call into question obliteration bombing was to call into question all bombing and the whole war effort itself.

V

Miss Brittain's protest grew out of her pacifism, and generally it was supported by pacifists; mainline Protestant churchmen either supported the existing bombing policy or kept silent. However, one systematic and penetrating Roman Catholic protest (in part stimulated by Miss Brittain's article) appeared in 1944 in a journal article entitled "The Morality of Obliteration Bombing," by Father John C. Ford, a leading Jesuit moralist. Like Miss Brittain, Ford distinguished carefully between the bombing of purely military targets and "the strategic bombing, by means of incendiaries and explosives, of industrial centers of population in which the target to be wiped out is not a definite factory, bridge, or similar object, but a large area of a whole city . . ." [18]

Ford outlined the basic Roman Catholic position on the immunity of noncombatants from direct attack, as it roots in the just-war theory. A war, to be justifiable, must be prosecuted by just means. This requirement includes respect for the distinction between combatant and noncombatant. While the former may be directly attacked, the killing of noncombatants is morally justifiable only if it is an indirect and unintended result of military action directed at combatants or a legitimate military target — and provided also that the unintended evil is not disproportionately large in comparison with the good being achieved. The killing of noncombatants by direct intention is equivalent to murder and is a clear moral wrong, even if undertaken as a means to a much greater good. In Catholic moral theory, it is not permissible to perform evil as a *means* to the achievement of good, no matter how great.

In accordance with this theory, then, the direct and intentional killing of five civilians would be simple murder. A bombing attack directed at a munitions factory by which 500 noncombatants would unintentionally but inevitably be killed

would be justifiable. However, the same attack would be unjustifiable if it killed 50,000 noncombatants, since in this case the
secondary evil probably would be disproportionate to the good
achieved by the attack.

Having established the fundamental moral theory, Ford proceeded to two questions relating to the application of this
theory to modern war. The first is a question of identity: do
civilians participating in a modern wartime economy qualify
as noncombatants in the traditional sense, or are *all* citizens
combatants in a state mobilized for "total war"? Ford insisted
that modern war has not rendered the traditional distinction
obsolete, and refuted those who would say, with one writer in
the *American Journal of International Law*, that "both in point
of fact and in theory the distinction has been so whittled down
by the demands of military necessity that it has become more
apparent than real." [19] It is true, Ford admitted, that no citizen
can escape from some involvement in the economy of a nation
at war — the farmer furnishes food for the support of the soldier at the front, and even the schoolgirl collects bottle caps for
the scrap drive. Yet mere cooperation in the economy is not
sufficient to qualify one as a combatant. This term applies
only to those under arms, or actively and directly engaged in the
prosecution of the war. Although it may be difficult to apply
this distinction to borderline cases (such as government office
clerks or transport workers), it is obvious that the vast majority
of civilians are not directly engaged in the production or supply
of armaments. Therefore a direct attack upon civilians is morally wrong.

The second question turns on the concept of double effect.
In Catholic moral theory it is not permissible to do an evil act
with direct intention, but it is permissible to allow the evil as
an indirect, secondary, and unintended result of a right act,
even if the unintended evil is known in advance to be inevitable.
Under this rule obliteration bombing, deliberately aimed at the

civilian population with the intent to undermine its morale, is clearly wrong. But in the case of a bombing attack obliterating a whole section of an industrial city for the express purpose of destroying its factories, can the civilian casualties be permitted as an indirect and unintended effect? "No," replied Ford. The killing of civilians is so intimately and inevitably connected with the attack that it is practically impossible for the airman "to let go his bombs, and withhold his intentions as far as the innocent are concerned." [20] In practice such an attack amounts to doing evil directly (killing civilians) in the hope that good (destruction of the factory and shortening of the war) will also be accomplished — which is not permissible. Ford concluded:

> Obliteration bombing, as defined, is an immoral attack on the rights of the innocent. It includes a direct intent to do them injury. Even if this were not true, it would still be immoral, because no proportionate cause could justify the evil done; and to make it legitimate would soon lead the world to the immoral barbarity of total war.[21]

VI

Despite the fervor of Miss Brittain's protest and the cold logic of Father Ford's arguments, both the pacifist and the Jesuit were essentially voices crying in the wilderness. Although there was some support of their views in church periodicals, there was no clear consensus among American churchmen (not to mention the general public) on the immorality of obliteration bombing. For example, the theologians of the Federal Council of Churches Commission on the Relation of the Church to the War in the Light of the Christian Faith reached an ambivalent position in their 1944 report. In one sentence, the theologians stated that "all of us agree" that "the massacre of civilian populations" is morally unjustifiable. However, the next sentence reads, "some of the signers of the report believe

that certain other measures, such as rigorous blockades of foodstuffs essential to civilian life, and *obliteration bombing of
civilian areas*, however repugnant to humane feelings, are still
justifiable on Christian principles, if they are essential to the
successful conduct of a war that is itself justified" (italics added).
How the "massacre of civilian populations" can be condemned
in one breath, and the "obliteration bombing of civilian areas"
condoned in the next, is not explained.[22]

And so it was that within seven years a radical change in
military practice and moral judgments had taken place. What
was universally condemned by churchmen and decent people
generally in 1937, and considered fit only for dictators in 1939,
was between 1940 and 1944 accepted as a "military necessity"
and a normal part of the procedure of war, both by the general
public and by the large majority of churchmen, both Protestant
and Roman Catholic.

VII

The climax to this movement, so far as the United States is concerned, came in March 1945. From their bases in the Mari-
ana Islands, our B-29's had begun bombing raids against Japan
in November 1944 which gradually built up in intensity. For
the first three months, the bombers delivered high-altitude daylight precision attacks against Japanese aircraft factories. High
winds and cloudy weather over Japan made the bombing "precision" in name only. In the first months of 1945, less than
17 per cent of the bombs were hitting within 3000 feet of
their targets. Results in terms of damage to the Japanese aircraft industry were disappointing.

> The effort to knock out the Japanese aircraft industry by high-
> altitude daylight precision bombing of carefully selected targets
> had failed. . . . Not one of the high-priority targets had been
> destroyed . . . Musashi [engine factory] had suffered only four

per cent damage after 835 B-29 sorties had been sent against
it . . .

Early in March 1945, General Curtis LeMay, who had taken
charge of the B-29 Bomber Command in January, summed up
the results of the efforts to date: "This outfit has been getting
a lot of publicity without having really accomplished a hell of
a lot in bombing results." [23]

LeMay decided to gamble on a bold change of tactics. Instead of sending his planes over Japan in daylight at high
altitudes, he decided to send them at night at low altitudes
(5000–9000 feet). Reducing the planes' armaments and low-
ering their altitude meant that bomb loads could be substantially increased. The planes were loaded with incendiaries rather
than the high-explosives typical of "precision" attack. On the
night of March 9/10, more than 300 B-29's dumped 2000 tons
of fire bombs on Tokyo. Fanned by a brisk wind, individual fires
quickly merged to form a huge conflagration that burned out
15.8 square miles of the city, including 18 per cent of the industrial area, 63 per cent of the commercial area, and the heart
of the residential district. So intense was the heat that the
water in the smaller canals was boiling. Japanese defenses were
completely overwhelmed. An estimated 100,000 persons died
from burns and suffocation in the fire storm.[24]

LeMay's gamble had paid off extravagantly. In quick succession, Nagoya, Osaka, and Kobe were attacked with the same
technique. Although the attacks had to be slowed down in
order to support the impending Okinawa invasion, LeMay continued as rapidly as his dwindling supply of incendiaries would
allow. By June 15 the first phase of his obliteration campaign
was completed.

> The six most important industrial cities in Japan had been
> ruined. Great factories had been destroyed or damaged; thou-
> sands of household and feeder industrial units had gone up in

smoke. Casualty lists ran into six figures. Millions of persons had lost their homes, and the evacuation of survivors had made it difficult to secure labor for those factories that remained.[25]

Thereafter, LeMay turned his attention to Japan's smaller cities, eventually raiding fifty-eight towns with fire bombs, in addition to continuing high explosive precision attacks on other targets.

Apart from the ineffectiveness of high-altitude precision attacks, there were two military justifications for the shift to massive incendiary raids. The first was the high vulnerability of Japan's concentrated and lightly constructed urban areas. So susceptible were the Japanese cities to this form of attack that a degree of economic collapse was produced in Japan within six months that took three years of bombing to produce in Germany.

A further justification lay in the organization of Japanese industry, in which large assembly plants depended for their supply of small parts upon many machinists working in small shops and in private homes. It was true in Japan, as it was not in Germany, that burning out the workers' residential district would directly interfere with production at the central plant. If war industry is a legitimate target for attack, it was argued, then it is permissible to attack Japan's urban residential areas directly. The effect of the incendiary raids upon Tokyo's "phantom industry" has been described by a Japanese newspaper writer:

> In Tokyo the raiders had struck most heavily where the human congestion was greatest and where there also was the greatest concentration of Japan's "phantom industry," where the piece work that fed the aircraft and other war industries was carried on. This was the section of small shops, of machine tools in homes, where families toiled endlessly to make small parts that went with their neighbors' daily product to produce the machinery of war. This was the root of the Japanese war

effort, and the Allies struck savagely at that root. In the heart
of the ordinary Japanese there was hatred and bitterness against
the American raiders who left an indiscriminate trail of the
blackened corpses of babies and grandmothers interspersed
with the wreckage of war machinery and the bodies of war
workers and soldiers.[26]

VIII

Although the March decision to shift from precision to obliteration bombing represented a decisive break with "orthodox
AAF doctrines," and constituted one of the major decisions of
the Pacific war, it was not made by America's political leaders.
Neither was it made by the AAF command in Washington, although the possibility of experimenting with fire raids had been
discussed there. The decision was made by General LeMay at
Guam. "For the change in tactics LeMay was responsible and
its success was to mark him as one of the very greatest of
operational air commanders of the war . . ." [27] The government did not hail the shift as a new policy; there was no out-
cry in the press; churchmen made no noticeable protest. Apparently the American people had become so accustomed to
news of destruction that they did not realize that America's
cherished doctrine of precision bombing had been abandoned
and the policy of obliteration bombing had taken its place.
The obliteration bombing of cities was accepted as a logical,
normal, and routine part of accomplishing the defeat of Japan.

IX

It is somewhat ironical that as LeMay's B-29's were razing
Japan's smaller cities as a "military necessity" for the defeat of
the Japanese, the United States Strategic Bombing Survey was
preparing a report on the bombing of European cities, in which

it disclosed that obliteration bombing had not contributed as much to the defeat of Germany as had been predicted. Of the total tonnage of bombs dropped on Germany, 24 per cent was dropped in obliteration raids on large cities — nearly twice the amount dropped on all manufacturing targets combined (9 per cent was dropped on oil and rubber targets, and only 2 per cent on aircraft factories). "In sheer destructiveness, these raids far outstripped all other forms of attack." The stated purpose of the obliteration attacks was "primarily to destroy morale, particularly that of the industrial worker" — to undermine the will-to-resist of the enemy population. While the psychological morale of the German people was affected by the bombing, the USSBS found that the effect of this upon behavior, that is, upon war production, was minimal: ". . . depressed and discouraged workers were not necessarily unproductive workers." German workers kept producing as long as they had the physical means to do so. The will-to-resist remained to the end: "at the end of the war local officials were attempting to repair [railroad] yards already under artillery fire from the advancing Allied armies." [28]

To their surprise, the investigators of the USSBS discovered that even in Hamburg, which suffered perhaps the most devastating obliteration raids of the whole war, war production returned to normal levels within a few weeks, and what had been a labor shortage was now relieved by former waiters, shopkeepers, and office workers seeking war employment.

> In reducing, as nothing else could, the consumption of non-essentials and the employment of men in their supply, there is a distinct possibility that the attacks on Hamburg increased Germany's output of war material and thus her military effectiveness.[29]

The USSBS reported that "the most important single cause of Germany's ultimate economic collapse" was the bombing at-

tack — not on her urban centers — but upon her railroad system, which transported raw materials, parts, and especially
coal, all of which were essential for continued production.[30]

In Japan, the USSBS found after the war, the effects of the
obliteration raids had been greater than in Germany, both upon
morale and war production. However, it was also discovered
that many of the factories destroyed by bombing raids had already been rendered ineffective twice over by sea blockade
(which cut off essential raw materials) and the progressive
breakdown of Japan's internal transportation system, upon
which factories were dependent for coal and for the moving of
parts and finished goods.[31]

In short, the careful postwar investigations of the USSBS
have made it plain that the massive urban raids, advocated in
the midst of the ignorance and uncertainties of wartime as a
military necessity, proved to be much less effective in destroying the enemy's ability to produce and to fight than precision
attacks upon his railroad system.

X

The general acceptance of obliteration bombing of cities as
standard procedure in the war against Japan had a decisive influence upon the choice of targets for the first atomic bomb.
In part, the nature of the weapon itself determined that its
target should be large; it was too powerful a bomb to "waste"
upon a single factory, no matter how big. The "dual target"
recommendation of the Interim Committee also pointed toward
an urban target. Yet what clinched the matter was that by
July 1945, when targets for the atomic bomb were chosen, the
word target had come to be synonymous with the word city, so
far as Japan was concerned. The loss of the distinction between military targets and urban areas can be seen clearly in
the accounts of those who chose the atomic bomb targets. The

choice of cities as targets for the atomic bomb was unquestioned and automatic.

The accounts of Truman, Stimson, and General Arnold betray a certain inconsistency between words and action. They frequently used the traditional language, which assumes a distinction between military targets and civilian areas. Thus Truman:

> In deciding to use this bomb I wanted to make sure that it would be used as a weapon of war in the manner prescribed by the laws of war. That meant that I wanted it dropped on a military target. I had told Stimson that the bomb should be dropped as nearly as possible upon a war production center of prime military importance.
>
> Stimson's staff had prepared a list of cities in Japan that might serve as targets. . . .
>
> Four cities were finally recommended as targets: Hiroshima, Kokura, Niigata, and Nagasaki. . . . The order of selection was in accordance with the military importance of these cities . . . Before the selected targets were approved as proper for military purposes, I personally went over them in detail with Stimson, Marshall, and Arnold . . .[32]

The President speaks of "the first use of an atomic weapon against a military target." He reports that he asked Stimson "which cities in Japan were devoted exclusively to war production." Afterwards Truman reported that the first atomic bomb had been dropped on a "military base," in order to "avoid, in so far as possible, the killing of civilians." [33]

Stimson, who had been championing international law and urging the restraint of war by morality for thirty years, had as recently as June 1 "sternly questioned his Air Forces leader, wanting to know whether the apparently indiscriminate bombings of Tokyo were absolutely necessary." The day before, he had cautioned the Interim Committee that our objective in using the atomic bomb was military damage rather than civilian lives.[34] Yet, in spite of the genuine concern of Truman and Stimson to minimize civilian losses, their unquestioning approval of a large city as target guaranteed maximum civilian losses; in fact it would be difficult to devise any use of the atomic bomb that could have taken more civilian lives.

Despite the use of language which had grown out of the traditional distinction between military targets and civilian areas, there is no shred of evidence in the accounts of Truman, Stimson, or General Arnold to indicate that any other target than a city was considered.[35]

XI

The degree to which traditional words and ideas can be shaped by a new historical situation is thus made clear. The Scientific Panel had recommended to the President "direct military use" of the bomb. In 1935 (and for several preceding centuries) these words would have meant that the bomb should be dropped on a military installation such as a fortress, supply dump, or naval base. In 1945 — just ten years later — the experience of the European war and the acceptance of obliteration bombing as standard procedure in the war against Japan, had so transformed the climate of opinion and men's ways of thinking, that these same words, "direct military use," meant something entirely different. They were understood to mean that the bomb should be dropped on the center of a large city.

Winston Churchill has written:

The historic fact remains, and must be judged in the after-time, that the decision whether or not to use the atomic bomb to compel the surrender of Japan was never even an issue. There was unanimous, automatic, unquestioned agreement around our table; nor did I ever hear the slightest suggestion that we should do otherwise.[36]

Just so, the choice of a city rather than a military or naval installation as a target for the first atomic bomb was "unanimous, automatic, unquestioned"; nor, apparently, was there "the slightest suggestion that we should do otherwise."

Only when "the force from which the sun draws its power" actually exploded over Hiroshima did most people awaken to question what they had accepted without question. The spectacular blast of the atomic bomb shattered men's shell of complacency — and suddenly made clear the direction of the path down which they had been walking, as if under hypnosis. After Hiroshima, men condemned not only the atomic raids because of their indiscriminate attack upon civilians but they also began to condemn the Tokyo fire raid. The Commission on the Relation of the Church to the War in the Light of the Christian Faith met again, and this time unanimously denounced World War II's obliteration raids, along with the destruction of Hiroshima. And a chorus of Roman Catholic moralists began to echo Father Ford's lonely condemnation of mass bombing.

16. The Political Failure

A THEME frequently encountered in churchly criticisms of the bombing of Hiroshima and Nagasaki is that Japan was already defeated, and therefore that the atomic bomb was unnecessary for winning the war. Churchmen citing these grounds varied from calling the bombing "unwise and unjust" to denouncing the bomb's "reckless and irresponsible employment against an already beaten foe." [1] Churchmen found support in the criticisms of scientists and military men. Albert Einstein wrote, "The war could have been won without it." Admiral Leahy, Chief of Staff to the President, wrote following the war, "It is my opinion that the use of this barbarous weapon at Hiroshima and Nagasaki was of no material assistance in our war against Japan. The Japanese were already defeated and ready to surrender . . ." [2]

Evidence cited above demonstrates that Japan was indeed essentially defeated in mid-1945, although her defending armies were still intact. But the evidence also indicates that Japan's military leaders, who dominated the government and controlled policy up to August 6, insisted upon defying the facts and definitely were not ready to surrender — and in fact maintained this position even *after* the atomic attacks. Therefore, the simple allegation that Japan was already defeated does not overthrow the main argument of Truman and Stimson. The recommendation implicit in this level of criticism is that the war should have been allowed to take its natural course. The war could certainly have been won by conventional means without the atomic bomb, but the cost in human suffering would have been greater than the cost of Hiroshima and Nagasaki, even had Japan surrendered prior to invasion.

Moreover, the evidence suggests the ironical conclusion that in the absence of the atomic bomb the invasion, although unnecessary, would have been inevitable. General MacArthur and General Marshall insisted that the invasion was necessary to bring Japan to surrender. No major power in the history of the world had capitulated and allowed enemy occupation of its homeland in the absence of an invading army; our military strategists could not conceive of Japan's doing so. Even General Arnold of the Air Force, although believing that bombing alone could bring Japan to surrender, wanted to invade Kyushu to obtain more and closer air bases. The Army view had prevailed among the Joint Chiefs of Staff, despite Navy misgivings. Preparations for the invasion were being pushed ahead; had not the atomic bomb precipitated Japan's surrender, it is very likely that these plans would have come to fruition in an assault on the Kyushu beaches.

In Japan, in the meantime, Army leaders were determined to hold out until they could meet the invader on the beaches and, it was hoped, inflict upon him severe damage. That Japan was already essentially defeated, with dwindling stocks of fuel and ammunition, was irrelevant to this stubborn determination. Japan's soldiers had shown themselves upon many earlier occasions to be capable of fierce resistance to the last man, even in the face of certain defeat. The strength of this determination in Japan's military leaders is indicated by the fact that it did not crack even after the dropping of two atomic bombs.

Thus, what was in reality unnecessary for the defeat of Japan was psychologically necessary for the Army leaders, both American and Japanese. The former were determined to invade, and the latter were determined to fight the invader on the beaches. Had the atomic bomb not cut short the war, the world might well have witnessed the disaster of two armies, each directed by its own shortsighted military prejudice, drawn irresistibly into a death grapple tragic for both.

II

Another group criticized the atomic bombing of Japan as unnecessary on deeper grounds. These critics pointed out that Japan was already known to be seeking peace by negotiation; had we skillfully capitalized on this knowledge, we could have achieved surrender by diplomatic means, thus eliminating the need for dropping the bomb.

A British historian of World War II wrote that by June 1945 only the obstacle of "unconditional surrender" prevented bringing the war to an end highly advantageous to Britain and the United States. Had the Allied leaders been truly interested in saving lives, then "all President Truman and Mr. Churchill need have done was to remove the obstacle of unconditional surrender, when the war could have been brought to an immediate end." Had the Potsdam Declaration stated clearly that the Emperor's status would be preserved, "there can be no doubt whatsoever that the ultimatum would have been accepted, in which case there would be no need to use the atomic bomb." [3]

Hanson W. Baldwin made essentially the same point:

> But, in fact, our only warning to a Japan already militarily defeated, and in a hopeless situation, was the Potsdam demand for unconditional surrender issued on July 26, when we knew Japanese surrender attempts had started. Yet when the Japanese surrender was negotiated about two weeks later, after the bomb was dropped, our unconditional surrender demand was made conditional and we agreed, as Stimson had originally proposed we should do, to continuation of the Emperor upon his imperial throne.

We were, therefore, twice guilty. We dropped the bomb at a time when Japan already was negotiating for an end of the war, but before these negotiations could come to fruition. We demanded unconditional surrender, then dropped the bomb and accepted conditional surrender, a sequence which indicates pretty clearly that the Japanese would have surrendered, even if the bomb had not been dropped, had the Potsdam Declaration included our promise to permit the Emperor to remain on his imperial throne.[4]

Is it true that Japan was seeking peace as early as May or June 1945, as some have stated? There were two independent moves in the direction of peace by Japanese attachés in Europe during the spring of 1945, but the initiative in these moves was undertaken by persons who had no authority to speak for the Japanese *government*, and all were ordered by Tokyo to cease their activities. Meanwhile, in Japan, War Minister Anami had four hundred persons thrown into prison for harboring antiwar sentiments. It was clearly not the official policy of the Japanese government to seek peace, until at the imperial conference of June 22 it was decided that overtures should be made to Moscow for the purpose of obtaining a negotiated peace. This change of policy (not known to the United States until the interception of the messages sent to Moscow beginning on July 12) meant only that negotiations should be sought, but did not determine the terms upon which a peace settlement would be acceptable to Japan's military leaders.[5]

The minimum that Japan's military leaders were willing to settle for (retention of the Emperor, plus three further conditions) was much more than Washington was willing to grant. Foreign Minister Togo recognized that the most Japan could hope for was capitulation barely short of unconditional surrender — and Prince Konoye understood that the purpose of his journey to Moscow was to get Japan out of the war on any basis whatever, so long as the Emperor was preserved.[6] In short, even during July the Japanese government, although agreed upon a policy of seeking a negotiated peace, was not agreed upon the peace terms to be sought. An Allied statement indicating that the Emperor might be preserved would have been reassuring, but would not have resolved the disagreement.

III

Meanwhile the United States government was having similar difficulty in reaching agreement upon the terms of surrender. The disagreement centered upon the proper interpretation of the formula "unconditional surrender." This formula was announced by President Roosevelt at a press conference at the conclusion of the Casablanca Conference in January 1943 — although the official joint communiqué from the conference contained no mention of unconditional surrender.[7] Did Allied adherence to this rather informally adopted formula prolong the war unnecessarily? In the case of Japan, the question turns upon the one condition essential for the Japanese, and upon which both the war and peace parties were in complete agreement: namely, the preservation of the Emperor and the imperial system.

The one condition that the Japanese agreed was most crucial was the very one upon which the Americans were unable to agree. United States officials had been wrestling with the problem of the Emperor for months. In response to inquiries from the War Department, which was to have responsibility for occupying and administering a defeated Japan, the Department of State prepared in May 1944 a report setting forth its policy recommendations on the postwar treatment of Japan. This report dealt at some length with the question of the Emperor and concluded that the United States should refrain from committing itself in advance regarding the Emperor's future status.

Secretary of State Hull summed up the State Department's position in these words:

> In general, we felt we should not make advance commitments which would prejudice the situation in favor of the Emperor institution, or against it. We did not want to come out against the institution lest this give the Japanese militarists live coals to blow upon and bring up a flame of last-man resistance. Nor did we wish to come out for the institution lest this discourage whatever popular movement there might be in Japan to erase it.[8]

Hull resigned in November of 1944 because of ill health, but his noncommittal policy continued to have influence.

When the final defeat of Germany became imminent, thoughts began to turn toward the surrender of Japan. In some quarters, it was felt (and, as we have seen, rightly so) that the unconditional-surrender formula was too vague; without more detailed specification of what unconditional surrender would mean for Japan, those in Tokyo favoring surrender would have great difficulty in countering the arguments of the military that unconditional surrender would mean — as Premier Suzuki put it — the "destruction" of the national polity and the "ruin" of the Japanese race.[9] Accordingly Captain Ellis Zacharias, of the Office of Naval Intelligence, drafted a presidential statement clarifying what unconditional surrender would mean for the Japanese people; Mr. Truman issued the statement on May 8, the same day that he officially announced the surrender of Germany:

> Nazi Germany has been defeated.
> The Japanese people have felt the weight of our land, air, and naval attacks. So long as their leaders and the armed forces continue the war, the striking power and intensity of our blows will steadily increase and will bring utter destruction to Japan's industrial production, to its shipping, and to everything that supports its military activity.

The longer the war lasts, the greater will be the suffering and hardships which the people of Japan will undergo — all in vain. Our blows will not cease until the Japanese military and naval forces lay down their arms in *unconditional surrender*.

Just what does the unconditional surrender of the armed forces mean for the Japanese people?

It means the end of the war.

It means the termination of the influence of the military leaders who have brought Japan to the present brink of disaster.

It means provision for the return of soldiers and sailors to their families, their farms, their jobs.

It means not prolonging the present agony and suffering of the Japanese in the vain hope of victory.

UNCONDITIONAL SURRENDER DOES NOT MEAN THE EXTERMINATION OR ENSLAVEMENT OF THE JAPANESE PEOPLE.[10]

It will be noted that the President's statement narrowed the unconditional surrender of Japan to "the unconditional surrender *of the armed forces*" (italics added). Zacharias, speaking as the "official spokesman" of the United States government, delivered a series of broadcasts to Japan emphasizing that "unconditional surrender is a military term, meaning the cessation of resistance and the yielding of arms. It does not entail enslavement. It does not entail the extermination of the Japanese people." These propaganda broadcasts were designed to allay the fears of the Japanese people, undercut the arguments of the military clique, and provide "ammunition" for the end-the-war party.[11]

Although he was aware that the question of the preservation of the Emperor was crucial for his Japanese hearers, Zacharias could not get authorization from his superiors to include in his broadcasts an assurance on this subject. He therefore resorted to the strategem of arranging for an anonymous letter to appear in the Washington *Post* in July which he felt sure the Japanese authorities would recognize as an unofficial expression of United States policy. The letter stated that the term "unconditional surrender" referred not to the content of the surrender terms but only to "the manner in which the war is terminated . . . namely, the acceptance of terms without qualifying counterarguments." As for the content of America's terms, they have already been explicitly stated in the Atlantic Charter, the Cairo Declaration, and President Truman's May 8 declaration. With regard to the concern of the Japanese people over their Emperor,

> If . . . their chief concern is over Japan's future national structure (Kokutai), including the Emperor's status after surrender, the way to find out is to ask. Contrary to a widespread belief, such a question can be answered quickly and satisfactorily to all those who are concerned over the future peace of the Orient and the world.[12]

Meanwhile, Joseph C. Grew (who had served as Ambassador to Japan from 1932 until Pearl Harbor, as Under-Secretary of State under Stettinius, and then as Acting Secretary of State), having originally agreed with Hull's noncommittal policy, became convinced that the time had come to speak out more clearly. To give Japan a definite and official assurance on the Emperor, he felt, would aid those in Japan who were struggling to facilitate surrender. On May 28, 1945 Grew, on his own initiative as Acting Secretary of State, went to President Truman and urged upon him the importance of reassuring the Japanese on this point. Grew proposed issuing a proclamation calling on Japan to surrender, but also stating that the United States was open to retention of the Emperor as Head of State. Truman considered this proposal "a sound idea" but asked Grew to sound out the opinions of our military leaders. The next day Grew presented his idea to Secretary of War Stimson, Secretary of the Navy Forrestal, and General Marshall, the Chief of Staff. They agreed that such a statement should be

issued, but recommended delay on the grounds that immediate proclamation (while the outcome of the battle for Okinawa was still in doubt) might be interpreted by the Japanese
military as a sign of weakness on our part. When Grew
brought the matter up with the President a second time on
June 18, Mr. Truman said that he had decided the proclamation
should be issued at the forthcoming conference of the Allies
at Potsdam in July.[13]

Other forces were at work, however. Grew was denounced
as an appeaser by those who felt that the imperial system was
the root of Japanese militarism. Admiral William F. Halsey is
reported to have recommended the bombing of Shinto shrines,
because of the evils of Shintoism, in which the Emperor is
regarded not only as the head of the state but also as divine.
The present writer clearly remembers the wartime atmosphere
in which Emperor Hirohito was considered on the same level
as Hitler and Mussolini, as one of the three Axis leaders who
must be overthrown. Many who did not subscribe to the proposed abolition of the Emperor were nevertheless hesitant to
give Japan a public assurance of the continuance of the Emperor, because of the frequent — and sometimes extreme — de-
nunciations of the Emperor made by U.S. officials during the
war. Admiral Halsey had vowed to add humiliation to defeat
by riding the Emperor's white horse through the streets of
Tokyo. Such statements had created a climate of opinion
within the United States, many feared, which would lead people to cry shame if our government reversed its field and guaranteed to preserve the man we had been denouncing as a war
criminal.*

Stimson's original memorandum of July 2 stated that Japan
would be more likely to accept the ultimatum if we gave some

---

* This incident suggests the degree to which a government, seeking to be
reasonable and flexible in negotiations toward viable objectives, may be hampered
by a total and unrestrained propaganda war of its own making.

assurance regarding the Emperor. Stimson continued at Potsdam to press for inclusion of such an assurance in the forthcoming warning to Japan. The Joint Chiefs of Staff also urged that the Emperor be retained, on the ground that only the authority of the Emperor could insure the prompt surrender of the hundreds of thousands of Japanese troops scattered throughout Asia and the Pacific islands. Nevertheless, when the Potsdam Declaration was issued on July 26 it contained no reference to the Emperor. The decision must have been made by Byrnes and Truman — but neither in his memoirs specifies the reasons for the omission.[14]

IV

Would the Japanese have accepted the Potsdam Declaration had an assurance regarding the Emperor been included? Certainly the silence of the Potsdam Declaration on this point aided the militarists and handicapped Togo's group; the latter could only argue on the basis of their *hope* that the United States would respond favorably *if asked* about the Emperor. A clear assurance on this point would have given Togo a formidable weapon with which to beat down the objections of the war party. Even so, it remains questionable whether such an assurance in the Potsdam Declaration would have produced surrender. As it was, Anami and his party insisted either upon adding further conditions or fighting to the death — even after the shock of the atomic bomb, Russia's entry into the war, and the receipt of Byrnes's message implying the retention of the Emperor. Only the Emperor's intervention a *second* time broke the deadlock and brought the Cabinet to acceptance of surrender. It is not obvious, to say the least, that the military extremists would have capitulated at the mere statement of Allied willingness to retain the Emperor — in the absence of the sense of emergency created by the atomic bomb and the Russian intervention which allowed the full weight of the Em-

peror's authority and influence to be thrown into the scales on
the side of surrender.

Another factor remains to be considered. As events actually
worked out, the influence of the Emperor was barely able to
thwart a military coup, following the final imperial conference's decision to accept surrender. At midnight on August 14
a group of Army fanatics attempted to take over the Imperial
Palace Guards; after a fruitless search for the phonograph record of the imperial rescript (which His Majesty had just cut)
scheduled to be broadcast the next day, the attempted coup
disintegrated. Groups of would-be assassins raided the homes
of Premier Suzuki and Privy Seal Kido, but failed to find their
victims. Navy planes flew over Tokyo dropping leaflets deny-
ing the validity of the imperial rescript and calling for continued resistance. It was only with difficulty that a group of
kamikaze fliers were prevented from carrying out their plan of
diving their suicide planes into the U.S.S. *Missouri* as it entered Tokyo Bay to accept Japan's surrender. The Emperor
had to dispatch his brother in order to pacify a group of mal-
contents at Atsugi airfield (where MacArthur subsequently
landed) who wanted to re-engage the Americans when they approached Tokyo.[15]

That these various attempts were quelled, and better organized attempts prevented altogether, was due to the unique influence of the throne, and to the fact that the Emperor had
personally announced his desire for surrender at two imperial
conferences and in the imperial rescript. This put the fanatics
in an awkward position: "To have acted against the express
wishes of an Emperor whom they had unceasingly extolled as
sacred and inviolable and around whom they had woven a
fabric of individual loyalty and national unity would have been
to destroy the very polity in perpetuation of which they had
persistently declared they were fighting . . ."[16] Had Foreign
Minister Togo been able to persuade the Cabinet to accept a

Potsdam Declaration (expanded to include an assurance on the Emperor) an extremist coup would have been quite probable. In the absence of the direct personal intervention of the Emperor (which would not have come about had the Cabinet reached its own decision), the coup might easily have succeeded, leaving the fate of Japan entirely in the hands of a fanatical clique determined to fight on for the "preservation of the Emperor" and the "glory of Japan." It was the crisis precipitated by the atomic bomb that rendered a successful military coup impossible.

In short, it is not self-evident, as claimed by the critics under consideration, that the inclusion in the Potsdam Declaration of an assurance promising the retention of the Emperor would have resulted automatically in Japan's surrender.

V

The "political failure" criticism may be made on a deeper level still: the Japanese cables intercepted on July 13 gave a clear indication of Japan's desperate desire to end the war — but our leaders failed to capitalize on this first-rate piece of intelligence. Could not a sensitive study of the cables and an imaginative diplomatic initiative have brought Japan to surrender and rendered use of the atomic bomb unnecessary?

Why did the intercepted cables have no effect whatever on the United States attempts to bring Japan to surrender? Apparently one reason is that American leaders accepted the "Japan-will-fight-on-rather-than-accept-unconditional-surrender" phrases of the cables at face value. Mr. Byrnes writes, "We could not rely upon Japan's inquiries to the Soviet Union about a negotiated peace as proof that Japan would surrender unconditionally without the use of the bomb. In fact, Stalin stated the last message to him had said that Japan would 'fight to the death rather than accept unconditional surrender.'" Other phrases in the cables, such as "unconditional surrender is the only obstacle to peace," which implied that Japan was ready to capitulate just short of unconditional surrender, were discounted. Yet the fact of making the overture itself, and the fact that the overture was addressed to Russia (which implied Japan's willingness to give up her claims in Manchuria and to settle there on Russia's terms), should have indicated clearly — to anyone bothering to analyze the cables seriously and sensitively — the urgency of Japan's desire for peace.[17]

At what level did analysis of the cables and their significance take place? Did Truman and Byrnes see the full texts of the cables at Potsdam and decide that the protests against unconditional surrender weighed more heavily than the urgent desire to end the war which the cables demonstrated? Or did Truman and Byrnes depend upon extracts or digests in which this interpretation had already been made by anonymous lower officials? The published evidence is not conclusive. Historian Herbert Feis concludes in *Japan Subdued* that "the contents" or "essential features" of the messages were transmitted to Stimson at Potsdam, and passed on by him to Byrnes and Truman. In his account Byrnes states that "the President had learned of the Japanese 'peace feeler' a day or two before our conference with Stalin [July 17] . . ." Five pages farther on he reports that on July 28 "Secretary Forrestal arrived and told me in detail of the intercepted messages from the Japanese government to Ambassador Sato in Moscow, indicating Japan's willingness to surrender." This latter remark suggests that prior to July 28 Byrnes's knowledge of the cables was not based upon a firsthand reading. (Certainly the difficult problems of reestablishing peace in Europe were making plenty of other demands upon his time for reading and thought!)[18]

Another reason that the interception of the cables did not result in a serious diplomatic effort to induce Japan to surrender was that Stalin was in a position to thwart the negotiations, and did so. By refusing to respond to Japan's request for his good offices, and by reporting the overtures to his Allies in a negative way, Stalin took steps to prevent Japan's getting out of the war before the Soviet Union could get in — and claim the rewards promised at Yalta!

Secretary Byrnes explains in his book *Speaking Frankly* that "agreement to negotiate could only arouse false hopes" [19] — presumably the hopes of the American people. Byrnes seems to have assumed that any negotiations with Japan would have to be announced publicly in advance; but there would seem to be no reason why Japan could not have been approached secretly. A channel for communicating with her independently of Russia had already been established in Switzerland by the earlier abortive attempts to negotiate peace through the Dulles OSS organization. Could not Japan have been notified through this channel that if she wanted to explore peace possibilities she might send a high official to (for example) Manila? Had Prince Konoye been allowed to make such a trip, he could have been given the text of the proposed Potsdam Declaration *before* it was broadcast to the world. He would have raised, undoubtedly, the question of the Emperor's status, and the Americans could have given substantially the same answer as that in Byrnes's actual reply. Robert Butow, the scholar who has studied more intensively than anyone else the struggle of Japan to surrender, concludes in *Japan's Decision to Surrender* that "it seems possible, even probable" that:

> Had the Allies given the prince a week of grace in which to obtain his government's support for acceptance, the war might have ended toward the latter part of July or the very beginning of August without the atomic bomb and without Soviet participation in the conflict. . . . If Prince Konoye had demonstrated that he was personally unwilling to entreat his government to accept the Allied terms or if the Japanese government had refused to accept the declaration in spite of Konoye's

possible representations in its behalf, the bomb could have been
dropped upon Hiroshima as scheduled. . . .[20]

Furthermore, had the Allies informed Konoye that they
would preserve the Emperor if Japan would surrender immediately, but could not give any assurance if Japan persisted in
fighting on, they could have transformed the Emperor issue
from a tool used by the militarists to *prevent* surrender into a
powerful tool in the hands of those working *for* surrender.
Further urgency could have been added by a frank and specific
description of a revolutionary new weapon that we had just
successfully tested and that would shortly be brought to bear
upon Japan unless she capitulated.[21] Ralph Bard, Under-Secretary of the Navy, made just such a suggestion in his memorandum to the Interim Committee; apparently it was never seriously considered. Instead of such a positive and imaginative
diplomatic effort "we relied upon the Potsdam Declaration" —
a political attempt foredoomed to failure because it ignored the
one issue crucial to the Japanese and (because of the way it
was publicized) was susceptible of being interpreted by the
Japanese as a mere propaganda stunt. Beyond that, we relied
upon the atomic bomb. It seems clear that had the attempt
to end the war by political and diplomatic means been undertaken sooner, more seriously, and with more skill, the decision
to use the atomic bomb might well have been rendered unnecessary.

VI

It may be possible to explain America's failure to seize the
diplomatic initiative partly in terms of the inexperience of her
leaders. With a new President (in office only three hectic
months) and a new Secretary of State (in office less than a
month and without previous responsibility in diplomacy or
foreign affairs), both pressed with momentous events and in-

volved in their first international conference, it would be understandable if the interceptions of the cables received less attention than they might have received in other circumstances.

But the root of the political failure reaches deeper. The handling of the Japanese surrender is related to a larger pattern of other events in which United States leaders tended to emphasize purely military means and purely military ends to the neglect of political means and political ends. A few significant examples will suffice to trace this pattern.

American leaders tended strongly to view the primary *aim* of the war purely in terms of military victory, and to ignore, or subordinate, the political objectives for the sake of which the war was being fought. President Truman reported that the political and economic matters discussed at Potsdam were subordinate in the minds of the American delegation to "one strictly military matter . . . the winning of the war against Japan. On our program that was the most important item." [22]

Stimson agreed. For him, "the dominant fact of 1945 was war, and . . . therefore, necessarily, the dominant objective was victory. . . . Surrender was a goal sufficient in itself, wholly transcending the use or nonuse of the bomb." [23]

The same attitude appeared in the controversy between the Americans and the British over the best strategy for ending the war in Germany. In Churchill's mind "Berlin was the prime and true objective of the Anglo-American armies" because of its political and symbolic importance. Further, he strongly advocated driving forward to "shake hands with the Russians as far to the east as possible," in order to restrict Russian postwar domination in eastern Europe to the smallest possible area. Once military victory was assured, political objectives took priority, in Churchill's view. Field Marshal Montgomery agreed with Churchill on the desirability of an Anglo-American drive to Berlin; he was therefore distressed to receive a message from General Eisenhower in March 1945 stating:

You will note that in none of this do I mention Berlin. That place has become, so far as I am concerned, nothing but a geographical location, and I have never been interested in these. *My purpose is to destroy the enemy's forces and his powers to resist* [italics added].

In Montgomery's view, "the important point was . . . to ensure that when that day [victory] arrived we would have a political balance in Europe which would help us, the Western nations, to win the peace." [24]

Eisenhower resented what he called "the intervention of political leaders in the development of broad operational plans." While he was aware of the political dimensions of the military campaign to defeat Germany, these "did not influence our military plans for the final conquest of the country. Military plans, I believed, should be devised with the single aim of speeding victory . . ." General Marshall, in answering Churchill's objections, supported Eisenhower's aims: "The single objective should be quick and complete victory." [25]

It was not only the *aim* of the war that was conceived in military terms; major policy decisions about the *conduct* of the war were assumed to be purely military questions that could be resolved by military officers without the aid of political or diplomatic advisers. This assumption was apparently shared by President Roosevelt, and even influenced his concept of his own role of leadership. Secretary of State Cordell Hull has described Roosevelt's delight in the military aspects of the war, and his tendency to think of the war largely in military rather than in political terms — even to the extent of thinking of himself as a military rather than a political leader:

He loved the military side of events, and liked to hold them in his own hand. Following Pearl Harbor, he preferred to be called Commander-in-Chief rather than President. He relished the title. He may have felt that this all-important position was now more important than that of President.

At a Cabinet dinner, probably in 1942, where I was to propose the toast, the President asked me, before I rose to speak: "Please try to address me as Commander-in-Chief, not as President." [26]

Roosevelt's penchant for treating wartime decisions as purely military matters is further illustrated by his dropping of Secretary Hull from the War Council:

. . . Prior to Pearl Harbor I had been a member of the War Council, composed of the President, the Secretaries of State, War, and the Navy, the Chief of Staff, and the Chief of Naval Operations, and I took part in its meetings. After Pearl Harbor I did not sit in on meetings concerned with military matters. This was because the President did not invite me to such meetings. I raised the question with him several times. It seemed manifest to me that, in numerous important instances, the Secretary of State should sit in on the President's war councils, particularly on those of a combined military and diplomatic nature, for it was obvious that scarcely any large-scale military operations could be undertaken that would not have diplomatic aspects.

I feel it is a serious mistake for the Secretary of State not to be present at important military meetings. I often had occasion to point out to the President that some developments of a military character, which undoubtedly had been decided at one of these meetings, also had a strong foreign affairs angle of which I should have been informed at the time.

The President did not take me with him to the Casablanca, Cairo, or Teheran conferences, which were predominately military meetings, nor did I take part in his military discussions with Prime Minister Churchill in Washington, some of which had widespread diplomatic repercussions. . . .

. . . I learned from other sources than the President what had occurred at the Casablanca, Cairo, and Teheran conferences. . . .

(One surprising thing that Hull learned about the Casablanca Conference was that there Roosevelt announced that unconditional surrender was the policy of the Allies; Hull, who opposed the idea of unconditional surrender, had not been consulted.)[27]

John J. McCloy, who served throughout the war as Assistant Secretary of War, also refers to "the habit of confining large questions on the conduct of the war to purely military considerations, which President Roosevelt instituted and which was almost unconsciously carried on by his successor. . . ."* To illustrate this habit, McCloy describes the June 18 meeting at which the Joint Chiefs of Staff presented to President Truman their plan for ending the war against Japan — and at which the idea of a political attempt to end the war came as an afterthought.

> Now this incident indicates that at the time everyone was so intent on winning the war by military means that the introduction of political considerations was almost accidental. . . .
>
> . . . .
>
> . . . We concentrated so heavily on the actual conduct of the war that we overlooked the need for political thinking. . . .[29]

The tendency to overemphasize the military aspects of the war and to overlook the nonmilitary was also reflected in a shift in attitude toward the atomic bomb as the war progressed. In the beginning the scientists had looked upon the development of the atomic bomb as insurance against its being used — by Hitler. The bomb was not looked upon as "just another weapon"; paradoxically, it was being developed precisely so that it would not be used. As the war progressed, however, the paradox was lost, and the bomb came to be regarded as merely a new weapon, "as legitimate as any other of the deadly ex-

---

* Stimson confirms what McCloy says about the exclusion of civilian officials under F.D.R., but gives Truman a more positive appraisal. He notes that although the State Department was not represented at the June 18 meeting, the very presence of the Secretary and Assistant Secretary of War "was a return to the procedure which Franklin Roosevelt had abandoned in 1942" and constituted "the beginning of the political actions which so greatly assisted in obtaining surrender."[28]

plosive weapons of modern war," and the question of the use of the bomb came to be subordinated to the question of military victory. Stimson writes that the "entire purpose" of the atomic project was "the production of a military weapon"; he emphasizes that "it was our common objective, throughout the war, to be the first to produce an atomic weapon *and use it*" (italics added). Truman reports that he "regarded the bomb as a military weapon and never had any doubt that it should be used." [30]

So it was that the question of the use of the atomic bomb came to be subordinated to the achieving of victory by military means. By the spring of 1945 the question was for all practical purposes settled: the atomic bomb, created under the auspices of a military organization, was essentially a bigger and better weapon, and should be used to secure victory by applying such overwhelming physical power to the enemy as to force him to surrender. Arthur Compton reports that in the discussions of the Interim Committee it appeared to be "a foregone conclusion" that the bomb would be used. Ralph Bard reports that as a member of the Interim Committee he came to the crucial May 31 meeting with no special preparation for making a momentous decision; he felt that the committee was merely giving formal approval to a decision already made. Had the identification of the atomic bomb simply as a military weapon still been open to debate, had the 1939 sense of paradox persisted until 1945, then serious and imaginative exploration of the possibilities of the new instrument might have led to employment less crude and more creative.[31]

Since the war was considered to be primarily a military matter, it was assumed that military men should make the most important decisions, and those on the basis of "military necessity." Thus the shift to obliteration bombing of Japanese cities (a major policy change) was decided upon by an AAF officer in the Pacific, not by top-level political leaders. Similarly, the decision to reduce the interval between the first and second atomic bombs from four to two days was made on purely tactical grounds by a front-line military officer.

This trend appeared to some degree even within the Cabinet. It is significant that the Cabinet member who was assigned the task of drafting a memorandum regarding the possibility of bringing Japan to surrender by political means was the Secretary of War — not the Acting Secretary of State, who had had many years of experience in Japan and knew Japanese politics and psychology intimately.

Finally, it may be noted that this general approach to war made itself felt in the choice of means to be used to accomplish a given end. For example, there was a choice of ways to convince the Japanese that we had more atomic bombs and were determined to use them. This could have been accomplished by military means (dropping a second bomb) or by political means (an explicit warning). We chose the blunt military means.

VII

We have seen that at a whole series of points, a military way of thinking shaped decisions affecting the later decision about the use of the first atomic bomb. It cannot be proved that a less military and a more political way of thinking, resulting in modifications all along this series, actually would have ended the war without the atomic bomb. What the military way of thinking undeniably did, however, was to close the door on a whole series of opportunities, any one of which *might* have made a difference, and which, taken all together, probably would have resulted in an outcome different from that which actually occurred — the killing of more than 100,000 people, and the crossing of the barrier into the dangerous world where a precedent exists for the military use of atomic energy.

17. Ethics in the Crucible of War

AT THIS POINT it may be appropriate to summarize briefly the results of our investigation into the various criticisms of the atomic bombing of Japan — and to offer certain reflections upon their significance.

The decision to use the atomic bomb took place within a historical situation with a peculiar political-military configuration. This context shaped the way in which policymakers thought about the bomb and its relation to the war, and heavily influenced the outcome of the decision itself. In particular, the gradual acceptance of obliteration bombing as a military necessity, until the mass-bombing of Japanese cities was regarded as standard procedure, largely determined that the atomic bomb — once it was decided to use it — would be dropped on the center of a large city, despite the professed concern of our leaders to avoid the killing of undefended civilians.

This particular decision took place within a larger context, a significant characteristic of which was the tendency on the part of American leaders (both military and civilian) to think of the war in purely military rather than in political terms. As a result, the goal of the war was military victory; the way to victory was the military defeat of the enemy armed forces; since the major decisions to be made were of a military character, policy formation was delegated to military men. The result was a whole series of decisions: to treat the atomic bomb as a bigger and better military weapon, to exclude civilian leaders from the highest war councils of the nation, to accept the judgment of generals that obliteration bombing was necessary for victory, to try a political method to end the war only as an afterthought, to ignore vital intelligence because it did not indicate that the enemy was ready to accept total surrender, to let a military commander decide on purely tactical grounds how much time the Japanese government should have to decide to surrender after the first atomic bomb — a series of decisions which tended to mold events in such a way that the atomic bomb would finally be used in a total and unrestrained military manner. Any one of these decisions, had the emphasis lain on the political rather than on the military way of thinking, *might* have precluded or tempered our use of the atomic bomb; the cumulative effect of making all these decisions on political rather than on military grounds could well have resulted in termination of the war by diplomatic means, and prevented the destruction of Hiroshima and Nagasaki.

Focusing more narrowly upon the specific decision to drop the atomic bomb — and taking as given the political failure and the war situation as it stood in mid-1945 — one cannot escape the conclusion that the atomic bombing of Hiroshima and Nagasaki caused less loss of life (and general human suffering and chaos) than would have come about had the new weapon been withheld and the war been allowed to continue by conventional means, with or without invasion of the Japanese home islands. Within this narrow context Truman and Stimson were right: the atomic bomb did cut short the war and save thousands of lives. Nevertheless, even within the situation as it had developed by August 1945, alternatives were still open — such as a demonstration of the atomic bomb against a large military installation in Japan, followed by a stern warning — which probably would have brought about Japan's surrender without the great toll of civilian lives resulting from atomic attacks upon two large cities.

II

It was noted in Chapter 4 that certain of the cherished ethical principles held by scientists were transformed under the impact of the threat posed to the civilized world by Hitler's emerging power. Something of the same transformation was wrought in the ethical principles of United States leaders, both military and political, during World War II. Our Air Force had entered the war proud of its Norden bombsight, and was committed to the superior morality and military effectiveness of daylight precision bombing of purely military objectives. Our government was on record as opposed, on humane grounds, to the bombing of civilian areas. The transformation both of practice and of official justification, under the demands of "military necessity," has been documented above. Churchmen proved only slightly more resistant than political leaders to this erosion of moral principles during wartime.

Henry L. Stimson's memoirs and diary record the feelings of one who was sensitive to this transformation and resisted it, yet found himself being swept along and finally participated in it. When the B-29's began their first raids over Japan, Stimson had struck from the list of targets the cultural and religious center of Kyoto, despite the fact that it was also an important center of war industry. He believed that air power could and should be used in a limited and discriminate way — and he extracted from Robert Lovett, his Assistant Secretary for Air, a promise that the B-29's would conduct "only precision bombing" against purely military objectives. His aim, as he put it, was to maintain "the reputation of the United States for fair play and humanitarianism." But then he found that our precisely dropped bombs were falling on soldiers, civilian workers, and children alike, that flames were devouring industry, commercial districts, and private residences indiscriminately. When Stimson called in Arnold to find out "the facts" and to hold him to "my promise from Lovett," the General told him that in the congested Japanese cities it was virtually impossible to destroy war output without also destroying civilians connnected with that output. The Secretary could only say that the promise he had extracted should be honored "as far as possible." [1]

Painfully Stimson realized that

> in the conflagration bombings by massed B-29's he was per-mitting a kind of total war he had always hated, and in recom-mending the use of the atomic bomb he was implicitly con-fessing that there could be no significant limits to the horror of modern war. The decision was not difficult, in 1945, for peace with victory was a prize that outweighed the payment de-manded. But Stimson could not dodge the meaning of his action. . . .[2]

Looking back over his five years of service as Secretary of War, he could say:

> . . . I see too many stern and heart-rending decisions to be willing to pretend that war is anything else than what it is. The face of war is the face of death; death is an inevitable part of every order that a wartime leader gives. The decision to use the atomic bomb was a decision that brought death to over a hundred thousand Japanese. No explanation can change that fact and I do not wish to gloss it over. But this deliberate, pre-meditated destruction was our least abhorrent choice. The de-struction of Hiroshima and Nagasaki put an end to the Japa-nese war. It stopped the fire raids, and the strangling blockade; it ended the ghastly specter of a clash of great land armies.[3]

III

Two fundamental ways of judging the morality of the use of the atomic bomb appeared during 1945 and 1946. The first was (in the broadest sense) utilitarian; the primary concern of those using this approach was the consequences of the act in question. Will the war be shortened? How many lives will be lost? Will long-term consequences be good or evil? The method is calculative: good and evil consequences are balanced one against the other, and the right act is that which produces the most good — or, at any rate, the least evil. America's leaders used this method in determining to drop the atomic bomb on Japan. It was the choice, made with awareness of its inherent horror, of the lesser evil. Yet the results produced by this method appalled many who were disposed to follow it. Once the result was faced for what it was — the deliberate bombing of two cities, resulting in death to more than a hundred thousand, and agonizing injury to as many more — many felt that the intrinsic character of the act in itself, completely apart from any consequences stemming from it, was so clearly immoral that any ethical system justifying such an act must be bankrupt. It is impossible to predict accurately the consequences of any major decision, or to calculate good and evil results numerically. This impossibility, together with the lack of any objective moral standard by which to judge the quality of an act, means in the end that a purely calculative ethical theory will permit the plausible justification of almost any atrocity, no matter how repugnant to man's innate sense of decency.

The second basic ethical approach to the question of the atomic bombing of Japan was formalistic: it was concerned with the rightness or wrongness of the act in itself. What determines the rightness or wrongness of an act is not its consequences but its inherent quality. If the act conforms to an objective moral standard, it is permissible; if not, it is forbidden or condemned. The standard to be applied in the case of Hiroshima may be summed up in the commandment "Thou shalt not attack noncombatants directly." If an act has the form of a direct and deliberate attack upon noncombatants — no matter how many or how few, no matter what the con-

sequences — it is a violation of the commandment and therefore wrong.*

For example, had the atomic bomb been withheld from use,
Hiroshima might have been attacked the same week by 500
B-29's dropping incendiaries; the center of the city could have
been burned to the ground, with the loss of 10,000 or 20,000
civilian lives. For Roman Catholic moral theory, such an incendiary raid and the atomic bombing of Hiroshima would be
on the same level of immorality. Both would equally be condemned as direct and indiscriminate attacks upon the innocent.

It may be noted, however, that despite its clarity of moral
theory the Roman Catholic Church probably would not have
specifically condemned such an incendiary raid upon Hiroshima
in the actual situation existing in August 1945. In spite of a
few lonely voices like that of Father Ford, and the often expressed concern of the Pope that aerial warfare respect the immunity of noncombatants, the fire raids had been going on
regularly since March. During this time the American Catholic
hierarchy had taken no forthright and united stand in opposition to mass-bombing (nor had the Protestant churches). The
leading American Jesuit theologian, John Courtney Murray, later
commented on the silence of the Roman Catholic Church regarding the incendiary mass-bombing attacks of World War II:

> Nor was any substantial effort made [by Catholic publicists
> or even bishops] to clarify by moral judgment the thickening
> mood of savage violence that made possible the atrocities of
> Hiroshima and Nagasaki. I think it is true to say that the tradi-
> tional doctrine was irrelevant during World War II. This is no

---

* As derived from Christian ethical theory, the proscription of direct military
attack upon noncombatants is not an external limitation imposed upon a supposed right of self-defense. Rather, it roots in Christian love for neighbor which
(1) imposes *as a duty* the physical restraint of an aggressor *for the sake of preventing him from harming the innocent*, and (2) at the same time prohibits direct
attack upon noncombatants and the fabric of civilian life — because protection
of these is the very reason for restraint of the aggressor in the first place.[4]

argument against the traditional doctrine. . . . But there is place for an indictment of all of us who failed to make the traditional doctrine relevant.[5]

Despite the immediate clarity of moral judgment provided by the formalistic approach to ethics, it is not devoid of dilemmas. In the example just cited it is too simple, in that it would leave out of consideration the consequences flowing from the two raids. An incendiary raid on Hiroshima, like those on dozens of other Japanese cities during the summer of 1945, would have advanced the end of the war somewhat, but only imperceptibly. In contrast, the atomic raid, as we have seen, was the decisive factor that brought the war to a halt within eight days. Although in one dimension (that of form) the two raids are morally equivalent, in another dimension (that of consequences) one is morally much better than the other. To be concerned only for form and to ignore consequences is to miss much of ethical significance; for certainly it was better on moral grounds that the killing and the disruption of Japanese civil life should stop than that it should continue.

Again, let it be assumed, for the sake of argument, that Truman's estimate of the alternatives before him was accurate: it was a choice between dropping the atomic bomb on Hiroshima and proceeding with the invasion of Japan. A formalist would be compelled to judge the atomic bombing of Hiroshima as impermissible, and therefore to recommend the invasion, which would be justifiable since it would proceed by conventional and discriminate attack on the military forces of the enemy. Having accepted as justifiable the killing of 317,000 Japanese soldiers in the Philippines campaign, and the killing of 107,000 of the total garrison of 120,000 on Okinawa, the Roman Catholic position would now forbid the killing of 110,000 civilians with the atomic bomb but condone a conventional invasion even though the preliminaries and the invasion itself took the lives of ten times that number of Japanese and Allied soldiers in Manchuria, China, and the Japanese home islands. In addition, it would reluctantly "permit" the death of many civilians and the destruction of many cities from battle causes, the freezing and starvation of refugee children during the approaching winter, and the complete breakdown and disruption of the fabric of Japanese civil life — provided only that all these evils were unintended and unavoidable effects of the direct attack of the invaders upon the defenders.

It must parenthetically be stated that Roman Catholic moral theology does specify that an act right in itself (such as an attack upon enemy armed forces in a just war) is not permissible if its unintended and indirect evil consequences are of such great magnitude as to be disproportionate to the good produced by the act. Yet the principle of disproportionate evil was not applied to the invasion of Germany, which resulted in just such death, suffering, and disruption of civil life; and there is no reason to believe that it would have been the basis of Catholic condemnation of the invasion of Japan (provided that generals considered invasion a military necessity).[6]

In contrast to a moral theory that would condone the greater evil consequences, provided only that they be produced by "legitimate" means, one cannot help feeling a certain respect for the elemental morality of Truman and Stimson in their determination to avoid the massive evil of invasion if humanly possible. They realistically surveyed the situation confronting them, estimated (probably correctly) that had they refrained from using the atomic bomb the war would have continued without much change in basic character — and then resolutely chose what appeared to them to be the lesser evil, regardless of the fine points of ethical theory.

It would appear, then, that just as a purely calculative approach to ethics has no inner principle to prevent the final bankruptcy of justifying an atrocity as "the lesser evil," so an ethical approach concerned exclusively with conformity to laws or norms, to the neglect of consequences, has its own peculiar form of bankruptcy. To forbid an atomic attack upon a city because of its indiscriminateness but complacently to recommend an invasion which, by "legitimate" means, would produce massive evil, death, and suffering borders on hypocrisy, or at least callousness.

The conflict between the calculative and formalistic approaches to the bombing of Hiroshima can be focused in a single question: is it right to perform an inherently immoral act in order to achieve a good end and avoid a massive evil? For the formalists the answer is easy — no, it is never permissible to do evil as a means to a good end. Considered in the abstract the problem is simple. But in a particular historical context the answer is not so simple.

The bare act of dropping an atomic bomb upon a city — considered in itself alone — is clearly immoral because it constitutes a direct attack upon noncombatants. Yet it is inconsistent to single out for condemnation the act of dropping an atomic bomb and at the same time implicitly to recommend continuation of a war that one knows will include direct attack upon noncombatants with incendiary bombs. In the midst of a historical context already compromised by past and present mass bombing of civilians, which would undoubtedly have continued in the future, can Truman justly be condemned for authorizing an atomic attack (no more and no less immoral than the fire raids) which promised to put an end to the whole badly compromised situation?

IV

The formal nature of the act in itself apart from its consequences, and the calculation of greater good and lesser evil —

concern with either one of these to the exclusion of the other leads only to corruption. Ethical theory that will stand the stress of the massive evils inherent in war must include *both* a calculation of consequences *and* a concern for the intrinsic morality of the act. Paul Ramsey, a Protestant moralist, has recently suggested that Roman Catholic moral theory (or, rather, the traditional *Christian* moral theory) at its best combines both. Calculation of probable consequences and the choosing of the greater good and the lesser evil are essential, but properly come only *after* determination of the intrinsic morality of the act itself.[7]

Thus in the case of bringing about the surrender of Japan in 1945: dropping the atomic bomb on a city would be ruled out at the start because of its violation of the immunity of civilians from direct attack. Among the remaining legitimate alternatives, a calculation of probable consequences would show that a diplomatic offensive, or even a military demonstration with the A-bomb, was morally better than invasion which, because of the enormous evil it would produce, could be considered only as a last resort.

The elimination at the outset of certain possible alternatives as inherently immoral does not remove the need for calculation of consequences among the remaining legitimate alternatives. It may stimulate more creative calculation and imaginative searching for a course of action which is both effective and morally acceptable. A firm policy decision not to indulge in mass fire-bombing of Japanese cities would probably have resulted in an early and systematic attack upon the extremely vulnerable Japanese railroad network — a course that the United States Strategic Bombing Survey suggests would have crippled Japan's entire war industry sooner and more effectively than did the incendiary raids.[8] It might also have led to an earlier re-examination of our policies regarding unconditional surrender and the status of the Emperor, and a careful use of diplomatic and political tools which, in the actual event, were never tried. Closing the door to immoral means may provide the opportunity for more creative use of legitimate means.

The failure of moral theory in those who made the decision to drop the atomic bomb was not that they failed to replace their dominant concern for "calculating the lesser evil" with a one-sided concern for the ethical principle of "noncombatant immunity, regardless of consequences." The failure lay in their inability to maintain simultaneously *both* a commitment to ethical principle *and* a realistic calculation of consequences in some such fashion as that suggested here. The tension between the two having been lost in the acceptance of obliteration bombing in March of 1945, it proved to be impossible to reestablish the tension in August.

v

While it is important to recognize the ethical failures in the making of a particular crucial decision, it is even more important to be aware of the ethical failures implicit in the unquestioned assumptions about the nature of war that were shared in 1945 by American leaders and people alike. The assumptions that war is primarily a military matter, that war is now total, that the purpose of fighting a war is to achieve military victory, and that war can end in victory only if the enemy is forced to surrender unconditionally — these came to be accepted as self-evident and unquestionable truths by the vast majority of the American people, despite the fact that such axioms stand in direct contradiction to the main stream of Christian ethical thought about war. Such general assumptions about modern war were at least as important — if not more so — in the shaping of the decision to drop the atomic bomb as were the ethical considerations consciously brought to bear upon that particular choice. What is required for the future is not only that proper ethical thinking be applied to the making of each particular policy decision affecting nuclear weapons. It is even more important that our whole style of thinking about war be such that these particular decisions are not — as in 1945 — morally compromised before they are reached.

IV

The Ethics of War in
the Atomic Age

1945-1950

18. The Scientists and the "Next War"

BEFORE HIROSHIMA, the scientists of the Manhattan project had begun to concern themselves not only with the question of the use of the new weapon against Japan but also with the changes to be introduced by their bomb into the nature of warfare, and the implications of these changes for international relations. The Jeffries Report of November 1944 predicted that until an international authority had been devised to control the production and use of atomic power, United States security would rest upon the fragile hope of deterring enemy attack by the fear of our retaliation. The report urged recognition of "the necessity for all nations to make every effort to cooperate now in setting up an international administration with police powers which can effectively control at least the means of nucleonic warfare." Niels Bohr, Leo Szilard, and James Franck drafted memoranda and talked with high government officials about the bomb's impact upon our relations with Russia and the necessity of averting an atomic arms race. The Franck Committee Report derived its specific recommendations regarding the use of the bomb in World War II from its primary concern for effective international control of atomic energy after the war.[1]

So acutely and universally felt were these concerns among the scientists, and so seriously did they take their newly felt social responsibilities, that within a few weeks of Hiroshima associations spontaneously sprang up at Los Alamos, Chicago, Oak Ridge, and other laboratories. By January 1946 these groups had consolidated to form the Federation of American

Scientists, and the scientists, who described themselves as "traditionally individualistic and non-political," launched forth upon a political career. Though inexperienced in practical politics, the members of the FAS nevertheless succeeded in defeating the May-Johnson bill (which would have maintained control of atomic energy within the hands of the military) and secured passage of the McMahon bill, establishing a civilian Atomic Energy Commission. But their primary concerns — concerns that won them the title "The League of Frightened Men" — were to awaken public opinion to the threat posed to civilization by an atomic arms race, and to urge the establishment of effective international control of atomic energy as the best means of averting the catastrophe of all-out atomic war.

II

The scientists' analysis of the threat posed by atomic weapons centered on a few key axioms, summarized in this section.

There Is No Secret of the Atomic Bomb. The first point made by the atomic scientists was that "the secret of the atomic bomb" is nonexistent. The basic scientific principles upon which the atomic bomb is based are the common property of scientists in all nations. The newspaper reports of the bombing of Hiroshima gave away the biggest secret, namely, that an atomic bomb could be constructed and would explode. The only secrets that remained were details of a technical engineering nature; any nation willing to devote scientific and engineering talent to the project and construct the necessary plants would be able to produce atomic weapons within a few years. Speaking as experts, the atomic scientists strongly warned against the illusion that America could gain military security by attempting to keep the atomic weapon secret.[2]

There Is No Defense against the Atomic Bomb. The scientists contended that the development of the atomic bomb had radically changed the traditional pattern by which every offensive weapon was soon adequately matched by a defensive weapon.

> Never has the offense become so entirely dominant. Never has there been a weapon whose first application in an attack will be almost certain not only to penetrate the defense, but also largely to demolish it. . . .
>
> The enormously greater destructiveness of the atomic bomb over that of any previous weapon means that an adequate defense must be designed to prevent a *very large fraction,* if not all, of the atomic missiles from reaching even the *vicinity* of their targets.[3]

The imbalance between offense and defense will give a decisive advantage to the unscrupulous aggressor who strikes without warning.

An Arms Race Inevitably Leads to War. The idea that an arms race will inevitably lead to war, although not one arrived at because of their special competence as scientists, was nevertheless widely accepted as self-evident by the atomic scientists. Leo Szilard stated in a magazine article that "if the arms race is permitted to continue . . . war will ultimately become unavoidable." Albert Einstein labeled the attempt to achieve national security by means of an atomic arms race "a disastrous illusion," and predicted that "in the end, there beckons more and more clearly general annihilation." The Emergency Committee of Atomic Scientists warned in 1947: "Once stockpiles of atomic bombs have been accumulated by two national blocks of a divided world, it will no longer be possible to maintain peace." [4]

Atomic Stockpiles Will Precipitate War. A corollary to the axiom that an arms race will inevitably lead to war was frequently stated as follows: a situation where two nations face each other, each in possession of substantial atomic power, will lead precipitously to war, since each side will be under irresistible pressure to strike the other before being struck. Said the Atomic Scientists of Chicago in 1946:

> Atomic bomb stockpiles increase the probability of war by creating an atmosphere of mutual suspicion among nations. They provide additional incentive to aggression by increasing the advantage of surprise . . .[5]

Scientists testified before the United States Senate in the same vein:

> The advantage of an undeclared war to an aggressor nation is enormous. The weapon is so effective against concentrations of people and industry that no fear of reprisals will be sufficient to prevent its use.[6]

Fear of retaliation by a country possessing more and bigger bombs will be insufficient to deter aggressor nations, since "there is no guarantee that the price of possible retaliation is one which they are unwilling to pay for the benefits they expect from administering the first effective blow." In short, "fear of reprisals cannot be counted on to prevent the use of atomic weapons." [7]

All Future Wars Will Be Atomic Wars. The atomic scientists proclaimed that in "the next war" atomic weapons would certainly be used. "Just as World War I ended with the airplane and World War II started with it, so we may expect that World War III may start with the atomic bomb which was developed at the end of World War II." Robert Oppenheimer stated in an address:

> Every American knows that if there is another major war, atomic weapons will be used, and that the problem we are dealing with is the problem of the elimination of war. . . . It is not thinkable that in any major future conflict, when the very life of a nation may be at stake, these weapons will not be used — they are much too effective for that.[8]

The Next War Will Begin with a Surprise Atomic Attack. The conviction that nuclear nations would be under heavy pressure to strike first before being struck, combined with the memory of the Pearl Harbor attack, produced what may be called the "Pearl Harbor complex": the scientists almost universally concluded that the next war would open with an atomic Pearl Harbor — a massive atomic air attack, or perhaps the exploding of atomic bombs secretly smuggled into a country.

> With rockets and mines available, the next war, the Atomic War, will probably start as a "push-button affair." Rather than mobilize armies and air forces and declare formal hostilities, an aggressor will one night set off a flight of rockets and the light of morning will reveal only ruins where the cities of the victim once stood.

Military men made detailed estimates of the number of atomic bombs that would be necessary to wipe out the United States in a single massive attack. Scientists vied with each other in describing the horrors of the first day to congressional committees, and testified that as many as one third of the entire population of the United States would perish on the first day of World War III.[9]

International Controls Are Essential to Prevent War. The conclusion drawn by the scientists from these axioms was that war was now so horrible that it was unthinkable — it must never be allowed to occur again. Because the secret of the atomic bomb is nonexistent and many nations will surely develop arsenals of atomic weapons, and since in a world where competing power-blocks face each other with nuclear armaments an atomic war is inevitable, drastic steps must be taken immediately to prevent an arms race from getting started. The scientists were convinced that the crisis caused by the advent of atomic weapons demanded a radical departure from the ordinary procedures of international relations, and a modification of the traditional concept of national sovereignty. Scientist after scientist testified before congressional committees that "international or world control of atomic energy is essential to the maintenance of peace." They proclaimed to the nation at large that "our highest national interest lies in co-operatively achieving effective international control of atomic explosives." The physicists of the Los Alamos laboratory pointed out the "absolute necessity of international control of atomic energy and atomic bombs if the people of all nations are to live in a stable, peaceful world." When Bernard M. Baruch presented to the United Nations Atomic Energy Commission the United States proposal for an International Atomic Development Authority for the development and control of atomic energy, the scientists applauded and rallied public opinion in support of the plan.[10]

Some scientists felt that international control of atomic energy would be only a first step toward the prevention of atomic war. The primary danger to man's security was not so much the bomb, which merely dramatized and heightened the central problem, but war itself. Attempts to control the atomic bomb by international agreement would be futile if wars were allowed to break out. "The problem we are dealing with," said Robert Oppenheimer, "is the problem of the elimination of war." "The great destructiveness of atomic bombs makes it necessary to find a way to avoid war," stated Arthur Compton.[11]

The method envisioned by the scientists for abolishing war was the establishment of world government: "Today it seems inescapable that within a relatively short time a world government must be established if we are to avoid the major catastrophe of a Third World War." [12] Dr. Albert Einstein believed that "a world authority and an eventual world state are not just *desirable* in the name of brotherhood, they are necessary for survival." Arthur Compton was convinced that "world government is now inevitable." [13]

III

What appeared to be self-evident to the scientists and to most thinking people in 1945 and 1946 can now be seen, after the passage of fifteen years, to be not quite so self-evident. True, certain aspects of the scientists' predictions (those closest to the area of their professional competence) have been fulfilled. The 1949 explosion of a nuclear device in the Soviet Union ended the United States' atomic monopoly; since then both Russia and Britain have built up nuclear stockpiles; France has joined the nuclear club; and other nations clearly have the scientific and industrial capacity to manufacture nuclear weapons should they choose to pay the economic price. Again, it is true, at least so far, that no sure defense against nuclear weapons has been developed, since effective defense would imply an almost 100 per cent interception of the bomb carriers. It appears that no nation is basing its national security on the assumption that it can fend off a massive nuclear attack without suffering incalculable damage.

Yet certain of the scientists' other assumptions have proved to be erroneous, or at least questionable. The "next war" proved to be neither atomic nor total. Since 1945 there have been bitter conflicts in Greece, China, Palestine, Korea, Indochina, Algeria, and Suez — conflicts that any other age would call wars — none of which has been a total or an atomic war, even though atomic powers have in some cases been participants. On the contrary, they have been fought by limited means and settled for limited gains.

The assumption that the next war would begin with a massive, sudden, and unannounced all-out nuclear attack, after the fashion of Pearl Harbor, now appears to be less an insight into universal truth about war than an opinion deeply qualified by recent experiences of World War II — the sudden and overwhelming blitzkrieg attacks of Hitler, and more particularly the

Japanese attack upon Pearl Harbor. The discussion about wiping out one third of a nation's population by a massive surprise nuclear attack proceeded on the assumption that the nature of the atomic weapon would alone determine the type of attack with which a war would open, as though the political purposes and ends to be sought by war were irrelevant. Further, the deterrent effect of fear of nuclear retaliation has proved to be more powerful than it was assumed to be in 1945: certainly United States strategists have been forced to re-examine their conception of American power in the light of the possibility of a Russian retaliatory strike that we are not prepared to absorb.

In a way it is strange that the belief that an arms race inevitably leads to war, which had been a pacifist axiom during the 1920's and 1930's, should have gained such wide acceptance outside pacifist circles after 1945; the classic example of an arms race leading to war was not World War II but what occurred thirty years earlier during the years leading up to World War I. Indeed, Winston Churchill, among many others, has made a strong case suggesting that it was the continued policy of weakness on the part of Britain and France, their very refusal to enter into an arms race against Hitler, which insured that war would inevitably engulf the Allies — and under the most disadvantageous circumstances.[14] Apparently it was the conviction that competing nuclear powers would be under irresistible pressure to strike first that reinforced the axiom of the 1930's to produce the widespread belief that an *atomic* arms race must inevitably lead to war.

However, it appears that the threat of retaliation has — at least thus far — prevented recklessness on the part of the nuclear powers, and a precipitous dash into all-out war. Certainly both Russia and the United States have, in view of the other's atomic power, exerted great caution in international affairs, avoiding outright military provocations and, when provocations arose, exercising restraint so as to avoid outbreak of nuclear warfare. Pacifists will doubtless insist that even though the war has not yet come it inevitably must come, unless the arms race is discontinued. Yet it seems that there is nothing built into the present arms race making war automatic. There is always the *possibility* that within the next few years the arms race could be discontinued and tension reduced (in which case, ironically, the acceptance of the pacifist's recommendation would refute his prediction). In short, the conclusion in Quincy Wright's massive *Study of War* appears to be correct: "Armaments races . . . constitute a form of international relations closely related to war and *often* [i.e., not *always*; italics added] ending in war itself." [15] The nuclear arms race is admittedly dangerous and might at any time, given the proper circumstances, break out into warfare; but there is no automatic mechanism insuring that it will inevitably do so.

IV

Despite what now appear to be obvious fallacies in the atomic scientists' analysis of war, a remarkable core of unanimity was reached in the early postwar years, not only among the scientists but among the leaders of the American community in general — politicians, educators, military men, and, as we shall see, churchmen. Not only pacifists and scientists believed that "if we have another war, it will be atomic war"; President Truman, speaking two months after Hiroshima, stated: "We can't stand another global war. We can't ever have another war unless it is total war, and that means the end of our civilization as we know it." The President of the University of Chicago warned those who talked lightly of settling international disputes by force that "force means war. War means atomic bombs. And atomic bombs mean suicide." [16]

That an arms race would degenerate into war was widely taken to be self-evident. "Atomic bombs and rockets in the separate hands of competing states would tend to precipitate total war, because of the mutual fears of annihilating aggression," pronounced the Executive Committee of the Federal Council of Churches. Many magazines agreed with the one that editorialized: "Nations which devote their energy to getting ready to fight, fight." A pamphlet distributed to servicemen by the YMCA described the situation that would result as rival nations armed themselves with atomic bombs:

> Is it hard to imagine the fear that would run riot throughout the world? Is it hard to foresee that governments would try to strike first with all the bombs possible, to prevent enemies from doing the same thing? The fact that the bombs are so destructive would not prevent war, but would push nations into aggression. . . . The more deadly the weapons, the more likely the outbreak of war.[17]

The conclusion to be drawn from this analysis was also obvious. Norman Cousins, in his widely read *Modern Man Is Obsolete*, stated it as a commonplace fact: "We are all agreed that war must be 'outlawed.' "[18]

Such ideas were not confined to uninformed persons who did not bear the responsibility of high office. On the contrary, our government's leaders based the nation's defense policy upon essentially the same presuppositions about the "next war" as those exemplified in the scientists' exhortations. "In case of another major war," testified Lieutenant General Raymond S. McLain in 1947, "the pattern would probably take the following form: First the blitz, using all modern means. If this should succeed, the war would be over. . . ." General Dwight D. Eisenhower based the Army's request for appropriations in 1948 upon the premise that "if global war comes to us again, the first blow will be struck not at Warsaw but at Washington; not at London but at Los Angeles; not even at Pearl Harbor but at Pittsburgh." Having assumed, under the influence of the Pearl Harbor complex, that the next war would begin with a devastating attack upon our cities (of course the United States would never strike first), our military strategists built up our air forces on the theory that our best defense lay in "our ability to strike back quickly with a counter offensive, to neutralize the hostile attack at its source . . . by striking at the vitals of the aggressor." [19]

The Administration accepted the scientists' prescription for the world's atomic ills by committing itself to international controls. The scientists, in the person of their wartime leader, Dr. J. Robert Oppenheimer, played an important role in drawing up the United States plan for an International Atomic Development Authority. And there were familiar echoes in the dramatic words with which Bernard Baruch introduced the United States proposal to the opening session of the United Nations Atomic Energy Commission:

> We are here to make a choice between the quick and the dead.
> That is our business.
> Behind the black portent of the new atomic age lies a hope which, if seized upon with faith, can work our salvation. If we fail, then we have damned every man to be the slave of fear. Let us not deceive ourselves: we must elect World Peace or World Destruction.[20]

An unspoken assumption underlying much of this discussion was that there was a continuous line of evolution from World War I through World War II, which when projected forward would determine the nature of war in the future. General MacArthur alluded to this evolution in his address on the deck of the U.S.S. *Missouri:* "The destructiveness of the war potential, through progressive advances in scientific discovery, has in fact now reached a point which revises the traditional concept of war. . . ." [21] War was assumed to be a self-existent entity, almost an organism with its own internal power of growth, and following a law of development independent of

the wills and decisions and purposes of the men who participated in it. It is beyond man's power to modify: ". . . let us
not deceive ourselves into thinking that war can be made humane. It cannot. It can only be abolished." [22] Men do not
have the power to influence or reverse the development of the
rampant weed of war; they can only pull it out by the roots.
Henry L. Stimson, looking back over forty years of public service covering both world wars, concluded:

> War in the twentieth century has grown steadily more barbar-
> ous, more destructive, more debased in all its aspects. Now,
> with the release of atomic energy, man's ability to destroy him-
> self is very nearly complete. The bombs dropped on Hiro-
> shima and Nagasaki ended a war. They also made it wholly
> clear that we must never have another war. . . . There is no
> other choice.[23]

To the leaders of American opinion, to makers of national
policy, and to the public generally, the truth about war seemed
unmistakably clear in 1945: conflicts during the twentieth century have grown progressively closer and closer to total war;
the advent of the atomic bomb guarantees that war has now
become total in its very nature. In all future wars there will be
no distinction between combatant and noncombatant — in fact,
it will be safer to be a soldier in the front lines than to be a civilian in the capital city at home. The next war will be total unrestrained atomic war beginning with a surprise all-out attack
upon major cities. Even the victor will have suffered such destruction that the term victory will have lost its meaning. Such
a catastrophe must at all costs be prevented from occurring.
International control of atomic energy is an immediate necessity to prevent an atomic arms race that will inevitably degenerate into an atomic war. Ultimately war itself must be abolished.

19. The Churches and Total War

THE CHURCHES' reaction to the problems posed by atomic weapons is best shown in a series of reports issued between 1946 and 1950 by commissions appointed by the various churches to study the implications of the advent of atomic energy. These studies are the result of deliberate and serious inquiry by leading theologians and moralists, and summarize the churches' understanding of the relation of Christian ethics to the major problems raised by war in the atomic era.

The churches found themselves in an anomalous position with regard to the idea of total war. Their immediate reaction was to reject it. The Church had always stood — and must continue to stand — in firm opposition to the unrestrained violence and indiscriminate destruction inherent in total war. The just-war tradition insisted that warfare was justifiable only if conducted by limited means and directed toward limited ends; and of course the pacifist tradition consistently rejected all war.

And yet, despite their rejection of the doctrine of total war, the churches accepted the common prediction that all future conflicts would in fact *be* total wars. Churchmen also echoed the generally accepted assumption that atomic weapons would tend to precipitate total war by placing a premium upon unannounced aggression, and the conclusion that the only solution was to abolish war altogether. Quotations from the American commission reports will demonstrate the high degree to which the churches were influenced by the presuppositions generally current in society at large.

A list of the major commissions and their reports will facilitate identification in the discussion that follows. (The two British reports, which will be discussed in the following chapter, were produced in dialogue with the corresponding reports of the American churches.)

1946 Calhoun Commission (Federal Council of Churches):
Atomic Warfare and the Christian Faith
1946 A British Council of Churches Commission:
The Era of Atomic Power
1947 Catholic Association for International Peace:
The Ethics of Atomic War
1948 A Church of England Commission:
The Church and the Atom
1950 Dun Commission (Federal Council of Churches):
The Christian Conscience and Weapons of Mass Destruction[1]

II

The Calhoun Commission, in its earlier report, *The Relation of the Church to the War in the Light of the Christian Faith* (1944), had insisted that the Church

must resist, by open criticism and persuasion, the theory and the attempted practice of "total war" . . . Total war is suited only for a totalitarian society, which as we have said is irreconcilable in principle with Christian faith in the sovereignty of God and the responsible freedom of man. No matter what the provocation, however great the extremity of military peril — even to the imminence of military defeat — the Church dare not approve a supposition that military expediency or necessity can ever rightfully become the supreme principle of human conduct.

. . . *The Church cannot acquiesce in the supremacy of military considerations even in war time, nor in the view that modern war may properly, even in the case of extreme peril to nation, church, or culture, become total war* . . .

The commission also rejected total war in the sense of total defeat of the enemy. The peoples of Germany and Japan must be provided, even after their defeat, "the basis for a normal, peaceable livelihood" and a "reasonable opportunity for peaceable intercourse with other peoples." [2]

In *Atomic Warfare and the Christian Faith* the Calhoun Commission, while reaffirming its opposition to total war, stated that with the advent of the atomic bomb, "the march toward total war . . . has been advanced a giant step further. For the new weapons are especially well suited to indiscriminate destruction." If another major war is fought, predicted the commission, "strategic bombing of key cities will have a still larger place from the very outset, and . . . rockets with atomic warheads, not piloted planes, will be the chief weapons for such attack. . . . All pretense of discrimination between military objectives and civilian homes would disappear. . . . The logical end would be total war in grim truth." The Calhoun Commission echoed the scientists' point that atomic weapons place a premium on "swift ruthless aggression," and pointed out the pressure upon nations to strike first before being attacked. In the situation facing us in the atomic age, therefore,

. . . the only mode of control that holds much promise is control directed to the prevention of war. We recognize the probable futility, in practice, of measures to outlaw atomic weapons while war itself continues. . . . Experience indicates that in a struggle for survival one side or the other will resort to whatever weapons promise victory, and its opponent will feel constrained to adopt counter-measures in kind. War itself must go.[3]

III

In *The Ethics of Atomic War,* Roman Catholic moralists explicitly rejected total war on the grounds that it involves indiscriminate attack upon the noncombatant civilian population: "Deliberate and direct attack on this portion of the enemy's people, no matter what the end sought, would be simple murder." Yet the moralists expected, as did everyone else, that "inasmuch as future warfare will probably be atomic warfare," it will be "total war in the fullest sense." The report mentions two further considerations which "confirm the conclusion that any future atomic war will be total war":

> The first is the assumption that no nation contemplating atomic warfare would have less than several hundred bombs, or, more probably, would even start a war unless it had a few thousand. The second assumption . . . is that a nation contemplating atomic warfare would launch most of its bombs without previous warning or declaration of war, and would launch them at once or within a few minutes. The nation against which so many bombs were used thus without warning would, in all probability, within fifteen minutes after the beginning of the war, find all its main centers of population and production pulverized and a large part of its people dead. . . . Thus would the concept of total war be brought to its final and logical conclusion.

A few pages later the committee again echoes the Pearl Harbor axiom of the scientists:

> Since any war that is started in the future will very probably begin with a large shower of atomic bombs and without warning, it is to be doubted that in the future any war at all will be a moral one . . . Moreover, it is unlikely that the military command in any large country will start a war without using atomic bombs immediately, since it will be presumed that the other side will use them as soon as it is attacked.

Since the next war is thus certain to be immoral, and since "an armament race is in itself a cause of war, and in the case of the atomic bomb may be the greatest cause," the Catholic re-

port concludes with an appeal for international control of
atomic energy to prevent such an arms race.[4]

IV

The Dun Commission Report, written five years after Hiroshima, made essentially the same two points about total war
as did its predecessors, although with significant modifications
in detail. While affirming the inescapability of total war in the
sense that in future conflicts "all human and material resources
are mobilized for war purposes," the commission rejected total
war in the sense that "all moral restraints are thrown aside and
all the purposes of the community are fully controlled by sheer
military expediency." The commission continued at some
length: "Military victory is not an end in itself. Just as death
is preferable to life under some conditions, so, too, victory at
any price is not worth having. . . . Military expediency, therefore, cannot be the sole test, but must be subordinated to
moral and political considerations." [5]

The Dun Commission echoed the earlier reports in predicting that any future major conflict would be total war: "If general war comes it will probably be a war for survival, not only
for the survival of a free civilization, but for the physical survival of peoples." One of the main points at which total war
threatens to burst through the "weak moral defenses erected to
keep war in some bounds" is the "widespread acceptance of the
bombing of cities as an inescapable part of modern war." The
report predicts that "if global war comes, and with it a resort to
still more powerful means of obliteration bombing, all of us
will be caught up in it, men, women and children . . ." "In
the harsh light of history," concluded the commission, "the
best hope of preventing a global atomic war lies in preventing
the recurrence of global war itself." [6]

The commission's choice of words indicates a significant

modification in expectation for the future, as compared with the earlier church reports. It is not predicted that *every* future conflict — but only every "global war" — will prove to be atomic and total. Doubtless the impact of the "police action" in Korea, which broke out as the commission was in the midst of its deliberations, helped to alter the conviction that every military contest must by nature be all-out, and opened eyes to the possibility of engagements that could be limited both as to means used and ends sought. Nevertheless this possibility, if it was in the minds of the members of the Dun Commission, found no explicit expression in their report. On the contrary, throughout the report, which dealt at great length with the possibility of war and the prevention of war, the commission did not mention a limited engagement such as that in Korea, but was preoccupied with the struggle for survival of "the free world" against "worldwide Communism." Despite the statement that the goal of the West is "not the conquest or forcible conversion of the Soviet Union," the only war that the report seriously considers as a possibility is all-out atomic war against Russia. The unintended effect is to imply that the war most likely to break out is total war.[7]

In another way the language used by the commission betrays total-war presuppositions. The word "victory" appears nine times on a single page; in another passage the word is "triumph"; elsewhere (in speaking of a possible future war) the report refers to "those we have conquered."[8] The members of the commission consciously and explicitly rejected total war; yet their use of words carrying all the overtones of World War II clearly indicates that unconsciously they were still thinking in terms of total war in the World War II sense — namely, that the national substance of the participating nations is at stake, and that at the conclusion of the war there are only the victorious conquerors and the prostrate vanquished.

Again, the commission very explicitly and at some length insisted that Christians cannot accept the supremacy of military expediency, even in wartime. Yet it seems that the dissenting criticism of one of the members of the commission is fair: when the report turns to practical recommendations, "the ruling assumption throughout . . . is that if 'we' are attacked, we must do whatever is needed to win" — including, it may be added, the use even of atomic weapons to "prevent the triumph of an aggressor." [9]

To point out these disjunctions between explicit statement and unconscious assumption is not to charge the members of the Dun Commission with hypocrisy; it is merely to note the degree to which even the most conscientious churchmen shared the pervasive but unexamined presuppositions of their countrymen regarding the nature of war.

At two points the Dun Commission made important departures from the generally accepted analysis current in 1945–1946. In a long section rejecting the possibility of preventive war, the commission specifically challenged the "faithless and defeatist idea that war is inevitable" because of the arms race or the supposed advantage of striking the first blow. "To accept general war as inevitable is to treat ourselves as helpless objects carried by a fated tide of events rather than as responsible men." The report envisions a prolonged cold war struggle between the West and the Communist world, during which "the avoidance of global war without surrender to tyranny" is at least possible.[10]

While agreeing that the best way of avoiding total war is to prevent war altogether, the commission jettisoned a second axiom of 1946. Having witnessed the dismal stalemate in the United Nations over controls, the commission had no illusions about preserving peace by effective international controls of atomic energy. It recommended instead that we "build up and maintain adequate strength in the free world"— military, economic, political, and moral — for "we believe that peace in our

world can be preserved only by the strength of the free world."
Specifically the commission urged strengthening democracy and
eliminating racial discrimination at home, technical assistance
to underdeveloped nations, and a deepened faith in God.[11]

V

Needless to say, the pacifists (who published no formal commission report during the period under discussion) agreed with
other churchmen that war had developed to the point where
any future war would be beyond moral restraint and would be
totally destructive. "Preparedness to wage war with these new
weapons will perpetuate anarchy among the nations and will
surely lead to a suicidal third world war if it is continued. It
will be sheer madness to engage in a race of atomic armaments." Pacifist writers tended to sum up the alternatives before
mankind in terms of a simple and clear-cut choice. "Total security or total extinction are the alternatives now. And there
is no security except at the price of the total abolition of war."
Or again: "A choice must be made and cannot be evaded: the
way of atomic war or the way of Jesus." [12]

Pacifists felt that international control of atomic energy did
not touch the root of the problem; the only real solution was
the complete abolition of war itself, and nothing short of
world government could accomplish this. "Nothing less than a
world government can meet the exigency of the bomb." John
Haynes Holmes was so carried away with the vision of a warless
world that he urged the establishment of "one sovereign government which shall be God's Kingdom upon earth."(!)[13]

In addition to moral indignation at the bombing of Hiroshima
and genuine horror at the prospect of an all-out atomic war,
one detects in the pacifist journal *Fellowship* a note of relief
and (if it is not unfair to say so) almost of rejoicing at the in-
vention of the atomic bomb. For this instrument of absolute

and indiscriminate destruction epitomizes and dramatizes the very essence of war. At last, what the pacifist has been saying about war for twenty years has been made unmistakably clear; even the most dense and the most callous can now see that war is impossible as an instrument of human purpose — and must be abolished. It seemed that the pacifist position and the pacifist movement had been vindicated by the ultimate weapon of war.

VI

It must be noted that in addition to sincerely held opinion about the course of future events, there was also a certain lack of disinterestedness in the churches' analysis of the "next war." Certainly the pacifists, but also to a large degree the churches generally, had a vested interest in peace. They were not merely reporting facts but promoting a cause. The churches have always opposed violence and war; an ingredient of overstatement may have crept into their analysis that tended to paint the next war so black that men would be motivated to choose peace instead. Something of the same ingredient may also have been present in the scientists' campaign: editor Eugene Rabinowitch has described the founding of the *Bulletin of the Atomic Scientists* as "part of the conspiracy to preserve our civilization by scaring men into rationality." [14]

The question of motive aside, it is clear that during the years immediately following Hiroshima, the churches with a high degree of unanimity had accepted essentially the position set forth by the scientists in their diagnosis of war in the atomic age. Protestants and Catholics, pacifists and nonpacifists all agreed that when the next war came it would be atomic war and total war. All implicitly assumed that it would be total not only in terms of the weapons used and the direct attacking of noncombatants, but also that it would be total in the same sense that

World War II was total: it would be a war for the survival of nations, waged for total victory and unconditional surrender. The World Council of Churches spoke for all when its Amsterdam Assembly said in 1948:[15]

> Warfare has greatly changed. War is now total and every man and woman is called for mobilization in war service. Moreover, the immense use of air forces and the discovery of atomic and other new weapons render widespread and indiscriminate destruction inherent in the whole conduct of modern war in a sense never experienced in past conflicts. In these circumstances the tradition of a just war, requiring a just cause and the use of just means, is now challenged.*

We now turn to an examination of the influence of these general ideas about total war upon the churches' specific recommendations regarding the use of atomic weapons.

---

* Of course, not all Roman Catholics would have agreed that the doctrine of the just war "is now challenged"; but a significant number did. The CAIP report, *The Ethics of Atomic War*, states in a footnote: "The Committee considers atomic war to be different in nature from ordinary wars and therefore not subject to the traditional rules applicable to ordinary aggressive and defensive war," p. 11.

20. Christian Ethics and Atomic Weapons

THE CHURCHES stated two things about war in the atomic age:
(1) that war in the future would be total; and (2) that total
war is immoral. There is only one logical conclusion to be
drawn from these two premises, and many nonpacifists joined
the traditional pacifists in affirming it: war must now be abolished — or, at least, the Christian must refuse to participate in
it. Yet when the question was raised about the morality of using atomic weapons in the world as it existed in the 1940's,
before war had been abolished, the answers given by the
churches were not so simple. Almost without exception the
major church pronouncements took a double position that involved a deep dilemma. On the one hand, to use atomic weapons would be inherently immoral because of their unlimited
and necessarily indiscriminate destruction of life and property;
on the other hand, statesmen have the responsibility to maintain stocks of atomic weapons and, if necessary, to use them in
defense of their nation, or of justice. The dilemma appears in
varying forms in the work of the several commissions.

II

The Calhoun Commission, in *Atomic Warfare and the Christian Faith*, pointed out that atomic weapons "lend themselves
to belligerent practices that are intolerable to Christian conscience. They make it harder than ever before to give real effect
to the traditional distinctions between combatants and noncombatants among the enemy, and between proportionate and ex-

cessive violence in conduct of the war. They tend to unlimited, indiscriminate destruction. . . . Hence, it is more than ever incumbent upon Christians to resist the development of situations in which [they] are likely to be employed." While the commission was unanimous in urging that manufacture of atomic bombs be stopped, and the government publicly affirm that the United States "will under no circumstances be the first to use atomic weapons in any possible future war," it was divided over the issue of whether — in the absence of international controls — atomic weapons could legitimately be used. Some members held that the bomb must be repudiated; others believed that "the way should be left open to regard the use of atomic weapons under some circumstances as right . . . in the present state of human relations, if plans for international control of aggression should fail, the only effective restraint upon would-be aggressors might be fear of reprisals, and that this possible restraint should not be removed in advance." [1]

III

Instead of being divided among themselves, the Catholic moralists who wrote *The Ethics of Atomic War* grasped both horns of the dilemma at once, apparently without being aware that it is a dilemma. To begin with, they affirmed essentially what Father Ford said about obliteration bombing — that it is impossible to release the bomb and withhold the intention to kill civilians, since when the atomic bomb is used over land "it is impossible to restrict its effects to a purely military target . . . the civilian population of the attacked country is inextricably involved in its effects, even if the bomb be intended solely against a military objective." Therefore the use of the atomic bomb over land must be condemned as violating the immunity of noncombatants.[2]

A few pages later, however, the committee asked the question: supposing that an enemy has just launched a massive nuclear attack against our cities, "will it be morally defensible on our part to send [our] bombs on his cities, even though it meant the loss of millions of civilian lives?" The answer: provided that the destruction of the enemy's cities is absolutely necessary for the purpose of "hindering him from the further act of sending an invading force to occupy our country and to enslave us," then

. . . a proportionate reason exists for our using our bombs in turn on his cities if these cities are the source of his military productiveness. Such a reason is to preserve our country and our whole remaining population from utter enslavement. . . . The evil wrought on the [enemy's] civil population is not intended, but permitted. What is solely intended is making impossible any further military effort against us. Hence, the use of the atom bombs against the enemy cities would under these conditions be permitted as being the *only possible* and *necessary* defense.

What is the difference between such a use of the atomic bomb and total war . . . ? It is true that if we can win the war by the use of one means which will incidentally and without intending it mean the death of 100,000 civilians or of another which in the same way will kill 1,000,000 civilians then we may not use the second and larger since the excess of evil is not required for the defense of our right. There is no proportionate reason. But if the second means is the only possible one, say by use of atom bombs, then since we do not intend the destruction of life but only of productive capacity, the permitted deaths of so many are outweighed by the good obtained, the salvation of the innocent country. This is not total war in the condemned sense.[3]

Thus the committee affirmed both the basic immorality of using the weapon against a city and the legitimacy of so using it if military necessity demands it.

IV

In *The Era of Atomic Power*, the British Council of Churches Commission likewise grasped both horns of the dilemma — but recognized that it was a dilemma. From one standpoint, the use of the bomb in itself seems clearly immoral: "The question has to be asked afresh whether the destruction of an entire population, including the aged and the young, is not an act so absolutely wrong in itself that no Christian can assent to it or share in it." From another point of view, however, the Christian must recognize that the statesman has the responsibility of protecting from ruthless aggression the Western democratic institutions which are "a profoundly significant transcription at the political level of Christian insight, and for this reason demand the active support of Christians." To refuse, in the last extremity, to have recourse to force for the protection of basic human liberties and rights would be a repudiation of the Christian's responsibility for his neighbor in the world. Since the atomic bomb "will inevitably take its place in the armoury of nations," and since "no effective means has thus far been suggested of deterring a would-be aggressor except the fear of reprisals," the atomic bomb "ought in the future to be used for one purpose, and one purpose alone, to deter by the threat, and if necessary by the execution, of reprisals a nation which attempted to use it for aggressive purposes." The commission recognized that manufacturing and holding the bomb for deterrence "is beset with grave dangers," including "the possibility of an occasion arising when the threat of reprisal would have to be put into action." But the commission felt it is necessary to accept that risk.

> To lay down in advance that a statesman, responsible for the defence of his nation and confronted by naked aggression, must, for moral or Christian reasons, refrain in all circumstances from recourse to atomic warfare would reduce to futility the argu-

ment that the use of the bomb as a deterrent may be the sole means of preventing war. . . . Circumstances may arise in which an adamant attitude, and a readiness to accept its consequences, may be the course best calculated to remove the danger of war.

From this point of view it is a serious question whether it is right for Christians to weaken the hands of their government by announcing in advance that, if hostilities take place, they will have no part in them. . . . If the supreme object of our endeavors is to save humanity from the appalling fate of atomic warfare, to assume that the best means of doing so is to renounce in advance the right of defence might well prove to be a serious political miscalculation.[4]

Having affirmed with equal clarity and sensitivity both the immorality of using the bomb, and the duty of being ready to use it, the committee declared, "We have no solution of the dilemma to offer," nor does the Church as a whole. For each side of the dilemma "is the expression of loyalty to one side of Christian obligation."

The one is a response to the claims of what presents itself as a moral absolute, and to an instinctive conviction that the future of the Church as the Body of Christ cannot be staked in a conflict in which there is no place left for mercy and the individual person counts for nothing at all. . . . The other decision is an attempt to discharge in the most desperate of situations the obligation which by God's appointment men owe to the temporal order; for those who make it the greatness of the crisis is a crowning reason why citizenship should be affirmed.[5]

V

The commission of the Church of England was appointed by the Archbishops of Canterbury and York to consider *The Era of Atomic Power* and to report to the Church Assembly: *The Church and the Atom* is the result. With regard to the use of the atomic bomb in warfare, the conclusions of the Anglican commission are very similar to those of the American Catholic moralists. The commission, having condemned the obliteration bombing of cities, rejects use of the atomic bomb as an instrument of obliteration: "The atomic bomb is inadmissible as a means of attack upon objectives in inhabited cities." Even against a purely military target the use of the bomb is questionable, since "it causes death and aggravates suffering needlessly." Yet on the other hand, "a national government has the imperative duty of maintaining adequate forces [and] adequate armament" for the protection of the community in which it exercises authority. It has the duty not only of resisting aggression, but also, if possible, of preventing it by deterrence. Does it have the right to reply in kind to a massive atomic attack by an enemy? The commission justifies a counterattack in these terms:

> . . . first, in all probability such an attack would, by threatening the existence of the community subjected to it, establish a "present imminent danger" which would justify all measures genuinely necessary to self-defence. Secondly, since in these circumstances the only hope of effective defence would lie in bringing overwhelming force to bear upon the enemy immediately, it seems that the use of atomic weapons would be genuinely necessary. Thirdly, since it would also be necessary to use these weapons in the most immediately efficacious way, whatever damage and casualties were inflicted in so doing could rightly be regarded as incidental to self-defence.[6]

VI

The Dun Commission avoided the dilemma by avoiding outright condemnation of the use of the atomic bomb. The report condemns the bombing of cities, the "mass destruction which is aimed primarily at the lives of civilians," and urges "restraint from destruction not essential to our total objectives" and the "avoidance of needless human suffering." Thus indiscriminate and excessive violence are condemned — but not the bomb, except by implication. The commission refuses to make a distinction in kind between atomic weapons and others, stating that "indiscriminate mass destruction may be caused by atomic bombs or by a fleet of armored tanks or by a ruthless army laying waste cities and countryside. We have found no moral distinction between these instruments of warfare, apart from the ends they serve and the consequences of their use." Indeed, "abandonment of atomic weapons would not eliminate mass destruction. . . . The real moral line between what may be done and what may not be done by the Christian lies not in the realm of the distinction between weapons but in the realm of the motives for using and the consequences of using all kinds of weapons." Thus the atomic bomb, as well as other weapons, may be used by Christians in the struggle for justice and freedom in the world, subject only to the restriction against excessive violence:

> If atomic weapons . . . are used against us or our friends in Europe or Asia, we believe that it could be justifiable for our government to use them with all possible restraint to prevent the triumph of an aggressor.[7]

VII

We have seen that all the major church studies between 1946 and 1950, whether Catholic or Protestant, adopted a double position regarding the morality of using atomic weapons. All condemned the act of dropping an atomic bomb in war as immoral in itself, because it would involve a violation of the immunity of noncombatants, or because it would be excessively and disproportionately destructive, or because it can be directly intuited that such violence would be incompatible with the spirit of Jesus Christ.

On the other hand, all (except pacifists) nevertheless condoned its use in certain circumstances of strict military necessity — despite their prior insistence that military necessity should not be the supreme criterion in wartime — whether for the purpose of national self-defense or the securing of justice and freedom against aggressive tyranny.

The internal contradictions in this double position reflect a deep-going confusion in the thinking of the churches, growing out of their unquestioning acceptance of the presuppositions of total war. Their condemnation of the use of atomic weapons reflected their conscious concern that all warfare be conducted only by limited, rather than unrestrained, means. Yet in answering specific questions about the use of atomic weapons, the churches unconsciously assumed a total-war situation in which unrestrained means were demanded. In part, this assumption is seen in the talk about "enslavement," the "invasion of our country," and "resisting aggressive tyranny," all of which recall a World War II type of conflict in which the ends sought threaten the national substance and even existence of the belligerents. The assumption is epitomized in the recurring question by which the churchmen posed to themselves the essential problem of using atomic weapons. The question specified an all-out attack on our cities, and in their answer the churchmen reluctantly permitted atomic counterattack — both in complete abstraction from any political purposes, limited or unlimited, being sought by ourselves or the enemy.

Their preoccupation with total war meant that during the years immediately after Hiroshima, when the churches were first struggling with the moral challenge posed by weapons of massive destructiveness, their attention was focused upon two extremes: either the abolition of all war, because now war is inevitably total, or use of the atomic bomb in conditions of extreme military necessity, which only an all-out attack on our cities could justify. Church moralists (and secular strategists) neglected the middle ground of limited military action directed toward limited political ends, which was in fact a much greater threat to United States interests in the struggle with world Communism than a massive atomic attack by the Soviet Union, and where their expressed concern for limitation upon the means of conducting warfare could have helped in the development of a relevant ethical-political theory for discriminate and responsible exercising of power in international affairs.

Church moralists, including those who consciously took their stand within the just-war tradition, concentrated their attention almost exclusively upon the question of whether use of atomic weapons would constitute an illegitimate *means* of warfare: they debated about intended and unintended injury to civilians, the indiscriminateness of the weapon, and its disproportionate destructiveness. It was not until 1948 that a major group of theologians and moralists remembered that the just-war theory also requires that war, to be justifiable, must be undertaken for a just cause, and thus in pursuit of a limited *end*.

VIII

In *The Church and the Atom* the commission appointed by the Archbishops of Canterbury and York applied the theory of the just war rigorously to the problems raised by atomic weapons; it discussed the legitimacy of the atomic bomb as a means of warfare only after a *prior* discussion about the proper ends of warfare. The concept of war for unlimited ends, including total victory and unconditional surrender, was firmly rejected by the commission:

> To seek the entire subjugation of the enemy, or the abolition of his sovereignty, or unrestricted control over his life, labour and property, is not permissible; for such aims transcend the limits set by justifying causes.

. . . no nation has the right forcibly to impose upon another the political system that it fancies, even if that system be
dubbed "democracy." Just war is a remedy for international
delinquency, not a means of making disciples of all nations.

The relation between a just cause and just means was then
pointed out:

It is patent that, unless the limitation of ends can be established, there is little chance of a hearing for the moral rules
that apply to the conduct of war.

The cause that warrants a state in making war determines
the proximate end it may justly pursue; the end thus determined sets bounds to the force it may justly use. . . . It is
always the duty of an agent to proportion means to ends. . . .

The commission concluded that "limitation in the methods of
warfare depends in the last resort on limitation in its ends." [8]

IX

It is significant that this first major statement explicitly applying to atomic weapons the doctrine of the just cause should
come from England rather than from the United States. Apparently it had little influence upon American church moralists,
for the Dun Commission Report, written two years later, made
no explicit mention of the idea of limiting the ends of warfare,
but on the contrary was obsessed with "global war" and "victory." The outbreak of the Korean conflict made a deep impression upon the members of the Dun Commission, and
doubtless was responsible for the passages in their report about
resisting aggression and the struggle with world-wide Communism. But the crucial fact that the Korean conflict was limited
in means because it was pursued for limited ends apparently
had little significance for Christian moralists in America.

The long-range impact of the Korean conflict was more important, however. Combined with the ending of the American monopoly of atomic weapons and the growing threat of nuclear retaliation by the Soviet Union, the experiences of limited military engagements in Korea and Indochina played a major role in forcing a rethinking of United States assumptions about total war. During the 1950's attention of military strategists shifted from the threat of an all-out push by the Red Army into western Europe, to the dangers of "brush-fire" wars in the "grey areas" around the perimeter of the Communist world; and a lively debate sprang up over the relation of nuclear "massive retaliation" to the achievement of limited political ends. A doctrine of limited war began to be formulated in such books as Robert E. Osgood's *Limited War* and Henry A. Kissinger's *Nuclear Weapons and Foreign Policy*.[9]

The debate among strategists was paralleled by renewed discussion among theologians about limited ends and their relation to limited means. The Jesuit theologian John Courtney Murray asserted that limited war is "a moral necessity"; since nuclear war "may be a necessity, it must be made a possibility." United States Atomic Energy Commissioner Thomas E. Murray, a Roman Catholic layman, denounced the apparent reliance of our military planners upon the deterrent effects of megaton weapons which, should the deterrent fail, could not be used either rationally or morally. In pointing out what he called the forgotten "equation between morality and security," Murray called for development of a wide range of tactical nuclear weapons of limited power, and "a flexible military policy based on a rational and moral use of these weapons — in a limited way to achieve limited objectives." Reinhold Niebuhr questioned whether the line between conventional weapons and tactical nuclear weapons could be so easily crossed without breaking down the barriers to a rapidly spreading all-out nuclear conflict; but he agreed with Murray on the necessity of using power discriminately in the seeking of limited political ends. A World Council of Churches provisional study document spoke of the "discipline which is capable of using armaments, whether conventional or nuclear, if at all, in a radically limited way only," and in pursuit of "limited objectives." [10]

The problem of limitation of warfare in the nuclear age has not been solved, either by strategists or moralists. But the universal acceptance of the inevitability of total war, which characterized the opening years of the atomic age, has successfully been challenged. As a result, the door is now open for serious ethical inquiry into the relation between moral and political ends and the discriminate use of military power. The doctrine of the just war, which many thought had been rendered obsolete by weapons of indiscriminate destructiveness and theories of total war, is now seen to have a new relevance.

V

Conclusion

21. The Need for a New Ethic

THE PURPOSE of this inquiry has been to gain some insight into the moral problems involved in the use of nuclear weapons, and some understanding of the role and relevance of ethical considerations in the making of major policy decisions. The method has been the detailed examination of certain specific decisions relating to the atomic bomb, and analysis of the ethical debate arising from the decisions. The major findings of our investigation as they are related to broader problems of ethics now confront us.

II

This study has confirmed the importance of historical context in the understanding and application of ethical principle. We have seen how conscientious men did in one historical situation what they never would have done in another, and how the very ethical norms they sought to follow in perplexing new situations were themselves understood anew, modified — perhaps transformed or even lost altogether — under the impact of the vivid and tragic experience of World War II. For example, the atomic scientists, confronted in 1940 with the threat of Hitler in sole possession of an atomic bomb, undertook as an urgent duty the building of an instrument of mass destruction — an act they would never have considered five years earlier and the consequences of which they found difficult to reconcile with their consciences five years later.

Americans entered World War II universally opposed on

261

moral grounds to the bombing of civilian areas. We have observed their gradual acceptance of obliteration bombing under the demands of "military necessity" and the transformation of ethical thought relating to such bombing. Some Christian moralists so modified their principles that they justified obliteration bombing; others held to the principle of noncombatant immunity — but kept silent.

We have analyzed the way in which men's experience during World War II shaped their later thinking about the nature of war, and deeply influenced the churches in their search for understanding about the moral problems raised by atomic weapons. And there would appear to be little doubt that the further experience of limited military engagements in Korea and Indochina, combined with the threat of growing Russian nuclear power, played an important role not only in stimulating a rethinking of American military and strategic doctrine but also in a resurgence of ethical inquiry into the relation between military power and political ends.

Just as important as the context of historical events is the context of ideas — the network of commonly held but unconscious presuppositions which gives subtle meaning to words and provides channels that guide the flow of conscious thought. During World War II the emphasis upon purely military considerations and the discounting of political considerations by United States leaders (and by the American public generally) prepared the way for the bombing of Hiroshima by so shaping the events and choices of 1945 that by August the decision to drop the atomic bomb "was not difficult." We have seen how the ethical considerations consciously brought to bear upon that decision were deeply influenced by the prior assumptions that the bomb was essentially a military weapon, that all other considerations must be subordinated to the one goal of victory-with-unconditional-surrender, and that the only method likely to achieve this goal was the further application of brute military force.

In findings such as these, this study has to some extent confirmed the contextual approach to ethics, at least as a description of what actually happens to men when they attempt to make their moral principles relevant to the difficult and shifting social problems confronting them in the course of history: a new historical situation does lead to a new and different understanding of previously accepted principles. The recommendation sometimes inferred from this by contextualists is that principles ought not to be held too firmly: the moral life is not merely the imposition of rigid ethical norms upon the richly varying stuff of life. The latter is undoubtedly true — but our findings suggest that the impact of new historical experience upon moral principles is so great that if the principles are held too loosely or too vaguely they may be lost altogether in the press of events. What is required is not only *a new understanding* of moral principles in each new historical context, but also a new understanding *of moral principles* in each new context. Because the impact of historical experience is so great, a firmer (though not rigid) grasp upon principle is necessary. A firmer grasp upon the basic insight underlying the principle of noncombatant immunity would have mitigated many of the excesses of World War II; and a stronger hold upon the ancient principle of the just cause in warfare might have averted much confusion in the thinking about atomic war in the years 1946-1950.

III

The decisions to make and to use the atomic bomb were viewed by those who made them as essentially choices of "the lesser evil." The limitations of a utilitarian ethical theory that depends upon prediction of consequences and calculation of the greater good and the lesser evil are clear.

Men, in their social decisions, are motivated not so much by the attractive power of a great good that they strive to achieve as by revulsion against a great evil that they seek to avoid. It was fear of Hitler's winning the war that started scientists on their quest for the bomb and led Allied people and leaders to modify their earlier principles regarding the bombing of civilians. The primary concern in the thinking of Truman and Stimson as they planned for use of the atomic bomb was to avoid "the ghastly specter of a clash of great land armies" in Japan. What injected urgency into the postwar campaign of the atomic scientists was their fear of a nuclear holocaust. Henry Stimson and James Franck arrived at opposite conclusions on the use of the atomic bomb against Japan not because they sought different ends. Both sought peace and security in the postwar world; both were conscientious and humane gentlemen. Seeking the same end, they differed because they were recoiling from different evils. For Franck the threat of atomic war in the future outweighed all short-run considerations; but for Stimson, a public official who felt keenly his responsibility to "the men in the armies which I had helped to raise," the threat of a massive and bloody invasion was much more pressing.

Ironically enough, subsequent events proved in every case that the fears, and the policies adopted in reaction to the fears, were exaggerated. The United States spent two billion dollars to insure against Hitler's nonexistent bomb. The obliteration bombing of cities, urged as a military necessity, contributed little to the defeat of Germany. The invasion of Japan was not really as inevitable as American leaders assumed. And the mutual fears of nuclear retaliation have (thus far) prevented the holocaust scientists were convinced would be inevitable if rival nations built stockpiles of atomic weapons in the absence of international control of atomic energy.

Such miscalculations could be taken for signs of American obtuseness, had not the Germans and Japanese made even more serious errors. The Japanese attacked Pearl Harbor on the assumption that the Americans would soon tire of war and settle for a negotiated peace; Hitler planned to knock Russia out of the war within a few months; Japan attempted to negotiate for peace through the Russians — who were racing to get into the Pacific war before Japan could get out!

This catalogue of errors proves not only that ignorance was well distributed on both sides during the war but also suggests the impossibility of predicting accurately the future consequences of a major social act. The issues facing statesmen in the modern world are so massive — the interrelationships of events so complex, the ramifications of acts so far-reaching — that any social ethical theory depending upon men's ability accurately to predict consequences and calculate good and evil effects must be called seriously into question.

Besides the limitations upon man's knowledge of the future, there are serious limitations upon his power to effect his will, once he has decided to act. The individual effort of Leo Szilard was instrumental in initiating the uranium project in 1939; but Szilard discovered in 1945 that his most strenuous exertions could not deflect from its course the juggernaut moving irresistibly toward the atomic bombing of Japan. Social institutions appear to take on an independence and a power of their own which defy the attempts of individual men to control them. General Groves has said of President Truman's decision to use the bomb: "Truman did not so much say 'yes' as not say 'no.' It would indeed have taken a lot of nerve to say 'no' at that time." [1]

One who studies the accounts of the participants cannot escape the feeling that throughout the atomic bomb project there was a twisting and a perversion of men's intentions. Scientists who undertook the quest to prevent Hitler's unrestrained use of the atomic bomb found that they were unable to restrain our own use of it. Those who planned to use the bomb on the supposition that the Japanese would take air raid precautions did not realize that the training tactics used by the 509th would lead the Japanese to neglect even minimal precautions for the protection of civilians. Those who insisted that they were interested in military damage and not civilian lives made a decision resulting in death for more than 100,000 civilians.

In short, no ethical theory is adequate which assumes that man, once he has determined the right course of action, can control events with the same precision with which the virtuoso controls his violin. Nor is an ethical theory adequate which assumes that men can accurately predict the consequences of major social decisions, and that good and evil results can mathematically be balanced one against the other. Life — at least the life examined in this study — is not so simple.

The inadequacy of calculative ethics apparently increases as the problems become larger. Who can accurately balance the evils of submitting to Communist tyranny against the risk of nuclear war inherent in resisting the spread of that tyranny? This inadequacy in the face of such issues has led one sensitive moralist to suggest that "calculative morality becomes less and less useful as the issue at stake becomes more and more momentous." Ethics, therefore, "must rediscover obedience in a situation in which calculation becomes less and less possible." To return to an ethics of obedience, in which the morality of the act is determined by its intrinsic nature, rather than its consequences, is not to eliminate calculation from ethics, he suggests. Calculation is no longer "a reliance," by which the morality of the act must somehow be determined; rather, calculation can become "a service" aiding in the implementation of an act whose essential morality has been determined on other grounds.[2]

It seems clear that an adequate ethic must include both formalistic and calculative elements. However, it may perhaps be suggested that an ethic including both elements, but concentrating negatively upon avoiding evil consequences and intrinsically wrong acts, will lead to pedestrian, if not negative, results. Perhaps the highest moments in man's moral life come not from an obsession with avoiding evil but rather from a positive attraction to good, which can release the powers of imagination and creativity.

It has been stated that Franklin D. Roosevelt had been planning as early as 1944 to put on a public demonstration with the atomic bomb before using it as a weapon against Japan.[3] Whether Roosevelt, whose political leadership had certain touches of creativity in it, could have made more imaginative or morally better use of the bomb than his successor must remain one of the unanswered questions of history. In any case it is doubtful that merely defensive or negative morality will prove sufficient to guide men through the perplexities and dangers of the atomic age.

IV

We have seen how the attitude of the American people toward war during the years 1946–1950 tended toward two extremes, to the neglect of the possibility of limited military engagements in pursuit of limited political ends.

World War II was thought of as a purely military matter, unrelated to questions of political policy; the sole end we sought was military victory. Therefore, as soon as victory was achieved, demobilization and a return to "peace" followed. With the Army demobilized, and a growing arsenal of atomic weapons, the nation was ready to fight a total atomic war, or no war.

This all-or-nothing approach to war is closely related to what Gabriel Almond has described as a tendency on the part of the American people to react to foreign affairs in terms of unstable and fluctuating moods — first of enthusiastic participation, then of withdrawal to a world of private concerns. The result is a flight from responsible exercise of military power as an instrument of national policy in time of peace, and acceptance of total and unrestrained military action in time of war.[4]

It was widely assumed that atomic weapons had determined that all future wars would necessarily be total. War was therefore denounced as wholly evil, beyond the scope of morality. "When a nation commits its destiny to the arbitrament of sheer might, it abandons all moral restraints," stated an influential church journal. "Its essential acts are judged, not by standards of right and wrong, but by military necessity. . . . The actual waging of war proceeds without benefit of any moral sanction and without the constraint of any moral law."[5] Since war was so evil as to be beyond redemption or restraint, all one could do was to abolish it — or pursue it against a wholly evil enemy.

And so in theory and emotional attitude, as well as in actual armaments, Americans were prepared for only two extreme possibilities: total atomic war or abolition of all war. They had neither adequate equipment nor adequate theory for conducting a limited military engagement designed to advance limited political ends. This lack of preparedness for limited military encounter explains much of the emotional frustration expressed by General MacArthur, and felt by the whole American public, over the "police action" in Korea.

And yet "brush-fire" wars and limited military skirmishes and infiltrations have presented in the past fifteen years, and will continue to present in the future, much the most active and serious threat to the national interests of the United States. In a world that includes both aggressive Communism and nuclear weapons, the two alternatives for which the American people are most prepared (withdrawal from all military commitments and the unrestrained use of nuclear weapons) are alike unsatisfactory, if not suicidal.

The role of the American churches from 1946 to 1950 was primarily to reflect and reinforce the inadequate ideas about war held by the American people. Inadequate and dangerous concepts should not be reinforced, but challenged. We need a new ethic that will provide relevant restraints upon both the ends and means of warfare, and will encourage the discriminate and responsible exercise of power — political, economic, and military — in support of enlightened and creative national goals. The development of such an ethic for the nuclear age is surely one of the most urgent tasks confronting both moralists and statesmen today.

Notes

Notes

CHAPTER 1 (pages 1-5)

1. The text of the Einstein letter is given in William L. Laurence, *Men and Atoms* (New York, 1959), 57.

CHAPTER 2 (pages 9-27)

1. Robert Jungk, *Brighter Than a Thousand Suns* (New York, 1958), 32-49.
2. Laura Fermi, *Atoms in the Family* (Chicago, 1954), 83-93; Jungk, *Brighter Than a Thousand Suns*, 60.
3. Jungk, *Brighter Than a Thousand Suns*, 61-66.
4. Fermi, *Atoms in the Family*, 123-39.
5. Jungk, *Brighter Than a Thousand Suns*, 67-68.
6. Arthur H. Compton, *Atomic Quest* (New York, 1956), 18-19.
7. Henry DeWolf Smyth, *Atomic Energy for Military Purposes* (Princeton, 1946), 28; Compton, *Atomic Quest*, 20.
8. Smyth, *Atomic Energy*, 45-46; Jungk, *Brighter Than a Thousand Suns*, 75-78.
9. Compton, *Atomic Quest*, 27, 43.
10. William L. Laurence, *Men and Atoms* (New York, 1959), 55-56.
11. Alexander Sachs, *Background and Early History Atomic Bomb Project in Relation to President Roosevelt*, testimony before a Special Committee on Atomic Energy, United States Senate (79 Cong., 1 Sess.), pursuant to S. Res. 179, November 27, 1945 (hereafter referred to as Sachs, *Testimony*), 557-59; Laurence, *Men and Atoms*, 58.
12. Sachs, *Testimony*, 556; text of the Einstein letter is printed in Laurence, *Men and Atoms*, 57-58.
13. Sachs, *Testimony*, 556-58; Nat S. Finney, "How F.D.R. Planned to Use the A-Bomb," *Look*, 14:26-27 (March 14, 1950).
14. Sachs, *Testimony*, 560.
15. Compton, *Atomic Quest*, 29-30.
16. Sachs, *Testimony*, 562-64.

17. Laurence, *Men and Atoms*, 61, 67.
18. Smyth, *Atomic Energy*, 49; Compton, *Atomic Quest*, 35-50.
19. Laurence, *Men and Atoms*, 64.
20. The foregoing discussion of technical problems is based upon Smyth, *Atomic Energy*, 27-35.
21. Jungk, *Brighter Than a Thousand Suns*, 90; Laurence, *Men and Atoms*, 41, 73-74; Compton, *Atomic Quest*, 23-24.
22. Jungk, *Brighter Than a Thousand Suns*, 111.
23. Compton, *Atomic Quest*, 6-8.
24. Compton, *Atomic Quest*, 59-60; Laurence, *Men and Atoms*, 53-54; Jungk, *Brighter Than a Thousand Suns*, 112.
25. Compton, *Atomic Quest*, 7, 49-53.
26. Smyth, *Atomic Energy*, 53-54, 71-73; Compton, *Atomic Quest*, 62-64.
27. Compton, *Atomic Quest*, 60, 194-95.
28. Jungk, *Brighter Than a Thousand Suns*, 76; Compton, *Atomic Quest*, 55, 8.
29. Henry L. Stimson and McGeorge Bundy, *On Active Service in Peace and War* (New York, 1947), 612-13.
30. Jungk, *Brighter Than a Thousand Suns*, 76; Compton, *Atomic Quest*, 283, 8.

CHAPTER 3 (pages 28-33)

1. Samuel A. Goudsmit, *Alsos: The Failure in German Science* (London, 1947), 3.
2. Goudsmit, *Alsos*, 7-8.
3. Arthur H. Compton, *Atomic Quest* (New York, 1956), 222-23.
4. Goudsmit's *Alsos* is the primary available resource for information on the Alsos mission.
5. Goudsmit, *Alsos*, 71, 87-127.
6. Werner Heisenberg, "Research in Germany on the Technical Application of Atomic Energy," *Nature*, 160:214 (August 16, 1947); Robert Jungk, *Brighter Than a Thousand Suns* (New York, 1958), 219.
7. Jungk, *Brighter Than a Thousand Suns*, 164.
8. Heisenberg, "Research in Germany," 213.
9. Goudsmit, *Alsos*, 177-81; Jungk, *Brighter Than a Thousand Suns*, 95-96.
10. Heisenberg, "Research in Germany," 214.
11. Goudsmit, *Alsos*, 3-5; Jungk, *Brighter Than a Thousand Suns*, 219.
12. Goudsmit, *Alsos*, xii.
13. Goudsmit, *Alsos*, 104-5, 137; Jungk, *Brighter Than a Thousand Suns*, 79; the same point is made by Hans Thirring in his book *Die*

Geschichte der Atombombe, 1946 (reviewed in *Nature*, 159:792, June 14, 1947).

14. For example, see Jungk, *Brighter Than a Thousand Suns*, 91-98.
15. C. F. von Weizsacker, "Do We Want to Save Ourselves?" *Bulletin of the Atomic Scientists*, 14:180 (May 1958).
16. Heisenberg, "Research in Germany," 211.
17. Jungk, *Brighter Than a Thousand Suns*, 89.
18. Henry DeWolf Smyth, *Atomic Energy for Military Purposes* (Princeton, 1946), 47-48.

CHAPTER 4 (pages 34-38)

1. Eve Curie, *Madame Curie*, trans. Vincent Sheean (New York, 1937), 203-4.
2. Quoted by A. J. Muste in "Conscience versus the Atomic Bomb," *Fellowship*, 11:209 (December 1945).
3. Arthur H. Compton, *Atomic Quest* (New York, 1956), 41-42.
4. Robert Jungk, *Brighter Than a Thousand Suns* (New York, 1958), 75-78; Henry DeWolf Smyth, *Atomic Energy for Military Purposes* (Princeton, 1946), 45-46.
5. Henry L. Stimson and McGeorge Bundy, *On Active Service in Peace and War* (New York, 1947), 613.
6. See Smyth, *Atomic Energy*, 47-54, 75-87.
7. Samuel Goudsmit, *Alsos: The Failure in German Science* (London, 1947), 76.
8. Jungk, *Brighter Than a Thousand Suns*, 87.

CHAPTER 5 (pages 41-47)

1. See Wesley Frank Craven and James Lea Cate (eds.), *The Pacific: Matterhorn to Nagasaki, June 1944 to August 1945*, Vol. V of *The Army Air Forces in World War II* (Chicago, 1953), 722, 725, and Samuel Eliot Morison, *Victory in the Pacific, 1945*, Vol. XIV of *History of United States Naval Operations in World War II* (Boston, 1960), 345.
2. United States Atomic Energy Commission, *In the Matter of J. Robert Oppenheimer: Transcript of Hearing before Personnel Security Board* (Washington, 1954), 326; hereafter referred to as *Oppenheimer Hearings*.
3. Arthur H. Compton, *Atomic Quest* (New York, 1956), 231-32.
4. Robert Jungk, *Brighter Than a Thousand Suns* (New York, 1958), 173-74; Bohr's text is given on pages 344-47.

5. Alice Kimball Smith, "Behind the Decision to Use the Atomic Bomb: Chicago 1944-45," *Bulletin of the Atomic Scientists*, 14:291 (October 1958).
6. Henry DeWolf Smyth, *Atomic Energy for Military Purposes* (Princeton, 1946), 225.
7. Leo Szilard, "A Personal History of the Atomic Bomb," in *The Atlantic Community Faces the Bomb* (University of Chicago Round Table Series No. 601, 1949), 14-16. The text of Szilard's memorandum is given in the *Bulletin of the Atomic Scientists*, 3:351 (December 1947). See also Smith, "Behind the Decision," 293, 296; James F. Byrnes, *All in One Lifetime* (New York, 1958), 284; Michael Amrine, *The Great Decision* (New York, 1959), 98.
8. Smith, "Behind the Decision," 293.
9. *Oppenheimer Hearings*, 14.
10. Compton, *Atomic Quest*, 234-35.

CHAPTER 6 (pages 48-69)

1. Henry L. Stimson and McGeorge Bundy, *On Active Service in Peace and War* (New York, 1947), 615-16.
2. Harry S. Truman, *Year of Decisions* (Garden City, N.Y., 1955), 9-10.
3. Truman, *Year of Decisions*, 11.
4. Truman, *Year of Decisions*, 85.
5. Stimson and Bundy, *On Active Service*, 635-36.
6. Stimson and Bundy, *On Active Service*, 616.
7. Elting E. Morison, *Turmoil and Tradition: A Study of the Life and Times of Henry L. Stimson* (Boston, 1960), 624-25.
8. Arthur H. Compton, *Atomic Quest* (New York, 1956), 219. The words are not Stimson's verbatim, but Compton's best recollection.
9. Interview with Arthur H. Compton, January 30, 1961. See also Los Alamos Scientific Laboratory, *The Effects of Atomic Weapons* (Washington, 1950), 24.
10. This and the preceding paragraph are based upon Compton, *Atomic Quest*, 234-37.
11. Los Alamos Sci. Lab., *Effects of Atomic Weapons*, 16-17; compare a "dud," which is a bomb that fails to explode at all. See also Henry DeWolf Smyth, *Atomic Energy for Military Purposes* (Princeton, 1946), 208-9.
12. Michael Amrine, *The Great Decision* (New York, 1959), 67, 84.
13. Compton, *Atomic Quest*, 237-38; James F. Byrnes, *Speaking Frankly* (New York, 1947), 261.
14. Compton, *Atomic Quest*, 238.
15. Byrnes, *Speaking Frankly*, 261; Compton, *Atomic Quest*, 238-39.

16. Compton, *Atomic Quest*, 239.
17. Compton, *Atomic Quest*, 239.
18. Henry L. Stimson, "The Decision to Use the Atomic Bomb," *Harper's Magazine*, 194:100 (February 1947).
19. "Was A-Bomb on Japan a Mistake?" *U.S. News & World Report*, 49:73-75 (August 15, 1960).
20. Leo Szilard, "A Personal History of the Atomic Bomb," in *The Atlantic Community Faces the Bomb* (University of Chicago Round Table Series No. 601, 1949), 14.
21. Compton, *Atomic Quest*, 242-43.
22. Alice Kimball Smith, "Behind the Decision to Use the Atomic Bomb: Chicago 1944-45," *Bulletin of the Atomic Scientists*, 14:299 (October 1958); Compton, *Atomic Quest*, 233-35.
23. The text of the Franck Committee Report is published in *Bulletin of the Atomic Scientists*, 1:1 ff. (May 1, 1946).
24. Compton, *Atomic Quest*, 236.
25. Compton, *Atomic Quest*, 239-40.
26. See the account of Foreign Minister Togo in Shigenori Togo, *The Cause of Japan*, trans. and ed. Fumihiko Togo and Ben Bruce Blakeney (New York, 1956), 315.
27. United States Atomic Energy Commission, *In the Matter of J. Robert Oppenheimer: Transcript of Hearing before Personnel Security Board* (Washington, 1954), 34.
28. Stimson and Bundy, *On Active Service*, 617.
29. Compton, *Atomic Quest*, 240-41.
30. Interview with Arthur H. Compton, January 30, 1961.
31. Arthur H. Compton and Farrington Daniels, "A Poll of Scientists at Chicago, July, 1945," *Bulletin of the Atomic Scientists*, 4:44 (February 1948).
32. Compton, *Atomic Quest*, 244.
33. Compton, *Atomic Quest*, 246-47.
34. Stimson and Bundy, *On Active Service*, 617.
35. The quotes by Stimson will be found in Stimson and Bundy, *On Active Service*, 613, 617, 629, 632, 629-30.

CHAPTER 7 (pages 70-81)

1. United States Atomic Energy Commission, *In the Matter of J. Robert Oppenheimer: Transcript of Hearing before Personnel Security Board* (Washington, 1954), 34.
2. James F. Byrnes, *Speaking Frankly* (New York, 1947), 261.
3. Winston S. Churchill, *Triumph and Tragedy*, Vol. VI of *The Second World War* (Boston, 1953), 638.

4. Wesley Frank Craven and James Lea Cate (eds.), *The Pacific: Matterhorn to Nagasaki, June 1944 to August 1945*, Vol. V of *The Army Air Forces in World War II* (Chicago, 1953), 614-17; Prince Naruhiko Higashi-Kuni, "Reasons for Defeat," *Vital Speeches*, 7:714-15 (September 15, 1945).

5. Robert J. C. Butow, *Japan's Decision to Surrender* (Stanford, 1954), 94.

6. H. H. Arnold, *Global Mission* (New York, 1949), 569, 566-67; Ernest J. King and Walter Muir Whitehill, *Fleet Admiral King: A Naval Record* (New York, 1952), 598, 605, 621.

7. Harry S. Truman, *Year of Decisions* (Garden City, N. Y., 1955), 416-17; John J. McCloy, *The Challenge to American Foreign Policy* (Cambridge, 1953), 40-41. For the details of the Army's planning, see Ray S. Cline, *Washington Command Post: The Operations Division*, in the *United States Army in World War II* series (Washington, 1951), Chapter 17, especially pp. 340-46.

8. Herbert Feis, *Japan Subdued* (Princeton, 1961), 11.

9. Cline, *Washington Command Post*, 347.

10. McCloy, *Challenge*, 42-43.

11. Henry L. Stimson and McGeorge Bundy, *On Active Service in Peace and War* (New York, 1947), 620-24.

12. Stimson and Bundy, *On Active Service*, 624-25; Truman, *Year of Decisions*, 417.

13. Joseph C. Grew, *Turbulent Era* (Boston, 1952), II, Chapter 36.

14. Stimson and Bundy, *On Active Service*, 626.

15. Byrnes, *Speaking Frankly*, 65-66, 204-6; Cordell Hull, *The Memoirs of Cordell Hull* (New York, 1948), II, 1593-94; Feis, *Japan Subdued*, 25-27.

16. Cline, *Washington Command Post*, 346.

17. Cline, *Washington Command Post*, 346.

CHAPTER 8 (pages 82-97)

1. United States Department of State, *The International Control of Atomic Energy: Growth of a Policy* (Washington, 1946), 106.

2. Herbert Feis, *Japan Subdued* (Princeton, 1961), 52.

3. Robert J. C. Butow, *Japan's Decision to Surrender* (Stanford, 1954), 130, 124. This and the following cables are quoted by Butow from *Proceedings* of the International Military Tribunal for the Far East, 23591-92.

4. James Forrestal, *The Forrestal Diaries*, ed. Walter Millis (New York, 1951), 74; see also pp. 75-76.

5. Butow, *Japan's Decision*, 103-11.

6. Butow, *Japan's Decision*, 130.

7. Feis, *Japan Subdued*, 57; James F. Byrnes, *All in One Lifetime* (New York, 1958), 292.

8. Both quotes from Marshall are found in *Military Situation in the Far East*, hearings before the Senate Committee on Armed Services and Senate Committee on Foreign Relations (82 Cong., 1 Sess.), May 3-August 17, 1951 (Washington, 1951), Part I, 562.

9. James F. Byrnes, *Speaking Frankly* (New York, 1947), 262.

10. Henry L. Stimson and McGeorge Bundy, *On Active Service in Peace and War* (New York, 1947), 617-18, 629.

11. Butow, *Japan's Decision*, 130.

12. Henry DeWolf Smyth, *Atomic Energy for Military Purposes* (Princeton, 1946), 247-50.

13. Feis, *Japan Subdued*, 60.

14. Feis, *Japan Subdued*, 72.

15. Harry S. Truman, *Year of Decisions* (Garden City, N.Y., 1955), 415; Byrnes, *Speaking Frankly*, 206.

16. Truman, *Year of Decisions*, 419; Winston S. Churchill, *Triumph and Tragedy*, Vol. VI of *The Second World War* (Boston, 1953), 638-39.

17. William Hillman, *Mr. President* (New York, 1952), 248-49.

18. Truman, *Year of Decisions*, 420. In a letter written January 12, 1953 (before his *Memoirs*), Mr. Truman described his concern over the choice of targets as follows: "I asked Secretary Stimson which cities in Japan were devoted exclusively to war production. He promptly named Hiroshima and Nagasaki, among others." See Wesley Frank Craven and James Lea Cate (eds.), *The Pacific: Matterhorn to Nagasaki, June 1944 to August 1945*, Vol. V of *The Army Air Forces in World War II* (Chicago, 1953), facing 712.

19. H. H. Arnold, *Global Mission* (New York, 1949), 585, 492; Stimson and Bundy, *On Active Service*, 625; see also the account in Feis, *Japan Subdued*, 73-74.

20. Craven and Cate, *Matterhorn*, facing 697.

21. Craven and Cate, *Matterhorn*, facing 712; Truman, *Year of Decisions*, 421.

22. Byrnes, *Speaking Frankly*, 207.

23. Truman, *Year of Decisions*, 387, 390, 396-97; Byrnes, *All in One Lifetime*, 296.

24. Shigenori Togo, *The Cause of Japan*, trans. and ed. Fumihiko Togo and Ben Bruce Blakeney (New York, 1956), 312-13; see also the discussion in Butow, *Japan's Decision*, 142-45.

25. Togo, *The Cause of Japan*, 313-14.

26. William J. Coughlin, "The Great *Mokusatsu* Mistake," *Harper's Magazine*, 206:31-40 (March 1953). See also Butow, *Japan's Decision*, 145-49; and Kazuo Kawai, "*Mokusatsu*, Japan's Response to

the Potsdam Declaration," *Pacific Historical Review*, 19:409-14 (November 1950).

27. Togo, *The Cause of Japan*, 313-14.
28. Butow, *Japan's Decision*, 148.
29. Stimson and Bundy, *On Active Service*, 625. See report in the *New York Times*, July 30, 1945, p. 1.
30. Byrnes, *Speaking Frankly*, 263.
31. Craven and Cate, *Matterhorn*, facing 712.

CHAPTER 9 (pages 98-107)

1. Details on the military preparations may be found in Michael Amrine, *The Great Decision* (New York, 1959), 58-63; and William L. Laurence, *Dawn over Zero* (New York, 1946), 196 ff.
2. Laurence, *Dawn over Zero*, 201; Herbert Feis, *Japan Subdued* (Princeton, 1961), 71.
3. Laurence, *Dawn over Zero*, 205-6, 211.
4. Laurence, *Dawn over Zero*, 212-21. See also Wesley Frank Craven and James Lea Cate (eds.), *The Pacific: Matterhorn to Nagasaki, June 1944 to August 1945*, Vol. V of *The Army Air Forces in World War II* (Chicago, 1953), 716-17.
5. Laurence, *Dawn over Zero*, 222.
6. Arthur H. Compton, *Atomic Quest* (New York, 1956), 257. See also Henry L. Stimson and McGeorge Bundy, *On Active Service in Peace and War* (New York, 1947), 630; and Karl T. Compton, "If the Atomic Bomb Had Not Been Used," *Atlantic Monthly*, 178:54 (December 1946).
7. Harry S. Truman, *Year of Decisions* (Garden City, N.Y., 1955), 423.
8. Laurence, *Dawn over Zero*, 226; Craven and Cate, *Matterhorn*, 718.
9. A facsimile of the note appears in Compton, *Atomic Quest*, 258.
10. Compton, *Atomic Quest*, 259.
11. For the details of the sortie, see Laurence, *Dawn over Zero*, 228-43; Craven and Cate, *Matterhorn*, 719-20.
12. Stimson and Bundy, *On Active Service*, 626.
13. The text of the Japanese statement is given in Robert J. C. Butow, *Japan's Decision to Surrender* (Stanford, 1954), 244.
14. Feis, *Japan Subdued*, 120-21; James F. Byrnes, *Speaking Frankly* (New York, 1947), 209.
15. The complete text is given in Butow, *Japan's Decision*, 245.
16. James F. Byrnes, *All in One Lifetime* (New York, 1958), 306.

CHAPTER 10 (pages 111-116)

1. "The Fortune Survey," *Fortune*, 32:305 (December 1945).
2. *Commonweal*, 42:468 (August 31, 1945); Leonard S. Cottrell, Jr. (ed.), *Public Reaction to the Atomic Bomb and World Affairs* (Ithaca, N.Y., 1947), Part II, ii.
3. Robert Jungk, *Brighter Than a Thousand Suns* (New York, 1958), 202; Laura Fermi, *Atoms in the Family* (Chicago, 1954), 245; Oppenheimer is quoted in *Time* Magazine, 51:94 (February 23, 1948).
4. Fermi, *Atoms in the Family*, 245.
5. See, for example, editorial in the *Presbyterian*, 115:4 (August 16, 1945).
6. Editorial, *Lutheran*, 27:2 (August 22, 1945).
7. The statement is printed in the *Federal Council Bulletin*, 28:6 (September 1945).
8. *New York Times*, August 8, 1945, pp. 1, 6, and August 9, 1945, p. 9.
9. *Christian Century*, 62:974, 1086 (August 29, September 26, 1945); *Commonweal*, 42:443 (August 24, 1945); *Catholic World*, 161:449 (September 1945).
10. *Fellowship*, 11:161 (September 1945); John J. Hugo, "Peace without Victory," *Catholic Worker*, 12:1 (September 1945).
11. *Atomic Warfare and the Christian Faith*, a report of the Commission on the Relation of the Church to the War in the Light of the Christian Faith (New York, 1946), 11-12; this was published as a supplement to the April 1946 issue of *Social Action*, Vol. 12.

CHAPTER 11 (pages 117-126)

1. Henry L. Stimson and McGeorge Bundy, *On Active Service in Peace and War* (New York, 1947), 631-32.
2. Stimson and Bundy, *On Active Service*, 620-21.
3. Stimson and Bundy, *On Active Service*, 617.
4. United States Atomic Energy Commission, *In the Matter of J. Robert Oppenheimer: Transcript of Hearing before Personnel Security Board* (Washington, 1954), 34; James F. Byrnes, *Speaking Frankly* (New York, 1947), 261.
5. United States Strategic Bombing Survey (hereafter USSBS), *Japan's Struggle to End the War* (Washington, 1946), 16-18.
6. USSBS, *Japan's Struggle*, 13.
7. Arthur H. Compton, *Atomic Quest* (New York, 1956), 237.
8. USSBS, *The Effects of Atomic Bombs on Hiroshima and Nagasaki* (Washington, 1946), 3.
9. USSBS, *Effects on Hiroshima and Nagasaki*, 15-20; see also Los

Alamos Scientific Laboratory, *The Effects of Atomic Weapons* (Washington, 1950), 201-19, 334-38.

10. USSBS, *Effects on Hiroshima and Nagasaki*, 6.
11. USSBS, *Effects on Hiroshima and Nagasaki*, 3, 40.
12. William L. Laurence, *Men and Atoms* (New York, 1959), 164.
13. Stimson and Bundy, *On Active Service*, 633.
14. United States Department of State, *The International Control of Atomic Energy: Growth of a Policy* (Washington, 1946), 107, 109.
15. Byrnes, *Speaking Frankly*, 264; Compton, *Atomic Quest*, 260, 284; Vannevar Bush, *Modern Arms and Free Men* (New York, 1949), 92.

CHAPTER 12 (pages 127-145)

1. Robert J. C. Butow, *Japan's Decision to Surrender* (Stanford, 1954), 248.
2. The following account is heavily dependent upon Butow's *Japan's Decision to Surrender*. This work is the most authoritative resource available on the history of the Japanese government in the summer of 1945, being based upon exhaustive study of the complete records (both published and unpublished) of the International Military Tribunal for the Far East, unpublished Japanese Foreign Office records, private diaries, and interviews with the participants. Butow supersedes and corrects earlier accounts, including USSBS's *Japan's Struggle to End the War* (Washington, 1946), Masuo Kato's *The Lost War: A Japanese Reporter's Inside Story* (New York, 1946), and Toshikazu Kase's *Journey to the Missouri* (New Haven, 1950), the latter being the account of a high Japanese Foreign Office official who participated in the events. Footnotes throughout the chapter will indicate only the major points of dependence and direct quotations.
3. Butow, *Japan's Decision*, 7-57.
4. Butow, *Japan's Decision*, 58-67.
5. Butow, *Japan's Decision*, 65.
6. Butow, *Japan's Decision*, 68-69.
7. Butow, *Japan's Decision*, 70-72.
8. Butow, *Japan's Decision*, 93-102, 112-20.
9. Butow, *Japan's Decision*, 121-28, 149-50, 153-54.
10. Butow, *Japan's Decision*, 142-44; see also Togo's account in Shigenori Togo, *The Cause of Japan*, trans. and ed. Fumihiko Togo and Ben Bruce Blakeney (New York, 1956), 312-13.
11. Arthur H. Compton, *Atomic Quest* (New York, 1956), 255; Butow, *Japan's Decision*, 150-51.
12. Togo, *The Cause of Japan*, 315.

13. Butow, *Japan's Decision*, 153-54.
14. Butow, *Japan's Decision*, 158-62.
15. Butow, *Japan's Decision*, 162-63.
16. Butow, *Japan's Decision*, 163-64.
17. Butow, *Japan's Decision*, 164-65, 170.
18. Butow, *Japan's Decision*, 165.
19. Butow, *Japan's Decision*, 167, 228-33.
20. Butow, *Japan's Decision*, 203, 232.
21. Butow, *Japan's Decision*, 168-75.
22. Butow, *Japan's Decision*, 175-76.
23. Butow, *Japan's Decision*, 176.
24. Butow, *Japan's Decision*, 177-78.
25. Butow, *Japan's Decision*, 245; compare James F. Byrnes, *Speaking Frankly* (New York, 1947), 209-10.
26. Butow, *Japan's Decision*, 193-202.
27. Butow, *Japan's Decision*, 199.
28. Butow, *Japan's Decision*, 203-7.
29. Butow, *Japan's Decision*, 207-8.
30. Butow, *Japan's Decision*, 248.
31. Butow, *Japan's Decision*, 231.

CHAPTER 13 (pages 146-161)

1. William Hillman, *Mr. President* (New York, 1952), 248-49; Harry S. Truman, *Year of Decisions* (Garden City, N.Y., 1955), 417; Henry L. Stimson and McGeorge Bundy, *On Active Service in Peace and War* (New York, 1947), 619; Erwin C. Lessner, "World War II," *Encyclopedia Americana* (1956 ed.), 29:559yy.
2. Lessner, "World War II," 29:559qq; Okinawa figures are given in the *New York Times* for July 7, 1945, p. 6.
3. Ray S. Cline, *Washington Command Post: The Operations Division* in the *United States Army in World War II* series (Washington, 1951), 346; United States Strategic Bombing Survey (hereafter USSBS), *Japan's Struggle to End the War* (Washington, 1946), 13.
4. USSBS, *Summary Report (Pacific War)* (Washington, 1946), 20.
5. William J. Coughlin, "The Great *Mokusatsu* Mistake," *Harper's Magazine*, 206:38 (March 1953); Lessner, "World War II," 29:559ww; Truman, *Year of Decisions*, 454.
6. *New York Times*, July 7, 1945, p. 6; Lessner, "World War II," 29:559qq.
7. Karl T. Compton, "If the Atomic Bomb Had Not Been Used," *Atlantic Monthly*, 178:54ff. (December 1946).
8. *New York Times*, August 7, 1945, p. 4; United States Department of

State, *The International Control of Atomic Energy: Growth of a Policy* (Washington, 1946), 107.

9. William L. Laurence, *Men and Atoms* (New York, 1959), 150.
10. Truman, *Year of Decisions*, 423.
11. Truman, *Year of Decisions*, 426.
12. "Talk of the Town," *New Yorker*, 21:24 (December 15, 1945).
13. Interview with Arthur H. Compton, January 30, 1961.
14. U.S. Dept. of State, *International Control*, 107.
15. Truman, *Year of Decisions*, 420; Wesley Frank Craven and James Lea Cate (eds.), *The Pacific: Matterhorn to Nagasaki, June 1944 to August 1945*, Vol. V of *The Army Air Forces in World War II* (Chicago, 1953), facing 712.
16. Interview with Arthur H. Compton, January 30, 1961.
17. Interview with Arthur H. Compton, January 30, 1961; interview with James B. Conant, December 1, 1960.
18. Truman, *Year of Decisions*, 418.

CHAPTER 14 (pages 162-169)

1. Robert Jungk, *Brighter Than a Thousand Suns* (New York, 1956), 354-56.
2. P. M. S. Blackett, *Fear, War, and the Bomb: Military and Political Consequences of Atomic Energy* (New York, 1949), 127-43; Norman Cousins and Thomas K. Finletter make the same charge in their article "A Beginning for Sanity," *Saturday Review of Literature*, 29:5-9, 38-40 (June 15, 1946).
3. The text is given in Robert J. C. Butow, *Japan's Decision to Surrender* (Stanford, 1954), 242.
4. Harry S. Truman, *Year of Decisions* (Garden City, N.Y., 1955), 411; see also Dwight D. Eisenhower, *Crusade in Europe* (Garden City, N.Y., 1948), 442.
5. Herbert Feis, *Japan Subdued* (Princeton, 1961), 77-78.
6. Truman, *Year of Decisions*, 381-83.
7. James F. Byrnes, *Speaking Frankly* (New York, 1947), 207-9.
8. Byrnes, *Speaking Frankly*, 205-7; Truman, *Year of Decisions*, 425; Ernest J. King and Walter Muir Whitehill, *Fleet Admiral King: A Naval Record* (New York, 1952), 611, 615; Robert E. Sherwood, *Roosevelt and Hopkins* (New York, 1948), 902; John R. Deane, *Strange Alliance* (New York, 1947), 275-76.
9. See, for example, Arthur H. Compton, *Atomic Quest* (New York, 1956), 247, 284; and Henry L. Stimson and McGeorge Bundy, *On Active Service in Peace and War* (New York, 1947), 633.

CHAPTER 15 (pages 170-189)

1. Federal Council of Churches, *Information Service*, Vol. 24, No. 34 (October 20, 1945).

2. *Bulletin of the Atomic Scientists*, 1:12 (May 1, 1946); Wilfrid Parsons, S.J., *et al.*, *The Ethics of Atomic War* (New York, 1947), the first of three reports in *Peace in the Atomic Age*, Catholic Association for International Peace, Pamphlet No. 38, p. 11.

3. *America*, 73:394 (August 18, 1945).

4. *Watchman-Examiner*, 33:791 (August 16, 1945); *Atomic Warfare and the Christian Faith*, a report of the Commission on the Relation of the Church to the War in the Light of the Christian Faith (New York, 1946), 12-13; this was published as a supplement to the April 1946 issue of *Social Action*, Vol. 12.

5. Lester Nurick, "The Distinction between Combatant and Noncombatant in the Law of War," *American Journal of International Law*, 39:691-92 (October 1945); address by Roosevelt to the American Red Cross, quoted by John Nevin Sayre in "American Postscript," *Fellowship*, 10:63 (March 1944).

6. B. H. Liddell Hart, "War, Limited," *Harper's Magazine*, 192:199 (March 1946).

7. Churchill is quoted in the London *Times*, January 29, 1940, p. 8; the Foreign Office is quoted in the *Catholic World*, 159:103 (May 1944).

8. United States Strategic Bombing Survey (hereafter USSBS), *The Effects of Strategic Bombing on the German War Economy* (Washington, 1945), 1.

9. USSBS, *Effects on German War Economy*, 1-2; Sir Archibald Sinclair, quoted by Vera Brittain in "Massacre by Bombing," *Fellowship*, 10:52 (March 1944).

10. USSBS, *Effects on German War Economy*, 2.

11. See, for example, J. M. Spaight, *Bombing Vindicated* (London, 1944).

12. The quotes are from Brittain, "Massacre by Bombing," 51-52.

13. H. H. Arnold, *Global Mission* (New York, 1949), 393-97; Winston S. Churchill, *The Hinge of Fate*, Vol. IV of *The Second World War* (Boston, 1950), 678-80; USSBS, *Effects on German War Economy*, 2.

14. Quoted in Brittain, "Massacre by Bombing," 51.

15. *Fellowship*, 10:79 (April 1944).

16. *New York Times*, March 7, 9, 1944, pp. 4, 16; "Bombing Protest Gets Nationwide Discussion," *Fellowship*, 10:76 (April 1944).

17. *Commonweal*, 39:531 (March 17, 1944); *Christian Century*, 61:340, 359-61 (March 15, 22, 1944).

18. John C. Ford, S.J., "The Morality of Obliteration Bombing," *Theological Studies*, 5:261-309 (September 1944); the quote is from p. 267.
19. Nurick, "Distinction between Combatant and Noncombatant," 680.
20. Ford, "Morality of Obliteration Bombing," 293.
21. Ford, "Morality of Obliteration Bombing," 308-9.
22. "The Relation of the Church to the War in the Light of the Christian Faith," *Social Action*, 10:68 (December 15, 1944).
23. Wesley Frank Craven and James Lea Cate (eds.), *The Pacific: Matterhorn to Nagasaki, June 1944 to August 1945*, Vol. V of *The Army Air Forces in World War II* (Chicago, 1953), 612, 573, 608.
24. Craven and Cate, *Matterhorn*, 614-17.
25. Craven and Cate, *Matterhorn*, 643.
26. Masuo Kato, *The Lost War: A Japanese Reporter's Inside Story* (New York, 1946), 8-9.
27. Craven and Cate, *Matterhorn*, 608.
28. USSBS, *Over-all Report (European War)* (Washington, 1945), 71, 97, 64.
29. John Kenneth Galbraith, *The Affluent Society* (Boston, 1958), 163.
30. USSBS, *Effects on German War Economy*, 13.
31. USSBS, *Summary Report (Pacific War)* (Washington, 1946), 18-19.
32. Harry S. Truman, *Year of Decisions* (Garden City, N.Y., 1955), 420.
33. Truman, *Year of Decisions*, 421; Craven and Cate, *Matterhorn*, facing 712; United States Department of State, *The International Control of Atomic Energy: Growth of a Policy* (Washington, 1946), 107.
34. Elting E. Morison, *Turmoil and Tradition: A Study of the Life and Times of Henry L. Stimson* (Boston, 1960), 633-34; Henry L. Stimson and McGeorge Bundy, *On Active Service in Peace and War* (New York, 1947), 632; Arthur H. Compton, *Atomic Quest* (New York, 1956), 237.
35. For Arnold's account see *Global Mission*, 492, 588-90.
36. Winston S. Churchill, *Triumph and Tragedy*, Vol. VI of *The Second World War* (Boston, 1953), 639.

CHAPTER 16 (pages 190-210)

1. John K. Ryan, "The Augustinian Doctrine of Peace and War," *American Ecclesiastical Review*, 116:416 (June 1947); "The Use of the Atomic Bomb" (statement by forty-nine religious and educational leaders), *Fellowship*, 11:161 (September 1945).
2. Albert Einstein, "The Real Problem Is in the Hearts of Men," *Reference Shelf*, Vol. 19, No. 2, p. 104; William D. Leahy, *I Was There* (New York, 1950), 441.

3. J. F. C. Fuller, *The Second World War: A Strategical and Tactical History* (London, 1948), 391-94.

4. Hanson W. Baldwin, *Great Mistakes of the War* (New York, 1949), 92.

5. Robert J. C. Butow, *Japan's Decision to Surrender* (Stanford, 1954), 56-57, 103-11, 75 (note 56).

6. Butow, *Japan's Decision*, 124.

7. Winston S. Churchill, *The Hinge of Fate*, Vol. IV of *The Second World War* (Boston, 1950), 686-87. See also Robert E. Sherwood, *Roosevelt and Hopkins: An Intimate History* (New York, 1948), 693-97; Elliott Roosevelt, *As He Saw It* (New York, 1946), 117.

8. Cordell Hull, *The Memoirs of Cordell Hull* (New York, 1948), II, 1589-93.

9. Butow, *Japan's Decision*, 69.

10. Ellis Zacharias, *Secret Missions: The Story of an Intelligence Officer* (New York, 1946), 401.

11. Zacharias, *Secret Missions*, 403.

12. Zacharias, *Secret Missions*, 371.

13. Joseph C. Grew, *Turbulent Era* (Boston, 1952), II, 1406-42; Harry S. Truman, *Year of Decisions* (Garden City, N.Y., 1955), 416-17.

14. Henry L. Stimson and McGeorge Bundy, *On Active Service in Peace and War* (New York, 1947), 623; Herbert Feis, *Japan Subdued* (Princeton, 1961), 64, 78-79; compare Hull, *Memoirs*, II, 1593-94.

15. Butow, *Japan's Decision*, 210-23.

16. Butow, *Japan's Decision*, 224.

17. James F. Byrnes, *Speaking Frankly* (New York, 1947), 211, 262; the excerpts of texts of the cables are given in Butow, *Japan's Decision*, 130, and Feis, *Japan Subdued*, Chapter 6.

18. Feis, *Japan Subdued*, 57-58; James F. Byrnes, *All in One Lifetime* (New York, 1958), 292, 297.

19. Byrnes, *Speaking Frankly*, 262.

20. Butow, *Japan's Decision*, 132-33.

21. Butow, *Japan's Decision*, 133.

22. United States Department of State, *The International Control of Atomic Energy: Growth of a Policy* (Washington, 1946), 106.

23. Stimson and Bundy, *On Active Service*, 629-30.

24. Winston S. Churchill, *Triumph and Tragedy*, Vol. VI of *The Second World War* (Boston, 1953), 456, 467; Bernard L. Montgomery, *The Memoirs of Field-Marshal The Viscount Montgomery of Alamein, K.G.* (Cleveland and New York, 1958), 296.

25. Dwight D. Eisenhower, *Crusade in Europe* (Garden City, N.Y., 1948), 396, 399, 402.

26. Hull, *Memoirs*, II, 1111.

27. Hull, *Memoirs*, II, 1109-10, 1570-71.

28. Stimson and Bundy, *On Active Service*, 620.

29. John J. McCloy, *The Challenge to American Foreign Policy* (Cambridge, 1953), 40-44.
30. Stimson and Bundy, *On Active Service*, 613; Truman, *Year of Decisions*, 419. Churchill confirms that the question of whether or not to use the bomb "was never even an issue" (*Triumph and Tragedy*, 639).
31. Arthur H. Compton, *Atomic Quest* (New York, 1956), 238; Alice Kimball Smith, "Behind the Decision to Use the Atomic Bomb: Chicago 1944-45," *Bulletin of the Atomic Scientists*, 14:297 (October 1958).

CHAPTER 17 (pages 211-222)

1. Elting E. Morison, *Turmoil and Tradition: A Study of the Life and Times of Henry L. Stimson* (Boston, 1960), 633-34.
2. Henry L. Stimson and McGeorge Bundy, *On Active Service in Peace and War* (New York, 1947), 632-33.
3. Stimson and Bundy, *On Active Service*, 633.
4. For a detailed exposition of the derivation of noncombatant immunity see Paul Ramsey, *War and the Christian Conscience* (Durham, N.C., 1961).
5. John Courtney Murray, "Remarks on the Moral Problem of War," *Theological Studies*, 20:54 (March 1959).
6. John K. Ryan, *Modern War and Basic Ethics* (Washington, 1933), 80-82; Cyprian Emanuel *et al.*, *The Ethics of War* (New York, 1932; Catholic Association for International Peace, Pamphlet No. 9), 28-30.
7. See Paul Ramsey, *War and the Christian Conscience*.
8. United States Strategic Bombing Survey, *Summary Report (Pacific War)* (Washington, 1946), 19. Compare USSBS, *The Effects of Strategic Bombing on the German War Economy* (Washington, 1945), 13.

CHAPTER 18 (pages 225-236)

1. Alice Kimball Smith, "Behind the Decision to Use the Atomic Bomb: Chicago, 1944-45," *Bulletin of the Atomic Scientists*, 14:291-96 (October 1958).
2. Los Alamos Scientists, *Our Atomic World*, ed. Robert E. Marshak *et al.* (Albuquerque, 1946), 24 ff.; Atomic Scientists of Chicago, *The Atomic Bomb* (Chicago, 1946), 14 ff.
3. Atomic Scientists of Chicago, *Atomic Bomb*, 21-22.

4. Leo Szilard, "America, Russia and the Bomb," *New Republic*, 121:11-13 (October 31, 1949); Albert Einstein, "Peace in the Atomic Era," *Vital Speeches of the Day*, 16:302 (March 1, 1950); editorial in the *Christian Century*, 66:1192 (October 12, 1949).

5. Atomic Sci. of Chicago, *Atomic Bomb*, 7.

6. Dr. John A. Simpson, in *Atomic Energy*, hearings before a Special Committee on Atomic Energy, United States Senate (79 Cong., 1 Sess.), on S. Res. 179, November 27-December 3, 1945, p. 305.

7. Atomic Sci. of Chicago, *Atomic Bomb*, 20, 7.

8. Harold C. Urey, *Atomic Energy: Master or Servant?* (Missoula, 1946), 8; J. Robert Oppenheimer, "The International Control of Atomic Energy," *Bulletin of the Atomic Scientists*, 1:1 (June 1, 1946).

9. Atomic Sci. of Chicago, *Atomic Bomb*, 20; U.S. Senate, Special Com. on Atomic Energy, *Atomic Energy*, 79-320 *passim*.

10. Atomic Sci. of Chicago, *Atomic Bomb*, 25; Los Alamos Scientists, *Our Atomic World*, 6.

11. Oppenheimer, "International Control," 1; Arthur H. Compton, "Atomic Power in War and Peace," mimeographed copy of address, October 5, 1945.

12. Urey, *Atomic Energy*, 13.

13. Albert Einstein, "The Real Problem Is in the Hearts of Men," *New York Times Magazine*, June 23, 1946, p. 7; Compton, "Atomic Power."

14. Winston S. Churchill, *The Gathering Storm*, Vol. I of *The Second World War* (Boston, 1948).

15. Quincy Wright, *A Study of War* (Chicago, 1942), II, 813.

16. A. J. Muste, *Not by Might* (New York, 1947), 1; Robert M. Hutchins, "Peace or War with Russia?" *Bulletin of the Atomic Scientists*, 1:2 (March 1, 1946).

17. "Statement on Control of the Atomic Bomb," *Federal Council Bulletin*, 28:6 (October 1945); *Christian Century*, 66:519-20 (April 27, 1949); Richard M. Fagley, *Brief Guide to the Atomic Age* (New York, 1945), 23-24.

18. Norman Cousins, *Modern Man Is Obsolete* (New York, 1945), 33.

19. Testimony before the United States House of Representatives Appropriations Subcommittee, quoted in Henry A. Kissinger, *Nuclear Weapons and Foreign Policy* (New York, 1957), 28-31.

20. Bernard Baruch, "Proposals for an International Atomic Development Authority," United States Department of State *Bulletin*, 14:1057 (June 23, 1946).

21. *New York Times*, September 2, 1945, p. 3.

22. Editorial on "Massacre by Bombing" in the *New York Times*, March 8, 1944, p. 18.

23. Henry L. Stimson and McGeorge Bundy, *On Active Service in Peace and War* (New York, 1947), 633.

CHAPTER 19 (pages 237-246)

1. Fuller details of the publishing of these five reports are given here. Commission on the Relation of the Church to the War in the Light of the Christian Faith, *Atomic Warfare and the Christian Faith* (New York, 1946), published as a supplement to the April issue of *Social Action*, Vol. 12; *The Era of Atomic Power* (London, 1946), a report of a commission appointed by the British Council of Churches; *The Ethics of Atomic War* (New York, 1947), published as the first of three reports in *Peace in the Atomic Age*, Catholic Association for International Peace, Pamphlet No. 38; *The Church and the Atom: A Study of the Moral and Theological Aspects of Peace and War* (London, 1948); *The Christian Conscience and Weapons of Mass Destruction*, a report of the Special Commission appointed by the Federal Council of Churches of Christ in America, reprinted in *Christianity and Crisis*, 10:162-68 (December 11, 1950), and also in *War and the Christian Church* (University of Chicago Round Table Series No. 670, January 28, 1951).

2. *Social Action*, 10:67-69 (December 15, 1944); italics are in the original.

3. *Atomic Warfare and the Christian Faith*, 8-9, 13-14.

4. *Ethics of Atomic War*, 11, 8, 16, 8-9, 11-12, 16.

5. *Christianity and Crisis*, 10:164.

6. *Christianity and Crisis*, 10:165, 163.

7. *Christianity and Crisis*, 10:166-67.

8. *Christianity and Crisis*, 10:164. Unfortunately, the slightly abridged version of the report appearing in *Christianity and Crisis* omits the passage that includes the word "triumph." The passage is included in the full text which appears in *War and the Christian Church*, p. 21.

9. *War and the Christian Church*, 21, 30-31.

10. *Christianity and Crisis*, 10:166.

11. *Christianity and Crisis*, 10:166-68.

12. Kirby Page, "Atomic Slaughter Confronts the Churches," in *The Church, the Gospel and War*, ed. Rufus M. Jones (New York, 1948), 157; A. J. Muste, "The Atomic Bomb and the American Dream," *Fellowship*, 11:169 (October 1945); Page, "Atomic Slaughter," 161-62.

13. John Haynes Holmes, "From My Standpoint," *Fellowship*, 12:2 (January 1946) and 11:186 (November 1945).

14. Eugene Rabinowitch, "Five Years After," *Bulletin of the Atomic Scientists*, 7:3 (January 1951).
15. World Council of Churches, *Man's Disorder and God's Design: The Amsterdam Assembly Series* (New York, 1948), IV, 218.

CHAPTER 20 (pages 247-258)

1. Commission on the Relation of the Church to the War in the Light of the Christian Faith, *Atomic Warfare and the Christian Faith* (New York, 1946), 13-14, published as a supplement to the April 1946 issue of *Social Action*, Vol. 12.
2. *The Ethics of Atomic War* (New York, 1947), 8, published as the first of three reports in *Peace in the Atomic Age*, Catholic Association for International Peace, Pamphlet No. 38.
3. *Ethics of Atomic War*, 12-13.
4. *The Era of Atomic Power* (London, 1946), a report of a commission appointed by the British Council of Churches, 52-56.
5. *Era of Atomic Power*, 56-57.
6. *The Church and the Atom: A Study of the Moral and Theological Aspects of Peace and War* (London, 1948), 45, 50, 52.
7. *The Christian Conscience and Weapons of Mass Destruction*, a report of the Special Commission appointed by the Federal Council of the Churches of Christ in America, reprinted in *Christianity and Crisis*, 10:162-68 (December 11, 1950), and also in *War and the Christian Church* (University of Chicago Round Table Series No. 670, January 28, 1951); see latter, pp. 20-21.
8. *Church and the Atom*, 33, 35, 111.
9. Robert E. Osgood, *Limited War* (Chicago, 1957); Henry A. Kissinger, *Nuclear Weapons and Foreign Policy* (New York, 1957).
10. John Courtney Murray, S.J., "Remarks on the Moral Problem of War," *Theological Studies*, 20:40-61 (March 1959); Thomas E. Murray, "Morality and Security — The Forgotten Equation," *America*, 96:258-62 (December 1, 1956); Reinhold Niebuhr, *The Structure of Nations and Empires* (New York, 1959), 279-81; World Council of Churches, Division of Studies, "Christians and the Prevention of War in an Atomic Age — A Theological Discussion" (mimeographed, 1958), 32-34.

CHAPTER 21 (pages 261-269)

1. Robert Jungk, *Brighter Than a Thousand Suns* (New York, 1958), 208.

2. Edward Leroy Long, Jr., *The Christian Response to the Atomic Crisis* (Philadelphia, 1950), 72, 63-64.
3. Nat S. Finney, "How F.D.R. Planned to Use the A-Bomb," *Look*, 14:24 (March 14, 1950).
4. Gabriel A. Almond, *The American People and Foreign Policy* (New York, 1950), Chapter 3.
5. Editorial, *Christian Century*, 62:1087 (September 26, 1945).

Index

Index